Big Government... Poor Grandchildren

Ty + Helen, I wish only the best for you and yours.

Orsham

Orsham W. Ellis

9-22-14

Big Government... Poor Grandchildren

How Democrats and Republicans Are Impoverishing You and Yours

Durham W. Ellis

Wealthy World Publishers
BIRMINGHAM, ALABAMA

First printing 2006

ISBN 13: 978-0-9767639-2-5
ISBN 10: 0-9767639-2-3
LCCN: 2005924541

Dedication

This book is dedicated to the memory of the men who wrote the two documents in the late eighteenth century whose influence combined to make us wealthy today: the Constitution of the United States of America (which mandated principles of limited government) and Adam Smith's *The Wealth of Nations* (which set forth the basic principles of capitalism). This book is also dedicated to the grandchildren of my grandchildren. May they all thrive and be wealthy in this constitutional republic that we mistakenly call a democracy.

About the Author

Durham W. Ellis

A 1964 graduate of the University of Alabama School of Law, Durham Ellis is a real estate broker living with his wife in Birmingham, Alabama, where they are closely involved with their children and grandchildren. As a student, Ellis was greatly disillusioned by the absurdly conflicting decisions and doublespeak "reasoning" he found in the constitutional law cases he studied. By contrast, he was influenced greatly by the clear, logical analyses of such libertarian and constitutional thinkers as Ayn Rand, Thomas Sowell, and Neal Boortz. This book is the result of over forty years of political analysis and discussion.

Acknowledgments

I thank my children for encouraging me to write this book and my wife for helping me actually finish it. I also want to thank W. Eugene Rutledge for sharing his invaluable knowledge of constitutional law and the federal judiciary.

I especially want to thank my editor, Allan Burns of Colorado Springs, for his incredibly insightful and excellent work. All therapists in Alabama are also most appreciative of Mr. Burns for the business opportunity created for them by the damage he caused to my ego as he prodded me to improve beyond my ability.

My wife, my children, my legal consultant, and my editor all want me to let you know they really tried but that, in the end, I was incorrigible and the opinions expressed in this book do not necessarily reflect those of anyone other than myself.

Table of Contents

Part II: Big Government vs. Freedom 73

Warning

> *"It is wrong always, everywhere and for everyone to believe anything upon insufficient evidence."*
>
> —W. K. CLIFFORD

> *"Most people can't think, most of the remainder won't think, and the small fraction who do think mostly can't do it very well. The extremely tiny fraction who think regularly, accurately, creatively, and without self-delusion—in the long run, these are the only people who count."*
>
> —ROBERT HEINLEIN

Do not assume that I have any ability to think just because my words are in print. I paid a printer to do that, so you will have to use your intellect and experience to evaluate every assertion I make.

This product is inherently dangerous, and no warranty is given or may be implied that it is suitable for any purpose. There is a risk that reading this book may be detrimental to your mental health, and all liability for its use and/or misuse is assumed by the reader. The reader is warned about the following specific misuses of this product, as they can result in serious physical injuries or death. This is a partial list and is submitted without limitation. The absence from the list of any misuse that you should discover could not possibly be my fault or yours. It must be the fault of someone else, maybe the government or my attorneys, and I suggest that you sue them instead of me for any such oversight.

1. You should not stack copies of it for use as a platform while smoking pot and cutting limbs from trees with a chain saw.
2. You should not set this book on fire and place it in your lap.
3. If it is on fire in your lap or elsewhere, you should not attempt to extinguish it with gasoline.
4. You should not eat it, with or without alcohol.
5. You should not use it as a club in an attempt to subdue an alligator.
6. You should not give it to anyone with a tendency of violence toward you.
7. In fact, even reading this book could cause your head to explode if you possess certain characteristics. Unfortunately, you will have to read it to find out if this problem applies to you. Good luck!

Part I

Big Government vs. Wealth

The Author Unmasked

Many have accused me of being a card-carrying member of the vast and sinister right-wing conspiracy since I disagree vehemently with many liberal positions, but these detractors are only partially correct. The problem is that I also disagree vehemently with many so-called conservative positions, so you could call me a part-time Liberal and a part-time Conservative. I am certainly an extremist, as I see no value in being a moderate who is willing to settle for being only moderately correct.

Maybe someday, someone will coin a label for people like me with a fundamentalist, unwavering faith in the absolute truth of every word in the U.S. Constitution. Until something better than "Born-Again Constitutionalist" catches on, I guess that the label "Libertarian" probably comes the closest to fitting me. However, individual Libertarians differ on some of the innumerable issues just like individual Republicans and individual Democrats do. All labels, including "Libertarian," are oversimplifications and often misleading, and this is probably a good thing. Hopefully, we will never stifle debate in this country and cause everyone to be stuck with the same "one size fits all" label.

But, before we get bogged down in a lengthy discussion of labels, we need to cover the innumerable ways our current big government violates the Constitution and the principles of free enterprise and how these violations destroy wealth—the wealth that your grandchildren will want to enjoy. First, let's establish some basics.

What Is Wealth?

I want to be rich, and everyone I know would rather be rich than poor, so why don't we do something about it? Collectively, we have control over our senators and congressmen, and they have the keys to the printing presses. Why don't we use our political power to get our government to print ten million dollars for each man, woman, and child in the country? Or, we could have the government hire all of us so that we could all quit our corporate jobs and small businesses and start controlling some activity in our society. The government could print enough money to pay each of us a salary of one million dollars per year. With each of us having so much money, we'd all be rich, right?

Sorry, dollar bills are just pieces of paper with words and numbers written on them, and they are worth only what they will buy. If there is no underlying wealth, they are worthless. For example, if you were cold and hungry after being stranded on a desert island for a few days, would you rather find a few tons of paper dollars, a few tons of gold coins, or some basic survival gear, including some matches, a knife, a fish hook, some fishing line, a blanket, etc.? The paper dollars would not help you start a fire any better than the leaves on the island, and the gold would not be any more nourishing than the sand and rocks there.

But better yet, wouldn't you really prefer to know that some intelligent and motivated people had invented and improved a gadget called a battery-powered radio transmitter and that you had one on that island that you could use to call for help? Would it really ruin your day to know that these people had gotten rich by selling a lot of these gadgets?

Well, is gold wealth? Yes and no. It is a useful metal just like iron and copper, and its price fluctuates according to the law of supply and demand just like iron and copper. The Spaniards proved this in the sixteenth century after they had stolen so much gold from the South Americans that it took more and more of their gold coins to buy goods and services than it had taken before their money supply increased and the value of each coin automatically decreased.

If there is sufficient underlying wealth and you have enough dollar bills, you are rich, but how much is enough? The answer is not simple, as dollars fluctuate in buying power and we have to acknowledge the permanent existence of the law of supply and demand. This law is one that simply cannot be rescinded or amended by humans.

Of course, we can always ignore history and try again to legislate prices. The French government passed a law after the revolution in the late eighteenth century, forcing people on penalty of death to accept its worthless paper money at face value as payment for valuable goods and services. It was one of the more dramatic attempts that did not work, but feel free to try again if your good intentions compel you to do so. You just might become famous by being the first one in history to succeed, but don't let your expectations get too high. Voters and politicians will accept the plan, but the marketplace has a nasty habit of enforcing reality and not accepting pipe dreams.

When we say that a widget costs $2.00, we have it backwards. The truth, in this hypothetical example, is that each dollar is worth one-half of a widget. When inflation causes that widget to cost $5.00, the value of each dollar has been reduced to one-fifth of a widget. Remember, it is the exact same widget; the value of the dollar is what has changed. Inflation occurs when there are more dollars in circulation chasing the same amount of goods and services. Each piece of paper with words and numbers on it is automatically reduced in value, and it takes more of them to buy a widget regardless of anything the politicians try to do.

In highly inflationary countries, such as Germany in the 1920s, there have been an abundance of currency and a scarcity of goods, so that reportedly it has sometimes taken a wheelbarrow full of pieces of paper with the right words and numbers written on them to buy one loaf of bread. We have seen many of the same effects in this country. At the end of the nineteenth century, a dollar a day was enough (barely) to survive on. When I was a child, salaries and wages were much lower than they are today, but it generally did not require two wage earners in one household to keep the bills current.

You have heard a zillion examples of inflation in this country, so I am going to mention only one. My parents could buy us a six-pack of Cokes® for 25¢. The huge increase in price for this product since the 1950s cannot be attributed to changes in the product because the only change in a standard Coca-Cola® was from 6 ounces to 12 ounces. Doubling the size would probably account for far less than a 10% change in price because so much of the total is in marketing, distribution, and other costs. With Pepsi® and other competitors breathing down their necks, Coca-Cola® could not get away with a huge increase in profit per unit sold.

So, just what did cause the increase in price of a Coke®? The answer is not simple because there are a number of reasons why it takes so many more pieces of paper today to buy the wealth of a soft drink, automobile, house, etc. With all due humility (if you think that a humble statement will ever follow that introductory phrase, remember that I am a real estate broker and have a bridge to Brooklyn that the tooth fairy has allowed me to offer to you at an incredible price), it is my considered opinion that one of the main causes of the higher cost of goods and services is the higher cost of government today. Somewhere along the way (the Great Depression?), we became afraid of the responsibilities of freedom and got the notion that government should solve every problem. Unfortunately, the government "solutions" were much more costly than they were beneficial. Instead of governments taking under 20% of the gross domestic product as they did for decades, they now confiscate about 40%, squandering most of the extra 20% on well-meaning but counterproductive meddling into our lives. The costs of an expanding government are not paid with magic money. It levies higher taxes, and you must pay them with real dollars. Then to stay in business or to keep feeding your family, you have to raise the price of your product or the amount of your wages. Otherwise, you will fail to survive as a business or as a person. Since everyone else is doing the same, you have to continue raising your prices and wages until the government stops increasing its expenditures. That is called inflation.

On the other hand, if government increases its expenditures without raising taxes, it simply prints more money. With more paper dollars chasing the same amount of goods and services, it takes more dollars to buy each product. That is also called inflation. Either way, more government expenditures cause inflation, and you pay more for that Coke®.

There is evil in the world, and there are plenty of legitimate needs for referees and protectors. Unfortunately, it costs in at least three ways to provide the necessary government workers to do the job:

1. They have to be paid and provided with office space, equipment, and supplies.
2. They are not producing new goods and services (wealth) with their efforts.
3. Workers in the private sector who are producing new goods and services have to divert a significant part of their time away from creating wealth and toward complying with the delays and paperwork demands of government regulations.

   Although it is vital that we pay into the government to support its necessary functions, it is also very costly to do so. However, allowing government to expand into unnecessary, undesirable, and even counterproductive areas causes additional expenses that we, as a society, cannot justify or afford:

4. When government performs functions that can be performed by private enterprise, the cost is always higher because of the difference in motivations. Government workers have to obey the regulations and are motivated to expand their private empires with as many workers and other expenses as possible to attain as high a pay grade as possible. Costs, prompt service, high quality, and general customer satisfaction are just not major issues. On the other hand, owners of private businesses want to provide their services as quickly as possible, with as high a quality as possible, and at as low a price as possible so that they will satisfy their customers and stay ahead of the competition. The small percentage of profits

they make on each transaction is vastly outweighed by the poor quality and inefficiency of the government bureaucrats attempting to perform the same functions.

5. After many of our resources have been dissipated on unnecessary and undesirable controls, we do not have adequate remaining resources for essential and desirable government functions such as national defense, intelligence gathering, public parks, and care for abused and neglected children.
6. Using competition to offset the natural tendency of most humans to be greedy results in the most efficient use of our finite resources that anyone has yet devised. Whenever government starts meddling with the law of supply and demand with wage minimums, price maximums, prohibitions against price gouging, etc., distortions always occur in the use of these resources. That is, we no longer get the most bang for the buck.

All of these necessary and unnecessary costs have to be paid by someone, and you are the one. You pay these costs directly in taxes, and you pay them indirectly in the form of higher prices for those widgets.

So, back to the question, what is wealth? Wealth is what money can buy, and the only way for the general level of wealth to rise is to increase the production of goods and services. One of the best ways to do this is to harness the creativity of millions of people, thereby creating new forms of wealth out of thin air. The best way to motivate millions of people to do this is to minimize controls and maximize persuasion through the free enterprise system. Since the opposition to free enterprise has not yet modified it out of existence in this country, we have been hugely successful.

In fact, at the same time that the price of many products has been rising, the price of many other products has been decreasing, and many products are being replaced by other products that are better, in the opinions of those making free decisions to buy them. That is, the buying power of our pieces of paper with words and numbers on them just does not stay the same from year to year or from product to product. A prime example is the personal computer. When my father was a child, computers of any type simply did not exist, and an infinite amount of money could not buy one. Then, large computers were invented so that it became possible to buy one with a huge amount of money. Later, a desire for profit caused small personal computers to be developed, and competition, mass production, mass marketing, and continuous modifications kept bringing the price of the vastly-improved product down to where it is today.

Wealth is not something lying around that the rich people have somehow grabbed for themselves. Wealth must be created, and people must be motivated to create it, because it takes a lot of risk and hard work to do so. Paradoxically, the selfless idealists who try so hard to help the unfortunate do far less good than those who are selfish enough to be motivated to produce something of value that they can sell to others for a profit. Idealists alleviate some suffering but only by spreading the wealth around and rarely by creating anything of value to add to the supply of wealth.

> *"The redistribution of wealth, after all, presupposes the existence of wealth to redistribute."*
>
> —ARCH N. BOOTH

Don't misunderstand me: The world needs all types of people, and more importantly, everyone needs an environment in which he or she can develop to the fullest. The point is that part of what each idealist needs is money, and there is a lot more of that available for all possible uses in a free enterprise economy. Also, those who devote their lives to the poor would be helped significantly if the free enterprise system were allowed to reduce the number of poor people needing assistance. Advocates of big government want the government to regulate everything. If you are as wealthy as you would like to be, if you are content with the amount of money available for all uses, and if you are content with the legacy that you are leaving your grandchildren, there is no reason to worry about the costs. Stay with the government system of excessive controls that we are steadily expanding.

> *"Where are we going, and why am I in this hand basket?"*
>
> —BUMPER STICKER

But if you are not satisfied with your current level of wealth and what we are doing to your grandchildren, there is a way out. Stop being a control freak and persuade others to do the same. When there are enough of us, we can change our government back to what our Founders intended—a system of limited government that increases wealth for all.

Open-Book Pop Quiz on Jobs

When you hear discussions about a desire for full employment, just what type of jobs do you want the bulk of us to have, in government or in the private sector? Does it matter? For assistance, see below:

Everyone wants full employment, so the "tax and spend" group complains whenever jobs are not being created under any given administration. Their solution? Fill up the government with as many people as possible and talk about all the jobs they created while in power. Unfortunately, very, very few of the government workers are creating wealth as they perform their official duties. Two of the exceptions would be teachers, as they provide the education necessary for others to create wealth, and postal workers, as they provide one of our communications systems, and methods of communication are forms of wealth. Any complaints you have about the quality of the services of these groups would quickly be reduced tremendously if they had to compete in the marketplace for the students and letters entrusted to their care.

In a business, the inventors, innovators, factory workers, and salespersons are examples of creators of wealth, and the accountants and security guards are examples of necessary expenses. In government, some employees are necessary expenses, but the balance of them are unnecessary or even counterproductive expenses. With rare exceptions, they are all expenses and not creators of wealth. The best way to reduce the nation's wealth (if that is really what you want to do to your grandchildren) is to hire as many government workers as possible and empower them to use government controls to drain our resources and stifle motivation.

It is now time for your answer. Do you prefer the bulk of American workers to be employed in (A.) the Private Sector or (B.) the Government Sector? Believe me: There is a right answer and a wrong answer to this question.

Correct Answer: (A.) Private Sector. The larger the percentage of the population creating wealth and the smaller the percentage of the population required to control others, the better.

> *"What this country needs are more unemployed politicians."*
>
> —EDWARD LANGLEY

In fact, in addition to measuring the number of employed Americans, the percentage of unemployment, the average income, and all of the other current measures of employment, we should measure the number and the percentage of the adult population that are engaged in creating wealth, either directly or indirectly. The percentage of workers who are getting paychecks but are engaged in protecting us from evil, keeping records, and other necessary and *un*necessary functions of control needs to be reduced to the absolute minimum necessary. Using the competition inherent in the free enterprise system is one of the most important tools we have to minimize the need for expensive government controls.

Force vs. Freedom

Why do I say that on most issues I am a Libertarian instead of choosing between Liberal vs. Conservative or Left Wing vs. Right Wing? I agree with others that those terms are very imprecise and prefer to choose between Ayn Rand's terms: Controllers and Persuaders. I consider Libertarians to be predominately Persuaders, as they acknowledge the existence of other opinions and attempt by reason to change them, and I consider both Liberals and Conservatives to be Controllers whenever they respond to their respective pet problems by saying, "There ought to be a law."

This stock solution of Controllers is based on the premise that people are inherently bad and/or stupid, and we therefore must resort to force to control their behavior. We accomplish this legally but immorally by passing laws directing our government officials to enforce our preferences on everyone. However, even the legality of these measures would be reversed if we were ever able to get a valid test of controlling laws against the higher law of the Constitution.

Pop Quiz: What does the current administration force you to do, refrain from doing, or support financially that absolutely infuriates you? Answer: All answers are correct, and there is a solution: Stop the government from meddling in everything. However, that solution will include some of your pet issues too.

The Democrats have made a big deal about the approximately $40,000,000 spent on what they have called the "coronation" of George W. Bush to his second term as president. The Republicans have responded that the Democrats would have done the same thing if they won the election and that most of the money was from donations and not from taxpayers. I say that both sides are dealing in half-truths. The Democrats would probably have done about the same, and some of the money probably was donated. My question is why any substantial money is ever donated to either winning side. Believe me, there is a reason, and I suggest that it is not a good one.

I suggest that our government has expanded past its amended charter into so many areas that it now has a lot of influence to sell, and those who want to get something from our government are constantly buying that something in the disguise of donations, campaign contributions, etc. Any money donated for the "coronation" went from the donors to the organizers and then back in some form from the government to the donors. Even many who donated to the losing side hedged their bets by supporting both sides. No one loses except the remaining taxpayers who are not in the loop.

Conclusion: Republicans and Democrats are impoverishing you and yours—that is, unless you are in the loop. Are you?

I vehemently disagree with the position of Controllers that government is the answer to every problem. Government certainly has its place and is an absolute necessity in its place, but government should be restricted to those functions it does best. There are other institutions that should be allowed to do what they do best, and the framers of our Constitution and Bill of Rights clearly stated what government was and was not allowed to do. They tried to keep all of the various institutions and even the three divisions of our government separated so that the powers of each would be diffused and limited.

For example, does any sane person believe that the Salvation Army should be in charge of our national defense, that Dow Chemical Company should be in charge of our environment, or that the Commerce Department should be in charge of developing new search engines for the Internet? Of course not. No one can maintain successfully that any of them should be abolished, but each of them should do only what they are good at doing. So why have we become so lazy? Why are we so afraid of the responsibilities that come with freedom? Why do we allow government to take such a large amount of available funds out of the economy so that it can "solve" all problems? Why have we sex-changed Uncle Sam into Mommy Dearest? For every problem, we turn down the TV just long enough to say, "Let the government solve it," and "There ought to be a law..."

Principles of Controllers

> *"Liberty is the prevention of control by others."*
>
> —LORD ACTON

Some of us are Controllers on some issues and others are Controllers on other issues, so a different mix of the following principles applies to each person. Which apply to you?

- You can stop water from boiling by putting a tight lid on the pot.
- Intentions are superior to results.
- Labels are more important than contents.
- Political correctness is more important than factual correctness and far more important than freedom of speech.
- The group has value; individuals do not.
- The group has responsibilities; individuals do not.
- Government should help all victims.
- Everyone is a victim. (Of course, this becomes a self-fulfilling prophesy for almost everyone in a country dominated by Controllers.)
- Congress can repeal the law of supply and demand.
- Wealth cannot be created, only divided.
- Dividing the pie fairly is more important than allowing incentives to bake larger and better pies.
- Profit is evil.
- All rich people are lucky and/or crooked.
- We need more laws and more government control to reach Utopia.
- There *is* such a thing as a free lunch, and the government provides it.
- Government bureaucrats following regulations care more for you than business people trying new ideas to get your approval and business.

- No government program is too expensive, too wasteful, or too counterproductive, provided that the crooked, lucky rich people pay their fair share of the cost—about 99%.
- The concept of limited government mandated by our Constitution is insensitive, outdated, and was not a major cause of the level of prosperity we enjoy today.
- Government is the answer to all questions.

Controllers in General

In spite of my numerous and vehement disagreements with Controllers, most of the ones I know are intelligent, educated, compassionate people. They generally have a true empathy for the downtrodden and want Utopia on Earth without wars, poverty, disease, violence, and all the other ills we have had to deal with for centuries. They wreak havoc on our freedom of speech with their political correctness guidelines only because they care about peoples' feelings and believe that they can best show their compassion by modifying the First Amendment into oblivion. They want to eliminate our freedom to bear arms only because they believe that enough laws can reduce the violence that some people cause with guns. They demand that everyone should have a right to "free" medical care because they see the medical miracles that are possible and want everyone to have access to them, regardless of the cost and regardless of who will have to pay the bill. They want to take from the rich and give to the poor because they sincerely believe that doing so will reduce the real problem of far too much poverty in the world. They do not seek changes to our Constitution by advocating the passage of amendments because the process is so cumbersome and they want to help some people right now.

Several decades after our country was founded, the Controller Karl Marx wrote a number of books and articles pointing out that the human condition was far from perfect on Earth and advocating his approach to controlling the symptoms. He meant well, but he failed to see the progress (not perfection) that was inevitable from the combination of Adam Smith's 1776 explanation of free enterprise in *The Wealth of Nations* and the principles of limited government mandated by our 1788 U.S. Constitution.

For another example of well intentioned but misguided Controllers, who could possibly disagree with the following goal of the Students for a Democratic Society? "We would replace power rooted in possession, privilege or circumstances, with power rooted in love, reflectiveness, reason and creativity." What human with blood in his veins could possibly be against such warm and fuzzy concepts as "love," "reflectiveness," "reason" and "creativity"? But then again, what human with a brain in his head could endorse this goal without some specifics? Without further elaboration, it is so vague as to be meaningless, and all agreements require a meeting of minds. Until there is a clear statement of whatever is being proposed, there is no way to evaluate any proposal and then to agree or disagree with it.

The main problem with the Controllers' proposed solutions is that they simply do not work. Controllers do not mean to ruin everything they touch; it just happens, generally according to the law of unintended consequences. They really try hard to turn idealistic fantasies into reality by passing laws, but their controls ignore basic human nature, address only the symptoms, and fail to solve the underlying problems. Since their motives are so pure and their goals are so high, they get frustrated by their lack of success. They know that they are right and push harder. They get more laws passed to control everyone's actions to "do it right" and make life fair.

The Democrat Controllers have taken credit for getting us out of the Great Depression with the New Deal, whereas the Republican Controllers say that the New Deal prolonged the problems and that World War II really did the job. So, where is the big difference? The only knight in shining armor that I see in either picture is big government. By accepting either the Democratic or Republican explanation, a huge percentage of people in our nation now have the mindset that we are individually helpless and that major involvement of a nanny government is the only way we can solve our problems. This is exactly the opposite from the principles on which our country was founded and became great.

Thomas Sowell is the first economist I have read who has called attention to the fact that Democrat President Franklin D. Roosevelt and his predecessor, Republican President Herbert Hoover, were both using the power of our government to enforce counterproductive trade restrictions, wage and interest rate minimums and, through the Federal Reserve System, to contract the money supply during a recession. Both presidents thereby contributed to the expansion of an ordinary recession into the Great Depression and its continuation for many years. The lesson is that big government is often the problem and should be considered as a possible solution only in those areas allowed by our Constitution as amended from time to time after full debate.

Another example of our mindset toward reliance on big government is the Marshall Plan, a U.S. taxpayer supported government program that has received well-earned recognition for helping Europeans to recover from the devastation of World War II. The problem is that very little credit is given to the efforts of millions of relatively free individuals in Europe who used the seed money from the Marshall Plan wisely. The government money helped them get started, but it was their hard work that made Europeans prosperous. Unfortunately, they too seem to have forgotten history and are looking more and more to a nanny government to solve the real problems that all humans have. Their unemployment rates have become far too high, and their post–World War II prosperity has already started to fade, just as ours will if we continue down the path we are on.

"From a practical perspective, you cannot legislate everyone's actions all day long," Dan Penning has noted, but the Controllers sure try to do so. Unfortunately, more laws and more government controls are totally ineffective in making hopes for Utopia materialize. In fact, most of their plans are counterproductive. They take huge sums of money out of the economy to mismanage all of their government programs. The controls and resulting disincentives stifle creativity and eventually lead to affordability problems (i.e., poverty) for all.

> *"For every problem there is one solution which is simple, neat, and wrong."*
>
> —H. L. MENCKEN

Controlling one symptom of a problem also causes other symptoms to develop. For example, a most honorable interest in our children expressed in a law mandating education until any given age often contributes to chaos in the classroom, as those who do not want to be there often disrupt the chance of educating those who do. Also, prohibitions against drugs and alcohol produce rich criminals. And, as elaborated elsewhere in this book, minimum wage laws contribute to unemployment and criminality, and price controls cause hoarding and sometimes lead to unnecessary suffering and even deaths.

The Controllers keep rewarding failure and penalizing success, which is not exactly what psychiatrists and psychologists say will work when dealing with humans. This system can only guarantee a nation full of failures, and that is not what I want for my descendants.

> *"The ultimate result of shielding men from the effects of folly is to fill the world with fools."*
>
> —HERBERT SPENCER

Controllers never seem to look at the absence of results and make adjustments. They just keep pressing for harsher enforcement of more detailed laws to make their system work, blaming others for the inevitable failures of their faulty system. They never seem to consider that if at first, second, and third, they do not succeed, to quit that approach and to try something else.

> *"...a man may do the wrong thing for the right reasons...or he may do the right thing for the wrong reasons....a man's reasons for doing something are less important than the ultimate value of what he does."*
>
> —MICHAEL CRICHTON

Persuaders are only slightly less idealistic and immensely more effective than Controllers. I am in favor of much less government control, and I can assure you that I am very idealistically concerned about the future of my country. I am passionate in my desire to promote governmental and economic systems that will give my children, grandchildren, and all of posterity a chance for the same prosperity that has been steadily increasing for both the rich and poor for as long as I remember in spite of the Controllers' attempts to "improve" the system.

That is, under the Persuaders' free enterprise system, most of the rich have been getting richer, and at the same time, most of the poor have been getting less poor for quite some time, in spite of concerted efforts of socialist Controllers to tinker with the capitalist system. One part at a time, we have been accepting each of the tenets of socialism in spite of the fact that it boasts a failure rate that approaches 100% as more and more of the program is accepted. Today's Democrats and Republicans have no idea just how much of the socialist program they have accepted. However, the leaders of the U.S. Socialist Party and the U.S. Communist Party understand fully that they now have very few unique proposals to offer and very few potential voters to attract. Their market niches have been decimated by the Democrats' and Republicans' acceptance of almost all of the planks in their platforms under the labels of liberalism and compassionate conservatism, respectively. If you believe that socialism is truly the compassionate "solution" that has actually solved problems and helped people create significant wealth, then go ahead and pass all of the economic proposals in the socialist platform. There is no reason to commit economic suicide on the installment plan.

On the other hand, "If it ain't broke, don't fix it." Persuaders, being more realistic than Controllers, tend to promote ideas that produce results and abandon those that do not. They noticed that Henry Ford got rich under the free enterprise system by developing the concept of mass production and that Fred Smith got rich by developing the Federal Express concept of overnight mail and package delivery. In the process, they and many others like them created huge amounts of new wealth out of thin air that benefited all of us.

So, Persuaders like the results of the free enterprise system and want to get rich too. They are not afraid of freedom and believe that they, too, can succeed. If their successes should result in a better standard of living for others, that is perhaps an insignificant bonus to them, but it is absolutely essential to us. All of us have benefited directly or indirectly from Ford's mass production and Smith's overnight deliveries, but my favorite example is the change in my lifetime from very painful to almost painless dentistry. All of the Kings Henry of England and all of the Kings Louis of France could never have pooled enough money between them to buy painless dentistry. Neither could they have bought an airline ticket, a personal computer, a telephone, an electric light bulb, central heating, indoor plumbing, television, radio, an automobile, or a penicillin shot.

According to a 2003 U.S. Bureau of the Census report, in the poorest 10% of U.S. households, 91% own color TVs, 74% own microwaves, 55% own VCRs, 47% own clothes dryers, 42% own stereos, 23% own dishwashers, 21% own computers, and 19% own garbage disposals. That is, many of the poorest people in this country now own items that were unavailable to everyone just a few generations ago. That is certainly not perfection, but it is undeniable progress.

In fact, our free enterprise system is far from perfect. Every few days, we hear that another drug company has just introduced a new wonder drug but at prices that very few can afford.

People will continue to suffer and die with those drugs just beyond their reach, and only because of money. That is not even close to a perfect system, and it is so tempting to exert some control over the drug companies to force them to reduce their prices to save lives. Surely, lives are more important than dollars.

Wrong! Or rather—the problem must be framed in a different way.

> *"For every action there is an equal and opposite reaction."*
>
> —ISAAC NEWTON

Price control has been proven over and over to be a disastrous concept. I assure you that every time you take that action, the control you exert costs you far more than you want to pay. The laws of economics do not notice any distinction between drugs and any other commodity like automobiles, computers, TV sets, and electricity. The first automobiles, computers, TV sets, and electricity were scarce and very expensive. Only the rich could afford them, and it was years before mass production and innovations brought them within reach of the masses.

One of the many reasons that today it costs more dollars (pieces of paper with words and numbers on them) to buy complete medical care (wealth) is that we have more types of medical care available to buy today, just like we have more computers now than before they were invented. Now that we can keep the majority of the population alive past sixty years old, we have chosen to pay the high price for the new drugs and equipment necessary to do so, and the situation is not going to improve. By the time that mass production and further innovations bring down the cost of what we are doing now, we will have learned how to keep the majority of the population alive past ninety years old, and it will cost even more for that technology than what we now have. Cutting edge technology in computers, medical care, and everything else is simply very expensive at first.

Just remember that King Henry VIII died of syphilis because no one had invented a cure, and his entire fortune could not help him. Once a cure was invented, only the rich could afford it for quite some time, and many more died of the disease. But now, the cure for syphilis has reached the masses, at least in this country that many in the United Nations consider to be so unprogressive. Remember that a price control on today's wonder drug will make it less likely that the cure for your great-grandchild's illness will be discovered and reach him or her in time. Your descendant will pay dearly for your short-term benefit of paying less for a pill today.

The United States may "lag behind" other industrial nations by not having government-provided medical care for everyone, and our pharmaceutical industry may generate what some feel to be obscene profits. However, as Thomas Sowell has pointed out, it is needless pain and suffering and preventable deaths that are truly obscene. Due to our system, we have far better and more accessible medical and surgical care, and our drug companies introduce far more life-saving medications than those "progressive" countries the Controllers want to copy.

When are those socialist countries or our non-profit organizations going to show us how to produce effective drugs more cheaply without those "obscene" profits? The answer is never. There is definitely a cause and effect relationship between incentives and results. I am personally very glad that the possibility of profits caused effective prescription drugs to be available for my wife's and my exposure to the poliovirus in the 1950s, my blood poisoning in 1960, my daughter's repeated bouts of pneumonia in the 1970s, my son's allergic reactions to bee stings in the 1980s, and my wife's breast cancer in 1990. Every one of these problems has caused numerous deaths in the past, and they could have been disastrous for me and mine if shortsighted Controllers of the past had been able to eliminate the motivation for doctors, researchers, and drug companies to develop cures for them.

Those problems were not disastrous for me only because some smart people had not been denied the motivation to get rich by creating wealth. (Remember that wealth is the supply of goods and services that are available to be bought using pieces of paper with the right words and numbers on them.) But, oh how the Controllers refuse to accept the concepts that new wealth can be created over time and that it can eventually benefit us all. One problem is that it often takes years for the costs to become affordable by the masses, and the idealism of Controllers does not permit patience. In fact, I would like it very much if more of Bill Gates' pieces of paper would come to me quickly so that I could enjoy more of the wealth that dollar bills can buy.

Alas, no system is perfect, and there is nothing that I can do about it. "God, give me patience, and give it to me right now." We have a goose that has laid some golden eggs, so the idealistic Controllers want to kill the goose and divide the eggs. They want us all to be wealthy right now. The fact that there will never be any more golden eggs coming from a dead goose just never crosses their minds. Or, if it does cross their minds, they suggest that we just impose some "reasonable" price controls. While we are dreaming, why don't we just make a wish upon a star to ensure that we can still get those golden eggs from a "reasonably" wounded goose.

Controls Produce Poverty

When I was a white Southerner coming of age in the "Civil Rights Sixties," it took a long time for one of the seldom-mentioned facets of human misery caused by segregation to penetrate my consciousness (lots of bone mass up there to penetrate). That overlooked area was the huge amount of effort that had been wasted by whites attempting to control blacks and thereby forcing blacks to spend huge amounts of additional time coping with and eventually resisting that control. People in Southern states would be much wealthier today if those millions of hours had instead been spent creating innovations and producing goods and services.

One of the reasons whites wanted segregation was that they did not want blacks to take away some of the good jobs that whites had been able to control for as long as they had been in this country. Whites acted on the belief that anything that someone else gets must come at the expense of someone else. This is the zero sum belief that jobs and wealth constitute a finite amount, and it has been proven to be false in the South, just like it has been proven to be false everywhere else it has been tested in the real world. As blacks started getting better jobs, there was a substantial amount of distress during the transition, but the total amount of wealth to divide has increased. Consequently, whites are now better off as a result of the changes, and blacks certainly are. For the benefit of all, there just needs to be more opportunities and no additional attempts to control.

The same principle applies to our international relations. Wealth is not finite, and the free trade agreement known as NAAFTA has not reduced the wealth of Americans. The "great sucking sound" of some jobs flowing out of our country to Mexico and Canada as predicted by Ross Perot was drowned out by the music of goods, services, and other jobs somehow flowing into our country in spite of all of the impediments against doing so caused by our excessive amount of government. There certainly have been hardships to some that have been caused during the transition to free trade, but the benefits are undeniable. There were also hardships to workers in the buggy whip industry that were caused by the transition from buggies to automobiles, but no one is advocating a return to buggies. Likewise, none of the reputable economists are advocating a return to restrained trade. That is a role for irresponsible politicians in response to their ignorant and vocal constituents.

The problems in our economy do not come from an experiment with too much free trade; they come from an experiment with too much government. We all complain strenuously when gasoline prices get higher than we like but fail to mention the excessive price of an oppressive and often counterproductive government. At least when the price of gasoline exceeds $2 per gallon, the product does not also make the car run backwards. Every zoning and environmental restriction costs money, and builders and developers attempt to pass those costs on to their customers in the form of higher prices. If they are unable to do so, they cease operations completely or move on to a different area. Either way, it takes more pieces of paper with words and numbers on them to buy the wealth of a home, because less construction in any area causes less supply there, and less supply causes higher prices. Either way, those with fewer dollars are pushed out of home ownership. That is, the poor are hurt the most. Of course, the Controllers will say that the fault lies with the "greedy" developers and builders and will try again to control the symptoms with some form of price control or quota.

Everyone in the world today would be wealthier today if billions of hours had not been wasted on various forms of excessive control. Some of those zoning and environmental controls are worth the cost, but some of them are not. We need a system that promotes more hours being spent creating wealth so that it would not take so many pieces of paper with words and numbers on them to buy a share of the goods and services that are somehow being produced in spite of all of the time that Controllers force us to waste.

Price controls contribute to poverty. Wage controls contribute to poverty. Election reform controls contribute to poverty. Poverty controls (welfare) contribute to poverty. Gun controls contribute to poverty. Drug controls contribute to poverty. Speech controls (censorship, political correctness) contribute to poverty. Controls of every kind when added together produce poverty. Some controls, such as those controlling abusive parents, bank robbers, and aggressive dictators, are necessary expenses, but so many of the other controls are optional.

It is your choice. Do you prefer for your grandchildren to live in a limited-government, free-enterprise United States or the modern equivalent of the controlled-economy and controlled-activity former U.S.S.R.? Do you prefer your grandchildren to be rich or poor? All you have to do to ensure their poverty is to continue the path of destruction the control freaks have set for us under the false flag of compassion. To ensure your grandchildren's wealth, you will have to work hard to change the current direction of our government, but you will not have to reinvent the wheel. Just pay attention to the Constitution and Adam Smith's principles of free enterprise and stop being a good-intentioned and foolish Controller.

> *"The totalitarian world produces backwardness because it does such violence to the spirit..."*
>
> —RONALD REAGAN

There is, however, another area of wealth vs. poverty that is much harder to measure than material goods and services. In many third-world countries, the governments are so controlling and repressive that some commentators refer to a poverty of dignity or a poverty of spirit among the people there. We even see some of that problem developing here with our multigenerational welfare recipients, etc. Since we know that controls cause this poverty of dignity, there is no reason for us to copy the systems being used in other countries that create the problem, or even worse, to repeat our own mistakes. To be truly compassionate, we need to observe the results of all systems and choose only those that work.

Controls Make Problems Worse

Some of the problems that Controllers are trying to control out of existence are poverty, prejudice, drugs, violence, inadequate education, and the purchase of political favors. These efforts at solving a problem by controlling the symptoms make the problems worse in a number of ways.

For example, gun control makes violence worse, and poverty control (welfare managed by government instead of by private charities) increases poverty. How can I make such politically incorrect assertions? Well, to begin with, I have no desire to be politically correct at the expense of factual correctness. In fact, political correctness is nothing more than another control, speech control, and it has created far more problems than it has solved. I avoid it whenever possible unless it also happens to be the truth. Second, my assertion is factually correct.

A prime example of controls making a problem worse is in poverty. Remember that poverty is an absence of wealth, and wealth is an abundance of goods and services that you can obtain with enough of those pieces of paper with the right words and numbers on them. The control system acts directly and indirectly to reduce the amount of goods and services available.

- Hours are spent writing all of the laws and regulations on how to take money away from producers and deliver it to non-producers.
- More hours are spent taking the money away and delivering it.
- Producers spend more hours complying with all the requirements.
- Motivation is reduced for producers to produce.
- Motivation is reduced for non-producers to become producers.
- None of the hours consumed by the control system are available for the creation and production of wealth.
- The creativeness of solutions to the problems of poverty is limited to the creative potential of bureaucrats working under the constraints, regulations, and incentives of their respective bureaucracies. Many of us will be less than ecstatic about that, but the poor will continue to suffer the most.

These same principles apply to the attempt to control every symptom of every problem. You probably already know that putting a tight cover on a pot of boiling water just makes an explosion. As another example, you have already heard—and the Controllers among you have rejected—the assertion that taking guns away from law-abiding citizens just makes it easier for criminals to take advantage of your weakness. The mainstream media has never told you about the prevalence of guns in peaceful Switzerland or the study in England concluding that deaths by handguns increased after they imposed strict gun control laws. Besides, the English probably just need to make the controls more stringent. If a system is not working, it obviously needs to be applied more forcefully. We just need to put tighter lids on pots to solve those unfortunate explosion problems. Sure!

Even if controlling the symptoms were a harmless response to problems, it would still cause harm since it is being used instead of developing and using effective remedies for the underlying causes. For example, patients can die from the use of harmless but inefficient medical remedies and the failure to use an available effective one.

Since some want to reduce the influence of money in politics, they have passed a law attempting to control the symptoms. The laws are very specific as to just what uses of money are prohibited in political campaigns. Very few hours are spent addressing the real problem that government has a lot of things to sell and there are many people willing to buy. If we reverted to the original plan of a limited government, there would be a limited number of things that the so-called special interests could buy and therefore far less temptation for those with money to buy them.

> *"Few men have virtue to withstand the highest bidder."*
>
> —GEORGE WASHINGTON

Likewise, trying to control guns diverts attention away from studying and solving the underlying causes of deadly violence in our society. Our current welfare system diverts attention away from studying and solving the causes of poverty. We simply must stop trying to control the symptoms of the real problems in our country. Instead, it is critical that we study and solve the underlying causes and stop making matters worse with a system that has never succeeded and never will.

Why are there so many acts of violence in this country? Why is there still so much poverty here? Why are there people here who are prone to racial and other prejudices? Why is there so much addiction to alcohol and other drugs? We sure are not looking for the answers. We are just wasting everyone's time and huge amounts of wealth trying to control the symptoms.

Social Non-Security

> *"Social security is a compact between generations."*
>
> —SOCIAL SECURITY ADMINISTRATION
> FORM SSA-7005-SM-S1(01-2004)

> *"Voters lavish approval on leaders who arrange for future voters to pay for current consumption of government services."*
>
> —GEORGE WILL

Some of those who do not object to "lies in advertising" for government activities say that Socialism Security is a "pay as you go" system. The truth only partially obscured by that label is that I will soon go as you pay. Democratic President Clinton said during his term of office that Social Security was in financial trouble, and Republican President Bush, the Younger, said that Social Security will be bankrupt by 2042 if we do not do something to keep it solvent. What in the world are they talking about? How stupid do they think we are? "THE EMPEROR HAS NO CLOTHES!" There is no money in the fund; Social Security is bankrupt today; it has been bankrupt for decades, and it will still be bankrupt in 2042 if it continues to exist at all. As Charles Krauthammer has said, "2042 is the fictional date for the financial bankruptcy of a fictional trust fund."

You already know that $24.00 "invested" in lottery tickets is most probably worth nothing, but what will $24.00 "invested" in the Social Security Trust Fund by a worker in his twenties be worth when he/she retires? Unless you can find any funds in this so-called Trust Fund, that $24 will be worth nothing then, just as it is now. The Democrats under President Johnson spent all of the money, and the Republicans have made no attempt to put it back since they took control of Congress and the Presidency. Now the Republicans and Democrats spend every dime that comes into the system, and the only "funds" you will find are the equivalent of a promise from the left pocket of the government to pay something to its right pocket *if* it should have the money to do so when the debt comes due. (Just try to do that the next time you run short, and see what response you get from your creditors.)

The reality is that you are part of a mandatory chain letter, and you can only hope that your children and grandchildren can pay you something in your old age because the "fund" has nothing in it. Incidentally, if you believe that you can attain social justice and equality through legislation, you need to know that white women have a better chance than black males of cashing in on this immoral scheme. At least, that is what the mortality tables indicate. So, while we are planning how best to save Socialism Security, maybe we could prop up the system by taxing black male workers even more so there would be more money available for elderly white women.

> *"Your estimated benefits are based on current law. Congress has made changes to the law in the past and can do so at any time. The law governing benefit amounts may change because, by 2042, the payroll taxes collected will be enough to pay only about 73 percent of scheduled benefits."*
>
> —SOCIAL SECURITY ADMINISTRATION FORM SSA-SM-S1(01-2004)

In spite of that reality, many politicians still make the claim that, unlike other possible investments, there is almost no risk in our Non-Security program because it has been guaranteed by our government. Unfortunately, there is no money in the fund, and there is always the serious risk that the flow of money from new suckers will be insufficient to fulfill the promises to older participants in the fraud. When that happens, the government responds with some combination of reducing benefits, deferring benefits, and raising taxes. In fact, this "investment" has been guaranteed by our government to be worthless, and the only risk we are avoiding is the risk of getting any return on our money. What we need is a system similar to those in Chile or formerly allowed to government employees in Corpus Christi, Texas, where individual workers have (or have had) the possibility of getting a real return on their investments.

For example, you would be amazed to know what the value would be in 2005 of the $24.00 in beads, cloth, and trinkets paid by the Dutch West India Company to the Manhattan Native Americans for Manhattan Island in 1626. If the payment had been in cash, if the Manhattan Native Americans had invested it wisely, and if they had reinvested all of the income that their investments produced, they would now have far more than it would take to buy Manhattan back with all of its buildings and income from tenants. Yes, it would even be free of all mortgages.

The following chart shows the accumulated value of only $24.00 invested for 379 years with various assumptions of after-tax rates of return, compounded annually. These returns could be from any combination of interest, dividends, rents, and appreciation in value of the investments.

Possible Returns from a $24.00 Investment

Rate of Return	*Comments*	*Accumulated Values*
No Return:		
Zero	No principal and no interest	Zero
	"Investments" in Social Security	Zero
	"Investments" in lottery tickets	Probably Zero
0%	All principal but no interest	$24
All Principal Plus Compounded Interest:		
1%		$1,042
2%		$43,619
3%		$1,760,000
4%		$68,500,000
5%		$2,576,000,000
6%		$93,569,000,000
6.621%		$856,300,000,000
	Value of all stocks on NYSE December 2003	$856,600,000,000
	U.S. Federal Expenditures 2003	$2,140,000,000,000
6.688%		$2,148,000,000,000
7.046%		$3,867,000,000,000
	U.S. Federal Debt 2003	$3,878,000,000,000
7.5%		$19,230,000,000,000
8%		$112,600,000,000,000
10%		$117,000,000,000,000,000
15%		$2,425,000,000,000,000,000,000,000
20%		$20,542,000,000,000,000,000,000,000,000,000

But, you say that you really did not plan to keep working for another 379 years. That is a valid point, and I too would like to retire before then. However, it is also valid that most workers in America "invest" more than $24.00 into the Social Security Ponzi Scheme before we do retire, and we should have some chance of a real return on our money instead of just hoping that our children and grandchildren will be willing and able to support us. Still, there is some good news and a reason to hope that this immoral program will die. As Dick Armey said recently, "Social Security has one foot in the grave and the other on a banana peel."

In a few more (okay, a lot more) generations, another 379 years will pass, and small returns accumulated over time would add up for you and yours if allowed to do so. Although inflation (caused by too many expenditures for too many government controls) will reduce the buying power of any paper dollars you should collect from the Socialism Security chain letter, that same inflation would account for a sizable increase in paper profits for many other investments. Don't forget that widget I mentioned that used to be worth $2 and then became worth $5 because the value of the dollar decreased and $2 could no longer buy an identical widget. Well, the same principle applies to all other goods and services including investments. The Controllers will make sure that excessive government spending will continue to reduce the value of each dollar, and we will be tempted to believe that our investments have experienced more real appreciation than they have. It will require a constantly increasing number of pieces of paper with words and numbers on them to buy these investments whether or not they have really increased in value.

The biggest problem in accumulating a substantial amount of assets is that the above chart refers to after-tax returns. I assure you that the Controllers will make sure that those returns will not be large because they need to confiscate huge sums of money from the public to squander on their counterproductive programs. The taxes will be heavy on anyone "lucky" enough to accumulate substantial riches over time by resisting the instant gratification of beads, cloth, trinkets, and a nanny government, so that he or she can invest for his or her future.

Since I have been so critical of our Social Non-Security system, I suppose that you now want me to suggest a painless way to get out of it. Sorry! I do not own a time machine, and I do not do miracles. This chain letter/pyramid/Ponzi scheme is going to end the way they all do: People are going to lose money, and in this case, a huge number of people are going to lose a huge amount of money. The crooks in charge of this scheme have followed the usual modus operandi of other Ponzi scammers and have already spent *your* money on something *they* wanted. In this case, they were politicians who bought votes and paid off supporters with "pork" projects. Our money has already been squandered, and therefore, it is already lost. The harsh reality is that there is only one remaining question—who will get stuck with the bill?

Democrats and Republicans are supportive of this mislabeled and unconstitutional Social Security program and are also quite willing to spend your money on unconstitutional purchases of votes from various special interest groups. They now should be consistent and authorize an unconstitutional commission for some artists to create statues to Carlo "Charles" Ponzi and grant him a bipartisan honorary citizenship posthumously. He is credited with developing the system of using money collected from current investors to keep earlier investors happy, and he would have been proud to know that the program that earned him a prison sentence is now an American institution, revered by hundreds of millions of people on both sides of the aisle for the perceived humanitarian benefits it bestows on so many. At the very least, our representatives should make the scam legal for those of us in the private sector and who are therefore not government officials, since the plan professes to be so beneficial, and all Controllers know that intentions are far more important than results.

While we are considering the effects on our lives as our government Controllers choose which facts to analyze and how best to spin those facts while presenting them to us, we need to recognize that the federal government owns a huge amount of furniture, equipment, artifacts, buildings, parcels of vacant land, etc. Anyone can easily research the amount of our federal debt, but no one is accounting for these real and personal properties. All of these should be considered as assets to offset the debt on an accurate balance sheet since correct accounting procedure requires the value of the national properties (assets) to be computed or the amount of the national debt (liabilities) would remain as meaningless as it is today.

Correct accounting procedure would also require the Social Security chain letter receipts and expenditures to be in the budget. Having them off budget is simply a lie just like it is a lie to refer to a Social Security Trust Fund when it has no funds. In a land of true equality, the "CEO" and "CFO" of the government would be sent to prison for this accounting fraud.

After correcting our current fraudulent national accounting statements, the best way to evaluate the significance of the annual national expenditures, annual national deficit, and total national debt is to compute them as percentages of gross domestic product. It should be obvious that a deficit of $100,000,000 would be disastrous for an economy generating only $100,000 in gross domestic product while the same deficit would be insignificant for an economy generating trillions of dollars each year. Also, the value of a dollar is not a constant. That is, $100,000,000 in 2005 does not have the same buying power as $100,000,000 had in 1905, so it is imperative to compute these numbers as percentages for them to have any meaning.

Government has almost no income in the sense that individuals and companies do, so there is no meaningful income and expense statement applicable to government. What we need is just an accurate expense statement to measure the costs of the "free" benefits that government provides us. Regardless of whether the national balance sheet, expense statement, and pertinent percentages are getting better or worse over time, "investing" in lottery tickets, chain letters, and excessive expenditures for our over-controlling government makes it harder for us to solve the real problem of too much poverty in this country. Similar activities by the totalitarian despots in other countries in our warm and fuzzy global village result in failures for them too. Big governments cause affordability problems (aka, poverty) everywhere, and government "solutions" make the problems worse here and everywhere else.

We've Gone Crazy

I once read a book by someone who maintained that we should form a government department of price controls. He explained in great detail how this department should operate for the "common good." The people hired to run this department would investigate the cost of everything, determine a "reasonable" markup on everything, and punish anyone who violated their dictates. His idea has been tried to a limited extent in every country in the world including ours, and it has always had disastrous results, but he truly believed that the concept should be developed to its logical extreme to be of maximum benefit.

First, it would take an infinite number of people to determine what everything "really" costs. Since the cost of everything affects the cost of everything else, the computations would defeat the best computers that the free enterprise system has made, and every error in computations would result in shortages of some products simultaneously with overages in others.

Second, it would take forever to establish a reasonable markup for everything, since each item involves a different degree of risk and marketing expense.

New products? You can forget ever seeing another innovation under this system. Just the thought of the paperwork involved in getting a new product to market would kill most ideas. If any new idea should somehow become reality, there would be the overwhelming complications of determining the cost of the new product, its markup, and its reasonable price. Then, the effect of the new product would have to be considered in re-pricing everything already on the market.

All the energy that would be spent by government officials controlling prices and all the energy we would spend conforming to those controls would leave little or nothing left for the actual production of goods and services, i.e., wealth.

The law of supply and demand smoothly handles all of these issues that are simply impossible for a government agency to control. We have abundance because we have at least partially agreed to deal with issues of pricing by letting everyone's personal greed be counterbalanced by everyone else's personal greed through competition. We need the system that allows rich people to keep their money because we need to give rich and poor people a motivation to create wealth for the benefit of all.

However, the Controllers want to "adjust" the free enterprise system so that it will be more "fair." And they also want to get involved in all of the other issues in our lives. They want a government agency to control everything. The fallacies in the control "solution" are glaringly obvious, but many idealists still believe that they can make enough modifications to this ridiculous plan to make it work.

"Opinions are like assholes; everybody has one," but do not make the mistake of believing that what I am saying is just my opinion. It is an historical fact, documented most dramatically by the social experiment of the U.S.S.R. after their revolution of 1917. While possessing incredible natural resources, they went from the impoverishing controls of the Czars to the devastating controls of their Communist replacements during a period of unprecedented increase in wealth in this country.

If you want more examples of devastating controls in the U.S.S.R. and other countries, including the United States, I suggest that you read a few chapters of *Basic Economics* by Thomas Sowell. Among other examples, he documents how our flirtations with rent control, gas rationing, and other controls have wreaked havoc in this country since we too are unable to repeal or modify the law of supply and demand. We're as crazy and reality challenged as the Controllers are if we agree with them. To paraphrase Denver City Councilman Charlie Brown, the United States is open for business, and I wish that we were not open for lunacy.

Fair Taxes

Taxes are not the problem; they are a red herring. Let me repeat that. Endless discussions of taxes are a very effective diversion that keeps your attention focused on the symptom of the problem and away from the underlying problem of too much spending for too much government. Back when the American public got conned into passing the constitutional amendment allowing income taxes, the functions of government were still being limited by the rest of the Constitution, and our bureaucracy did not need a huge additional source of money. Since only the super-rich (primarily Northeasterners, who were also known as Damn Yankees by some voting for the amendment) were going to be affected by this new income tax, the masses did not object. Now that the government has expanded its functions to meet its expanded ability to raise money, many of the masses have been unpleasantly surprised to find that they are also feeding the insatiable beast that bears little resemblance to the government designed by our Founders.

> *"Government does not tax to get the money it needs; government always finds a need for the money it gets."*
>
> —RONALD REAGAN

However, Americans love to discuss the red herring of fair taxes. "We" are always paying too much, and "they" are never paying enough. We never stop to consider that when the government spends money, we all get the bill in one form or another.

High taxes and high prices for goods and services, also known as inflation, are the inevitable results of the problem of spending too much money for too much government. What we are doing with excessive government spending is making it harder for all of us to buy goods and services, and the inability to afford goods and services equals poverty. We need to spend less time discussing how much tax others should pay and more time on eliminating the cause of those high taxes we all pay.

So, what should we do about spending? All we need to do is to cut government activities back to the basics as outlined in our Constitution. What is so hard about that? Remember that there should be a huge number of government employees who would no longer be wasting their time and our money "working" at the nonessential and/or counterproductive government functions that would be eliminated. These people can stop interfering in our lives and being a drain on the treasury, and they will be available for jobs that produce wealth and some tax revenues of their own.

President George W. Bush caused a furor in 2005 when he presented a budget that proposed cuts in spending for 150 U.S. governmental programs. 150! Just how many total governmental programs do we now have in this "limited" form of government our Founders created? Another question: I agree not to raise any corn again next year, and I'll even agree not to sell any real estate. Where do I go for my checks?

While we allow unlimited spending and only dream of fiscal responsibility, our control-based mandatory tax system is resulting in open class warfare. Everyone wants to receive more "assistance" from the public treasury at the expense of someone else, especially when those paying will be our children and grandchildren. (Thanks a lot, AARP, but you can stop sending me any further solicitations at your earliest convenience. I have gray hair, but I am not interested in supporting your efforts to use the ballot box to put more debt on my grandchildren for my benefit.)

We spend far too much time trying to increase our slice of the pie at someone else's expense, and we spend far too little time baking pies. We somehow even find a reason to debate whether the rich should get tax cuts whenever they are made. Why shouldn't tax cuts go to taxpayers? Since the rich pay most of the taxes, why shouldn't they get the bulk of the reductions on those rare occasions when reductions are made? Whose money is it anyway? Have we reached the point where the people and their money belong to the state? God help us if that is so.

If you are paying less than $1,000.00 per year in income taxes, don't expect even a 100% reduction in tax rates to reduce your taxes by more than $1,000.00. Unless a tax law includes some provision for you to receive some welfare checks mislabeled as tax relief, whatever you pay in taxes will be the maximum savings you can expect from any "cut." If you want some dramatic results, you first need to make yourself more valuable to an employer or directly to the public so that they will pay you more money and you can start paying hundreds of thousands of dollars in taxes. Then and only then will you see those hundreds of thousands of dollars in your taxes be reduced by enough to put a few zeros before the decimal point, but when you are one of those rich people, your taxes will still far exceed that $1,000.00 or whatever you are paying now.

The Democratic Party is openly promoting plans based on socialistic goals to reduce the number of taxpayers at the lower end of the scale while soaking the rich to pay for social programs and the employees to run them. Two obvious techniques being used are the constantly increasing amounts allowed for exemptions and standard deductions on your Form 1040. You can check this assertion simply by comparing the exemptions and standard deductions from as many of your past tax returns as you choose. To get you started, the following chart applies to single persons or married persons filing separately:

Year	*Exemptions*	*Standard Deductions*	*Total*
1997	$2,650	$4,150	$6,800
1998	$2,700	$4,250	$6,950
1999	$2,750	$4,300	$7,050
2000	$2,800	$4,400	$7,200
2001	$2,900	$4,550	$7,450
2002	$3,000	$4,700	$7,700
2003	$3,050	$4,750	$7,800

They increase every year, which means that more taxpayers are being taken off of the rolls each year. We real estate brokers are so proud of how we have used our political power to defend the itemized tax deduction for interest spent on home mortgages, but there is more than one way for Congress to skin a cat. The value of itemized tax deductions for home mortgage interest keeps going down as the difference continues to narrow between the total itemized deductions that can be claimed by homeowners and the constantly increasing standard deduction.

Neal Boortz has said that the Democrats will have a monopoly on government once they are successful in taking 51% of voters off of the tax rolls, as they will have bought permanent loyalty from that 51%, and with it they will have total control of the government. It will probably require more than 51%, because some people in the group will not vote and some will agree with Republican values and vote for candidates of that party. However, the principle is sound, and by the way, this will be accomplished with your money. As we go to press, the top 50% of income earners pay 96% of the income taxes, so the Democratic plan is well on its way.

Consequently, the Republicans are responding with their plan, which is to give only lip service to fiscal conservatism and to buy your vote with your own money by outspending the

Democrats. They have certainly done exactly that since President Clinton retired and President Bush was elected. The problem for Republicans is that their voter base is fully aware that high taxes reduce business activity and thereby contribute to poverty for all. So, the Republicans have resorted to the shell game of reducing taxes and using deficit spending to pay for the excessive growth in their government activities. That is, they are not buying your votes totally with your own money; they are also relying heavily on money borrowed (i.e., stolen) from your descendants.

Unfortunately for all of us, the supporters of neither of these political parties will be able to enjoy any success for long, because every cause has an effect. The wealth in this country will go into a rapid decline shortly after the Democrats get the power to charge the "rich" whatever they desire to fund whatever programs they choose to provide. Likewise, the wealth in this country is already in serious jeopardy as the Republicans borrow and spend without any thought of the limitations our Founders placed on government. In this race to be the party to destroy us first, the winner will soon preside over a national disaster that will affect all of us, but it will affect the poor the most. No longer will the average poor person in this country be on the level of the average average person in Europe.

At that time, the Republicans or the Democrats can try to blame the other for the disaster but only with the same absence of success as President Nixon's attempts to blame his need to resign from office on losing his power base in Congress. We will still have a national disaster, and it won't be any of the likely scapegoats at fault. It will partially be the fault of Democratic and Republican Controllers, but it primarily will be your fault for failing to understand where the Controllers of the major and most of the minor political parties are leading us and for failing to stop them in the voting booths. And do not give me the cop-out that you are tired of voting between Brand X and Brand Y as the Controller that might be the lesser evil at best. Remember, there is always the federal courthouse, as most of the powers grabbed by these Controllers are unconstitutional, and even the politically appointed "Your Honors" in our U.S. Supreme Court would eventually have to respond to a deluge of assertive challenges under the Tenth Amendment.

Starting with the basics of our current system, a 0% tax rate will not produce any revenue for the government to perform its essential functions, its nonessential functions, and its counterproductive functions. At the other extreme, a 100% tax rate makes us all slaves, a condition that is not exactly conducive to hard work and a total barrier to taking risks and bringing innovations into the marketplace. In between 0% and 100%, it gets much more complicated. There have been many instances when a reduction in the tax percentage (but not all the way to zero) resulted in an increase in the tax dollars collected. Likewise, there are instances where an increase in the tax percentage has resulted in a decrease in tax revenue. For an example from my personal experience, some of my relatives inherited some shares of stock in a corporation. For twenty years, and with a capital gains tax rate of not less than 20%, they never sold a single share of that stock. Shortly after the rate was reduced to 15%, they sold it all. The government collected 15% of the profit instead of continuing to collect zero, but the revenues did not stop there. The salesperson earned a new commission and paid income taxes on it. He also added that commission to others generated by the same tax "cut" and was in a position to buy a newer car or a bigger house. The providers of that car or house made money, paid income taxes, built another car or house, and bought other goods and services. Some of the unemployed were offered jobs to help provide those goods and services. Those that accepted the opportunity were taken off of the welfare roll and placed on the taxpayer roll.

The multiplier effect of the revenue generated by that capital gains tax "cut" and those generated by "cuts" in income taxes was phenomenal. The reason is simple human nature. We work harder and are more motivated to buy and sell when we feel that we are going to get a fair share of what we produce, and we do less when we feel that what we produce will be confiscated (stolen legally but immorally) by those with enough power (votes) to do so. We instinctively look after our own survival and well-being, and we work in groups whenever doing so is to our advantage, but only to the extent that those groups advance our personal interests.

Controllers do not like that aspect of humans, but all of their laws and controls have failed to change us. Persuaders, being more realistic, seek curbs on criminal excesses, but otherwise work within the natural human motivations and limitations.

Would it hurt Bill Gates to be taxed at a higher level so that more could go toward universal healthcare? Philosophically considered, unless he stole that money, it is his, and it is none of our damn business what he does with it so long as he does not hurt others. Even considering the direction our country has been taking, "we, the people" still do not have the power to vote on what amount we consider to be a "reasonable" return on Mr. Gates' efforts and then to confiscate 100% of the excess. (One should note that he has freely chosen to give some of his money to charities of his choice in addition to paying the taxes required by government to support its mandatory charities.) Practically, Mr. Gates would be able to continue to eat just as high a quality of steak as he chooses, but we would be able to afford only a lower and lower quality of hamburger, because motivation for everyone to create wealth would be reduced, and our lifestyles would suffer as a consequence. Our existing healthcare problems would become even worse as bureaucrats would get even more control over the product than they currently have. To add insult to all the injuries of these negative consequences, the government's tax revenues would decrease once the tax percentages got too high and destroyed the incentive for people to create wealth.

Earnings vs. Take-Home Pay

Since many taxes have already been deducted before you get your paycheck, you have been conned into believing that what you take is what you make. If you want to know what you really pay in taxes for the "free" governmental services you receive, fill in the following form adapted from the one provided by Bliss & Laughlin Industries to their employees in the mid-1970s.

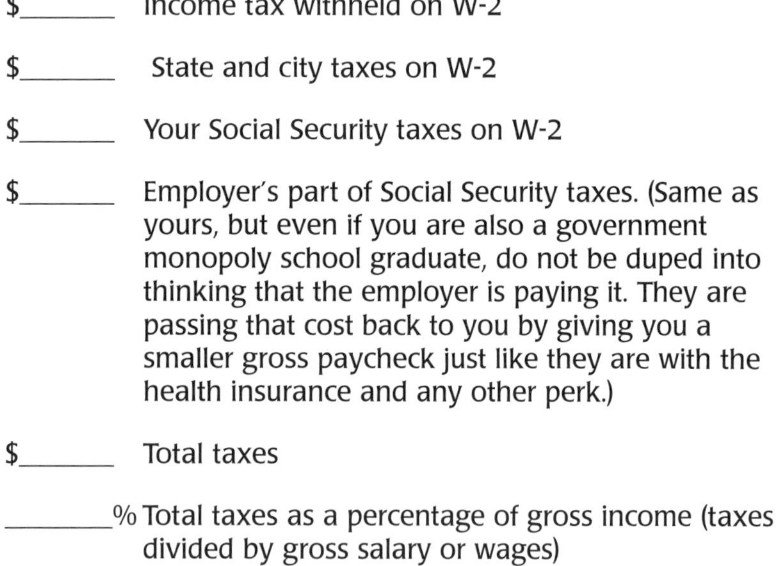

$______ Income tax withheld on W-2

$______ State and city taxes on W-2

$______ Your Social Security taxes on W-2

$______ Employer's part of Social Security taxes. (Same as yours, but even if you are also a government monopoly school graduate, do not be duped into thinking that the employer is paying it. They are passing that cost back to you by giving you a smaller gross paycheck just like they are with the health insurance and any other perk.)

$______ Total taxes

______% Total taxes as a percentage of gross income (taxes divided by gross salary or wages)

However, if you really want to know what your governments are costing you, add in sales taxes, real estate taxes, and all the other taxes. Don't forget the mother of all tax nightmares, inflation. That hidden tax comes into your life like a thief in the night and costs you the most of all.

Corporate Taxes

Although a national sales tax may be preferable to our complicated and time-consuming income tax system, I will leave that issue to others and repeat that high taxes are only a symptom of too much government and that we need to cut government back to its necessary functions. However, there is another alternative that keeps being presented, namely higher income taxes on corporations. Although a sales tax is highly visible, payroll withholding taxes and taxes on corporations have the unfortunate disadvantage of being largely invisible. With either of these forms of taxation, "we the people" are not constantly reminded just how expensive our government has become. Anyway, this is how higher corporate taxes would work if we should use this method to raise money for the necessary, the unnecessary, and the counterproductive functions of our overblown government:

> Since businesses either pass all of their costs on to their customers or cease to exist, they effectively do not pay any taxes or any other expenses for that matter. They are merely conduits for this money. Therefore, all individual taxes could be eliminated and all business taxes could be raised sufficiently to make up the difference. When these corporate expenses are in turn passed on to the public in the form of prices, the tax burden would be spread in a way that is almost as equitable as the Libertarian fee system. The huge amounts of time currently spent preparing individual tax returns would be released for other activities such as additional wealth production. Even the "soak the rich" graduates of government monopoly schools would be ecstatic in the fallacious belief that they are making businesses and their rich owners pay their fair share.
>
> With the unconscionable tax burden kept invisible and spread fairly, higher corporate income taxes must be the answer to keep everyone happy. It is just too bad that all domestic corporations with foreign competition would probably cease to exist as their higher taxes would require them to charge prices that could no longer compete

in the world marketplace. Oh well, that would at least benefit the local environment.

So, just what is a "fair tax" plan? Sorry, that is a trick question—discussing the issue is merely a distraction, and the answer is, "none of the above." None of the plans will ever be fair so long as we keep trying to control the symptoms and ignore the cause. The burden of government in the forms of taxes and inflation will remain onerous for all of us until we get back to the concept of limited government mandated by our Constitution.

Voluntary Fees vs. Mandatory Taxes

> *"Taxation is the price we pay for civilization."*
>
> –SUPREME COURT JUSTICE OLIVER WENDELL HOLMES

> *"Taxation is the price we pay for failing to build a civilized society. The higher the tax level, the greater the failure. A centrally planned totalitarian state represents a complete defeat for the civilized world, while a totally voluntary society represents its ultimate success.... The triumph of persuasion over force is the sign of a civilized society."*
>
> –MARK SKOUSEN

So, who is right and who is wrong, Justice Holmes, the Controller, or Dr. Skousen, the Persuader? Supreme Court Justice is an impressive label, but we still need to examine the contents. Libertarians, including myself and possibly Dr. Skousen, propose that we pay taxes to support only national defense, operation of Congress, and the short list of other absolutely essential functions. For all of the optional services, such as civil law suits and funding for stadiums (also known during the declining years of the Roman Empire as coliseums), we should charge user fees for services requested and provided. With this plan, the marketplace will determine which services are worth the cost, and the total taken out of the economy by government will be less than our current plan because those services with little public participation will automatically be reduced in size by lack of support.

The logistics are intimidating in changing from our current mandatory tax system dominated by the Controllers to a predominately volunteer fee system as proposed by the Persuaders. However, the benefits would be incredible to the extent that we are able to accomplish the transition. Until that is politically feasible, we should focus on reducing government expenses to the basics and then establish rates that provide only enough money to support those absolutely essential functions of government.

Since we Libertarians advocate voluntary fees to fund as many government services as possible instead of the imposition of mandatory taxes, just how would such a system work? Well, in some cases, it would not work at all, such as the absolutely necessary funding of the various departments of national intelligence and defense. The natural tendency of humans is to do as little as possible and to let others do as much as possible when the benefits apply to the general public and are hard to measure on an individual basis. Allow me to repeat that sentence for the edification of those among us socialistic enough to be "progressive." The natural tendency of humans is to do as little as possible and to let others do as much as possible when the benefits apply to the general public and are hard to measure on an individual basis.

However, to get back to taxes, many government programs could be optional as they are not essential for our national survival, and it is easy for each individual to measure the benefits. The Federal Housing Association (have I mentioned that my day job is real estate broker?) is an excellent example of the voluntary fee system at work. As it was originally conceived, the only taxpayers who paid into this government program were those who chose to do so, and they voluntarily paid large amounts for the correspondingly large benefits they received. Each homebuyer had the option of choosing a traditional method of financing the purchase, or he or she could pay some fees to the Federal Housing Association. If the homebuyers chose to pay FHA and could meet FHA's standards of down payment, credit worthiness, etc., it in turn would insure a lending institution against the potential that the borrower would fail to make the payments. The fees that the FHA charged homebuyers for the mortgage insurance were sufficient to cover the costs of the inevitable losses that occurred when some of the borrowers failed to pay. That is, FHA received fees and paid claims, lenders made profits with minimum risks from insured loans, real estate brokers earned commissions, lenders and brokers paid taxes, and renters became homeowners. Win, win, win, win, win.

Since FHA produced value, it flourished and was even copied by entrepreneurs in the private sector. The program had value as determined by those writing the checks instead of being judged only by those receiving the checks. Otherwise, it would have survived only with supplements from taxpayers. There are numerous government programs in existence today that would fail if put to the test of the marketplace, but FHA was one of the exceptions until it was merged into the welfare system called the Department of Housing and Urban Development (HUD). The original FHA provides the pattern that should be copied in all of our optional government programs.

Zero Sum?

Is there anything wrong with the following scenario repeated in our country daily? After cost overruns and graft, the politicians and contractors in Massachusetts get rich while the taxpayers in New York and elsewhere get soaked for a major public improvements project in Massachusetts financed by the federal government and known as the "Big Dig." Then, the reverse happens with the taxpayers in Massachusetts and elsewhere taking the hit for graft in New York.

After multiplying this process thousands of times all over the country, does it all even out? Is there a zero sum to all of the exorbitant taxes and exorbitant illicit gains? (The ripoff is not worthy of being called just a high profit or gouging.) Is it therefore okay that government is completely incapable of and disinterested in cost controls?

Hell, no! In addition to the fact that some individuals pay excessively while others steal the excess with impunity, there is the issue of the failure to create wealth using this system. The thousands of bureaucrats required to mismanage the transfer of money are not available to add to the supply of goods and services. They do not create wealth and simply consume it. Thus, they contribute to the poverty suffered by the poor that the Controllers claim to care for and accuse the Persuaders of ignoring.

All Rich People Are Crooks?

The socialist subspecies of Controllers make a big issue of the fact that the average income of the richest 20% of the world's people was thirty times that of the poorest 20% in the 1960s and that this has increased to be 224 times as large today. They also point out that it now takes the national incomes of the poorest forty-nine countries to equal the combined incomes of the world's three richest people or the combined incomes of the poorest three billion people to equal the combined incomes of the richest 225 people.

These socialists are horrified by the difference in incomes between the richest and the poorest and want to impose controls on the symptoms to effect a different result. Their "Alice In Wonderland" reasoning goes something like this: People in free enterprise countries have more money than people in socialist countries. Even the poor in the capitalist countries are not as poor as those in most of the socialist countries. We must change this "unconscionable" disparity in incomes by using government powers to take from the rich and give to the poor. That is, we should use socialism to cure the problems caused by socialism. Huh?

Since so many governments represented in the UN agree that socialism is more benevolent than capitalism, it appears to me that they had some difficulties in ranking the success rates of countries in a recent UN study. The problem was that the country with the highest average income was the United States, which also is still among those with the highest level of political and economic freedom, even though those freedoms have been decreasing. In my opinion, the authors of the study decided to spin the facts to meet the desired conclusions that controls are good and capitalism is bad, and to do so, they chose which statistical measurements to employ.

As Mark Twain or Benjamin Disraeli observed, "There are three kinds of lies: lies, damn lies, and statistics." At the same time that the authors of the study used measurements that tend to dilute purely materialistic considerations, they also used measurements that support the conclusion that we should adopt a socialistic approach to address the failure of others to adequately address those same materialistic issues. That is, the study tends to support the opinion that we should use socialism to cure the economic problem (i.e., poverty) caused by socialism. Huh?

First, they listed some valid statistics showing that the U.S. needs to improve in the areas of violence, life expectancy, infant mortality, deaths from malnutrition, and percentage of population in prison—substantially as a direct and indirect result of our misnamed "war" on drugs. They also pointed out that we have a large number of children living under the poverty level, but I am not sure whether the definition of "poverty" had been skewed to reach a desired conclusion, and I certainly challenge the opinion that capitalism is the cause of the poverty that does exist in this country and elsewhere.

Their study included material possessions per person, mean wealth, and average income, in all of which categories the U.S. ranks first, but the masterstroke was to give significant weight to median income as contrasted with mean income. Although median is a valid measurement that gives an accurate evaluation of some situations, the UN Controllers must consider it abominable that the United States has the greatest disparity in the entire world between the wealthy and the poor. That is, they seem to feel that we must get our Controllers busy putting ceilings on people to limit the returns on their abilities. Then, we can redistribute those confiscated high incomes to decrease the differences between our highest and lowest incomes, thereby improving our subjective rating at the UN in our standard of living. It would also improve our standing at the UN if we would place our troubled healthcare system under the enlightened control of our politicians and bureaucrats.

Even after the authors of the UN study chose which facts to report and how to evaluate them, the country recognized by everyone to have one of the most nearly free and capitalistic systems of all 191 governments represented in the UN still finished number eight, higher in the ratings than 183 of the remaining 190.

Unfortunately, we do not rank number one on the list of countries with the greatest economic freedom and the lowest levels of government interference in the economy. We have even slipped out of the top ten according to the 2005 issue of the Heritage Foundation/*Wall Street Journal Index of Economic Freedom*, which places us in a tie for twelfth place with Switzerland. It is significant that countries that have done the most during the last nine years to improve their scores on the index's ten measures of economic freedom have, in general, experienced the highest rates of economic growth, and the message is clear. Unless you stop our out-of-control government and get us moving in the correct direction again, your children will remember the good old days when it took some selective reporting and spin for a UN study to rank our standard of living no higher than number eight.

Dilemma: How to continue the successful operation of the "benevolent," "progressive," and "benign" socialist countries in the world once the United States completes its transition to becoming the same. At that time, the U.S. will no longer be able to respond as generously to disasters in other countries, create significant sources of new wealth to benefit everyone, or enforce the American version (conquer and set free) of Pax Romano by acting as the world's policeman. Somehow, those "successful" socialist countries will have to motivate or force their citizens to generate enough wealth so that they can assume more responsibility for these issues. One hope is that they will learn from our mistakes and do a better job than we have. Our performance certainly fell short of perfection, and our critics jumped on every single shortcoming. I am ready to sit back and do nothing but criticize their efforts for a while.

Rampant poverty in the presence of incredible wealth is not a big issue; it is huge. It is horrible that there are millions of people in the world today who live on the equivalent of less than $2 per day. Furthermore, we know the answer, and it could be argued that we have a moral obligation to help them. However, our obligation is not to perpetuate their misery by destroying ourselves but to help others implement the solution too. The solution is not to penalize the rich for their successes by dividing the assets and incomes equally because this only has the inevitable result of a somewhat equal division of poverty. The solution is to spread limited government and capitalism to the poor countries. Poor people in socialist countries are not the victims of the free enterprise in our country; they are the victims of the lack of free enterprise in their own countries. What they need is to be freed from the stifling controls that keep them poor.

After a change by any country to limited government and capitalism, the incomes of different individuals will continue to show major disparities, but this will not be an unjust distribution as the socialist Controllers maintain because some individuals will accumulate more wealth than others only because they have done something to earn it. Simultaneously, the poor will become less poor as everyone becomes wealthier. And there is no need to worry that the successes resulting from the spread of capitalism to other countries will come at our expense. Success is not a zero sum game. When the peoples of the world start enjoying the successes of capitalism, we too will get some of the benefits of the wealth they create.

With the few exceptions of some successful thieves in and out of government, the people with large incomes are the natural results of preparation, application, and the luck to live in countries with some version of a free enterprise economic system. On the other hand, the poorest 20% are predominately in countries with some form of socialism. As an aside, do we really want those forty-nine totalitarian governments in the UN with the worst track records of impoverishing their populations to vote on issues that affect our well-being? I sure as Hell don't.

Larry Page and Sergey Brin made a fortune developing Google, so they must be crooks or at least just very lucky, right? If you believe that, you probably also believe that wealth cannot be created and therefore it must be divided fairly. Well, there surely has not been an equal division of money between Page, Brin, and myself, so do I have a complaint that I was treated unfairly?

I do not know of anything they did that was illegal or immoral, and you may notice that there are some very weak points in the case for an equal division of income between Page, Brin, and myself. I was not smart enough and motivated enough to create Google, and they were. Their success did not cost me anything, and in fact, they created wealth that came to me much faster than predicted by the highly questionable "trickle-down" theory of economics. The wealth they created came to me very quickly in that their search engine made it much easier to do a large number of jobs, including the research for this book. Therefore, I certainly do not begrudge them the money they made from their innovation. In fact, I hope that the People's Republic of Washington, D.C., lets them keep enough of their profits so that many others will notice Google's success and be encouraged to try to get rich from their own ideas too—because I want the benefits that will flow down to me from those additional innovations.

You are free to disagree. If you believe that wealth cannot be created and that all of the money accumulated by one person must have come from someone else, don't let the facts confuse you. Just press ahead and document the manner in which Google's success took food off of your table and how a system closer to socialism is superior. Also, since everyone knows that Socialists care more than Capitalists about the general good, be sure to list the millions of people they have recently helped escape the tyranny of people like Adolf Hitler, Saddam Hussein, and the military leaders under Japanese Emperor Hirohito. While you are on a roll, you can explain how the success of the economic system in this country caused failures in many other parts of the world.

I am particularly interested in your thoughts about how our success harmed the citizens of those warm and fuzzy totalitarian states of the right, left, and church that are so well represented in the United Nations. Or was the damage to those people caused by their economic systems and the despots ruling those countries, contrary to the opinion of so many in this country? Leaders of both major parties have helped to install and support many of those despots, and many in this country respect them highly and seek their approval desperately. Or were those failures merely the unfortunate result of bad luck instead of bad economic and governmental systems? We certainly would not want to upset the despots of the world by making a politically incorrect statement of the unvarnished truth.

No one is asking you to ignore the natural tendency of most humans and almost all businessmen to be greedy. The question is how best to deal with the negative aspects of that greed. Controllers see none of the positive potential of natural human greed and try in vain to control the symptoms of it, thus eventually causing poverty for all. Our government has already become large enough to cause affordability problems for many in the middle class and is on the way toward causing problems for the rich. Once it becomes as "progressive" as the former Soviet Union, even Bill Gates will feel the pinch.

On the other hand, Adam Smith, author of *The Wealth of Nations* in 1776 (the same year as our Declaration of Independence), recognized and discussed the "mean rapacity" of businessmen. However, he showed how wealth could be created for all by harnessing the natural human characteristics and by using the competition inherent in the free enterprise system to control the negative aspects of human nature. Of course, we have to get the power of governments involved whenever the mean rapacity of businessmen results in activities that defeat competition or otherwise injure others. Pollution of air and water by dumping automobile exhausts and factory wastes by the cheapest manner available are examples of business activities that hurt people and that are not effectively controlled by competition, so we must get governments involved.

However, the issue of how to deal with monopolies is not as simple, and we need to pause before invoking government intervention in this area. Quite often, and especially if the company with a dominant market share has prices that are truly too high, the marketplace, by competition alone and without any government intervention, will defeat that company's attempt to create a monopoly. For example, any attempt to corner the buggy whip market would have been destroyed by the introduction of automobiles, and any monopoly on typewriters would have been destroyed by the introduction of computers. If we had gotten down to only one American automobile manufacturer, it still would have run into serious competition from newly created Asian and European automobile manufacturers. A&P, Montgomery Ward, Sears, and K-Mart have all had dominant market shares for long periods, and then they have all seen their dominance diminish dramatically due to new ideas from new competitors.

As to the so-called, "trickle-down" economics, money does trickle down to some extent, but the reality is much better than a trickle, and it goes both ways. If smart people are allowed to keep enough of what they create, they will be motivated to take risks and work hard. Then, the wealth they create will rush down, and pieces of paper with the right words and numbers on them will trickle up to the creators of that wealth. It is only after a huge number of upward trickles becomes a fortune that a creator of wealth can become one of those hated rich people who was "a crook" or "got lucky."

When Isaiah Berlin stated, "Freedom for the wolves means death for the sheep," he missed a number of points, at least to the extent, if any, that he was referring to capitalists. First, we human wolves would really prefer to be called businessmen or entrepreneurs, and some of the human sheep would probably prefer to be called something else too. Even some of the real wolves and sheep would probably take offense at being compared with humans if they had a voice. However, in spite of the protestations of the political correctness Controllers, our constitutionally guaranteed freedom of speech trumps all desires for a freedom from being offended, so let's all get over it and move on.

The main problems with applying Mr. Berlin's quotation to capitalism are (1) the failure to acknowledge the exorbitant, poverty-producing costs of maintaining a force of government shepherds, and (2) the lack of understanding of the nature of human wolves operating under free enterprise. The system ensures with its competition and rules that there will always be a pack of human wolves constantly trying to become smarter and tougher than the leader and constantly looking for ways to take the lead. Some are criminals who break the rules and rightly deserve more punishment than they usually get. However, most are simply looking for better ways to provide goods and services to the human sheep and other human wolves, thus making a profit. If the profit ever gets too high, the rest of the pack will pounce. That is, attacks on the sheep are cut short as the pack pounces on the lead wolf and takes his business away.

Remember that if all rich people are crooked, you and all other Americans must also be crooked because by the standards of the "progressive" totalitarian countries in the United Nations, all Americans are rich. However, there is one significant way in which all Americans truly are lucky. Those of us alive today had nothing to do with creating the economic and governmental systems we inherited, but we have a lot of opportunities to defend or destroy them. We also have a lot of opportunities to help the people of other countries to change their systems to those that work.

Wage and Price Controls

The best way to deal with fluctuations in wages and prices is to treat them with careful neglect, to let the marketplace deal with the problems. For example, allowing the price of whale oil to soar to "unconscionable" levels led to the utilization of kerosene, gasoline, heating oil, and other petroleum products. The result was far better for humans and whales than price controls could possibly have been. If we let the price of gasoline soar to "unconscionable" levels, something else will be developed. I do not know what it will be, but the marketplace will find it if we just back off and leave it alone. In fact, the free enterprise marketplace is the only way to find it.

All wage and price controls are futile attempts to negate the law of supply and demand, and all of these controls result in unintended and undesirable consequences. One example of these problems caused by wage controls took a few decades to mature. The wage controls imposed during World War II caused employers to look for perks other than wages to attract the best workforce possible under the circumstances. After looking at possible benefits to add, employers did not start paying any significant amounts to their employees for groceries, rent, utility bills, life insurance, or automobile insurance, but they did start adding substantial employee healthcare benefits.

Today, we are faced with an unintended consequence of that attempt by employers to recognize the market value of a good employee in spite of another futile attempt by government to control symptoms. We now have a national mindset that employers have the moral and sometimes the legal obligation to pay for healthcare. At the same time, we do not have the national mindset that employers should pay for other necessities and luxuries for their employees, and until government makes another attempt at wage control, a "right" to those additional forms of payment for work performed probably will not develop and become entrenched. The "right" to healthcare has increased the demand for medical services, and an increased demand has been one of the major factors in the increased price of healthcare.

In summary, wage controls failed to control and only contributed to a number of problems, including the creation of an entrenched entitlement. The "free" benefits led to higher usage of that particular service. Higher demand contributed to higher prices for that service. And now, proponents of big government propose to solve a problem that big government caused by repeating the process with more of the same. Duh?

Price Gouging

> *"Anyone who sells above the set prices, let him be marched off to a concentration camp."*
>
> —ADOLF HITLER

I keep thinking that Hitler must have said something correct during his lifetime, but I have never found it, and this statement of his is wrong too. Many of you fellow graduates of government monopoly schools will disagree, thinking that Hitler finally got something right and that Adam Smith's free enterprise ideas missed the point in the serious area of gouging the poor and infirm after a disaster.

Wrong! Exorbitant prices being charged by one rapacious businessman are best left to competition from other rapacious businessmen who will quickly enter such a wide-open field, increase the supply, and force down the prices. You may already realize that supply and demand set prices in a free economy, but it is also true that prices plus demand affect supply. But first, we need to establish some basics, and once again we run into the problem of labels vs. contents. The crimes of looting and deceptive trade practices, such as "bait and switch" after disasters, are not the same as unusually high prices during such periods. Also, we tend to call it a disaster when our picnic is rained out, but examples of real disasters are when hurricanes or earthquakes injure and kill people, turn children into orphans, destroy real and personal property, make travel extremely dangerous, and make it difficult to impossible for the survivors to obtain food, electricity, and water. In the areas affected by the devastation of a real disaster, there are desperate needs (high demand) coupled with a rapidly diminishing amount of goods and services (low supply).

These are the problems, and the only question is how to address them. If we allow the marketplace to respond, there will be high prices for a while, even to the extent that Controllers would describe them as "gouging," but the normal marketplace response is the lesser evil as compared to price controls. High prices not only reduce hoarding by the early customers, but far more importantly, they motivate other rapacious businessmen to make extraordinary efforts to sell their goods and services in the wide-open field. With so many greedy entrepreneurs attempting to cash in on the situation, the supply rapidly gets back to normal, and prices also come back down quickly. This speed is especially important to the poor who need the basics of life immediately and a return to a normal marketplace as quickly as possible so that they can buy what they need at the best prices possible.

On the other hand, you can operate from the insulting premises that everyone is stupid but government officials and that we all need to be protected from our own stupidity. If you use the power of government to regulate prices after a hurricane, you may get a good feeling from the knowledge that you have "done something about the problem," just like all Controllers seem to feel after they have passed yet another law in another vain attempt to control the symptoms of all of the real problems in our imperfect world. However, the devastating effects of the real disaster still exist, and there is still the problem of how to address them. The area affected is still faced with extraordinarily high demand coupled with extraordinarily low supplies. The only differences between the approaches of free enterprise vs. government control are how the few supplies will be distributed in the face of the overwhelming demand and how fast the previous level of supplies will be reestablished.

With price controls, the first ones to the store will buy all of the supplies and hoard them. The others will do without, so the Controllers have to add another control—rationing. Since prices and hoarding are only symptoms of the real problem of shortages, and since the costs of all of these efforts to control those symptoms will be charged to your credit card, you might want to review the six types of expenses you will be forced to pay for the government "solution" as discussed in the chapter "What Is Wealth?" You might also want to evaluate the effectiveness of the suggested controls on these symptoms to see if you are getting your money's worth, because there are a lot of things that you will not be able to buy with your credit line after it has been exhausted on well-meaning but counterproductive purchases.

Hoarding can be very subtle and difficult to detect and control. For example, at one set of prices, a shopper will buy one more loaf of bread and rent one of the scarce motel rooms, making it less likely that someone else will be able to buy bread or rent a room. At another set of prices, that same person will buy one less loaf of bread and stay in his damaged but livable home, leaving those items available for someone to whom they may be critical for survival.

While the Controllers are depleting your grandchildren's possibility for wealth with these extraordinary measures to control the symptoms of the problem, no one will be motivated to expend extraordinary efforts to increase the supply and get the marketplace back to normal. Controllers are good at devising tight lids for boiling pots, but they never seem to figure out how to move the pot or to turn off the stove, and their only solution for the resulting explosions are tighter lids that buy some time before they result in bigger explosions.

Consumers do not like high prices even for short periods, but we also do not like the absence of goods and services, particularly when those supplies are matters of life and death. Remember that extraordinarily high prices will reduce hoarding, save lives, and result in extraordinary efforts to add to the supply. The prices will come down quickly because the marketplace will recover quickly if allowed to do so. So, before you feed your feelings of moral superiority by criticizing the "unscrupulous profiteers who take advantage" of the unfortunate victims of real disasters, tell me how many times you have stopped your normal operations, loaded your pickup truck with life-saving merchandise, and driven in the dark and rain across downed electric wires and around washed-out sections of roadway to sell that merchandise to those victims at prices set by the Controllers.

Am I saying that price gouging after a disaster is desirable? Of course not! I am saying that disasters are much worse than a rained-out picnic. Real disasters are horrible, and high prices for the scarce supplies are a facet of the devastation. However, gouging is a lesser evil than allowing Controllers to disrupt the process of recovery and to cause even more suffering and deaths. Their only proposal is to attempt to control the symptoms of the real but temporary problem of extraordinary scarcity by trying to eliminate the law of supply and demand. The fictitious Don Quixote was a delightful, idealistic eccentric who did no harm and even some good, but the real-life modern-day well-meaning idealists cause major suffering for you and yours. When they strap on their rusty armor and start tilting at windmills, they hurt you, because as the Southernism claims, "What goes down in the well comes up in the bucket."

To summarize, we know that:

- Supply and demand set prices in a free economy.
- And I just gave examples of how prices plus demand affect supply.
- In turn, this effect on supply satisfies demand.
- And this satisfaction of demand affects prices.
- But there are still other causes and effects. For example, the combination of supply and prices affects demand as when ample supply and low prices encourage waste and excess consumption. Also, merely a consensus of opinion about future supply affects prices, such as when releasing oil from the Strategic Oil Reserve fails to reduce gasoline prices at the pump to any significant extent if the marketplace perceives that such a solution to an inadequate supply will be only temporary.

The interactions of supply, demand, and prices are extremely complicated, and the "dog-eat-dog" marketplace has proven itself to be much more efficient in breaking down all of the issues into manageable parts than government Controllers have. Adam Smith's free enterprise system of competing greedy businessmen is the absolute best method ever formulated to supply our needs and allocate our limited resources among their various potential uses. Mr. Smith's principles apply in good times and are especially needed in the bad times.

Incidentally, do you believe that it is gouging for an especially talented musician to charge what the market will bear for his performances? There is only one of him, and he is in high demand, so his free market price will be high. How about that movie star? The football star? And now for the tough one, so try to be consistent. What about the CEO of that big corporation that we hate so much? It is just too bad that businessmen have not been exempted from "truth in advertising" laws like the politicians. We would like CEOs and their corporations a lot more if they too could make us false promises of Utopia instead of just providing us jobs, goods, and services.

Control over pricing in any area, including salaries for CEOs, is just not an area for effective government intervention, especially during a disaster. This is mainly due to the limitations of any government, which can only try to control the symptoms of the real problems. It is also partially due to the fact that the people who would create and administer the government programs would be those among us whose levels of aptitude for creative problem solving qualify them to be politicians and bureaucrats. Those who are bright, creative, and caring are stymied by all of the bureaucratic regulations, or they leave big government for other jobs where they can use their talents to the fullest. We need them to venture from their field of expertise and "solve" our economic problems about as much as fish need chain saws and chewing tobacco.

Regulatory Agencies

Once a law is passed by the Legislative Branch, it must be administered by one of the regulatory agencies of the Executive Branch. This costs huge amounts of money and takes time away from the creation of wealth. Therefore, a new law should be the last option to be considered in dealing with a problem instead of being the knee-jerk first response because, as Jesus of Nazareth said, "a bad tree cannot produce good fruit."

For those well-meaning Controllers who think that laws are the magic solution to make problems disappear, I remind them that it is never possible to meet every possible need, and various economic systems merely use various approaches that try to do the best we can with what we have. All systems require us to deal with limited resources and alternative possibilities. Every benefit has a cost, and all of life is a series of tradeoffs.

I also recommend the book *Out of Bounds, Out of Control: Regulatory Enforcement at the EPA*. In his book, James V. DeLong conclusively documents one prime example of how laws designed to control complicated problems quickly become a severe drain on our nation's wealth. After passing any new law, the first step of the big government "solution" for any problem is the expansion of old agencies or the creation of new agencies to address it. According to Mr. DeLong, the Environmental Protection Agency (EPA) had, as of 2003, 18,000 employees and a budget of $8,100,000,000. To restate these facts, 18,000 people were not creating wealth and instead were reducing by $8,100,000,000 the amount that producers have available to buy the goods and services that are somehow being created and produced by them. And this is only one agency! The "solution" is quite expensive. Are you getting your money's worth?

But calculating the costs has just started. The next step for these thousands of employees is to write extremely complex regulations on enormous amounts of paper (from trees that were part of the EPA's area of influence, i.e., our environment). The complexity of these regulations requires the millions of businesses under the EPA's control to hire attorneys, engineers, and other experts to attempt to interpret them, another huge expense for this "solution." And I do mean attempt to interpret, because the EPA's volumes of regulations create enormous difficulties for making good faith attempts at compliance. With all of the ambiguities and contradictions, technical violations are guaranteed to occur.

As Adam Smith observed, no individual corporation or corporate leader can be entrusted with any aspect of the public welfare. He did, however, point out that the free enterprise system of competing rapacious businessmen can be entrusted with many aspects of public welfare due to the competition inherent in the system. One area that is not protected by competition is our environment, and the EPA is therefore one of our most needed agencies of government control. Because of that, it is not the best example of how good intentions are just not sufficient to overcome the inherent problems of a system based on control. However, it is an excellent example of how good ideas once given to bureaucracies will tend, automatically, to be expanded to their ridiculous and often counterproductive extremes and also of how the inherent inefficiencies of bureaucracies mean that we pay a huge price for the benefits we get. We cannot afford to pay the same huge prices for controls in other areas that could be substantially controlled by competition, such as prices. And we absolutely do not need to pay the same huge prices for controls in other areas that create more problems than they solve, such as over-restrictive zoning laws that simply increase the cost of housing and move congestion from the cities to the highways. I surely do not want politicians and bureaucrats making decisions about any aspect of *my* healthcare. Laws attempting to control symptoms of problems unfortunately result in more problems, extreme costs, a new set of victims, and thousands of people employed in ways other than in the creation of wealth, the wealth your grandchildren will need but that will not exist.

By the way, monopolies also create problems for us as they stifle both competition and ingenuity, and the next regulatory enforcement action we really need is for the trust busters in the Federal Trade Commission to eliminate the government's virtual monopoly on schools. But that is just a fantasy; the Executive Branch of our government is not organized in such a way as to control its own growth. We are going to have to accomplish that result a different way. As discussed in more detail elsewhere in the book, I strongly believe that we should abolish the entire Department of Education and give control over educational decisions to the consumers of the product by issuing education vouchers to the students or their parents.

Minimum Wage Laws Hurt You

> *"The real minimum on wages is zero."*
>
> —THOMAS SOWELL

The first step is for enough well-meaning Controllers to notice a situation and to apply enough pressure on legislators to "do something about it." Then the legislators, recognizing that their jobs can be lost at the next election, set an artificial minimum on wages so that "greedy" employers will be forced to pay all workers living wages that allow them to support families of four or whatever. Then, due to the artificially high wage level, employers buy as many machines as possible, hire as few people as possible, and attempt to hire the best workers they can find at the price they have to pay. The young, uneducated, and unskilled (usually without a family of four to support at age 18–22) remain unemployed and collect wages at the real minimum of zero per hour. Being unemployed, they also are unable to obtain job experience and skills to advance into higher-paying jobs as they get older. As they age, they gradually become unemployable. Realizing they are being permanently shut out of the job market, at some point they resort to various forms of crime. We then fail to connect the causes and the effects and complain about those worthless people who won't get a job (usually focusing on a minority group).

While the politician gets reelected for his courageous compassion in controlling wages, we pay in numerous ways for another futile attempt to negate the law of supply and demand. We suffer due to the crimes that result, and pay police, prosecutors, judges, and jailers to control the symptoms of our stupidity. But worst of all, the unfortunate teenagers caught in the system have their entire lives destroyed as attempts to control one symptom of a problem only contribute to additional symptoms and additional problems.

Can we solve the problem of street crime by eliminating minimum wage laws? Of course not. However, these well-meaning laws are one of the underlying causes of street crime and need to be eliminated as we continue to look for other causes and other solutions. We can stop causing so many unintended disastrous consequences if we only stop "caring" so much that we keep trying to rescind the law of supply and demand. And if so many of us were not relegated to the substandard education and political correctness guidelines provided by our government monopoly schools, more of us would focus on how we could best capitalize on the true worth of our time, talents, and intellects and be less concerned about the current minimum starting wage.

Compassionate Conservatives

> *"Compassion is the use of public funds to buy votes."*
>
> —THOMAS SOWELL

Many fiscal conservatives are on the defensive. As a result, you will often hear a politician say that he or she is a compassionate conservative. What that means is that they want your vote and know that you, being fellow products of government monopoly schools, truly believe the lie that socialist Controllers care more for the poor than the free enterprise Persuaders do. They know that the liberal news media is a formidable force and that it will be extremely difficult to persuade you as to just how wrong your opinion is. Therefore, they have conceded the validity of the false belief that socialists are more compassionate than believers in freedom, and they have agreed to approach the "ideal." To show this compassion, do they open their wallets? No, they point the government's big guns at your head and force you to open your wallets whether you want to support their program or to do something else.

Just how compassionate is it to make conditions in our country closer to those in Cuba, Iran, or any other country you can name that has serious "big government" controls? Are the poor better off in Mexico or North Korea than they are here? Of course not, and there is a reason, a controlling government of the left, right, or church. If you are interested in making sure that your grandchildren do not become as poor as the poorest in a South American dictatorship, organize and vote for less control and more freedom right here and right now. Also, remember that our Constitution mandates a limited government, and you can also sue to remove many of the controls since they are unconstitutional.

However, you will hear some politicians at every election stating that they care for you in spite of being a member of the group that "everyone" knows is the epitome of callousness—the fiscal conservatives. The truth is that the compassionate conservatives, along with those who are unequivocal about being fiscally liberal, only care enough for your vote to destroy the wealth of your country and make everyone poorer. Their programs will make all of us poor regardless of whether the definition of poverty is established by local advocates of big government or by the inmates of the poorest totalitarian country in the UN.

> *"The inherent vice of capitalism is the uneven division of blessings, while the inherent virtue of socialism is the equal division of misery."*
>
> —WINSTON CHURCHILL

In spite of the fact that those at the top of a socialistic society are "more equal than others," there is a lot of truth in Mr. Churchill's observation. However, do not make the mistake of believing that he meant that wealth is something out there that capitalism divides one way and socialism divides another way. He was fully aware that wealth is something that individuals have to create by clear thinking and hard work. Capitalism merely provides people the incentive to do so while socialism only causes people to pretend to work while the system pretends to pay them in return. Churchill was saying that one system, capitalism, with one set of incentives has one net result, an uneven division of blessings. At the same time, a different system, socialism, with a different set of incentives has a different net result, a division of misery that is roughly equal except for a few at the very top.

Controllers truly believe that "the rich keep getting richer and the poor keep getting poorer." It is a catchy phrase with some elements of truth in it, but it also contains a lot of fallacies.

The only rich people who keep getting richer are those who continue to live in a free enterprise system and who keep doing the smart things that created their fortunes in the first place. How many wealthy Rothchilds or Medicis alive today can you name? There are innumerable examples of families going "from rags to riches to rags in three generations," and the same can happen to our entire country too. It has happened to other countries, and we are not immune to an attack of terminal stupidity.

As for the poor in the United States, there are a number of different situations for different poor individuals:

- Some of the poor are truly and permanently unfortunate.
- Some are truly but temporarily unfortunate.
- Some are young or recent immigrants and have not yet reached their potential.
- Some are old and past their primes or retired.
- Some are between jobs.
- Some keep doing the stupid things that cause poverty.
- Some prefer to live off of the dole instead of doing the work that millions of immigrants risk their lives to come here to do.
- All are helped somewhat by the current system whereby the government provides them with various forms of assistance and puts the expenses on your tab.
- All are also hurt substantially by the current system that consumes so much of the available money and charitable impulses of Americans and produces so few benefits. This system ignores the causes of poverty, does not create solutions to the underlying problems, and merely attempts to control the symptoms.
- All are helped by the increasing level of wealth that is created by those motivated to become rich and that keeps flowing down to them in spite of all that the Controllers do to impede progress with well-meaning but counterproductive measures.

Do my proposals (really those of Adam Smith and the authors of our Constitution) support big corporations and the wealthy? You're damned right they do—just as much as they support small businesses and those who want to become wealthy. These proposals support those who have money just as much as it does those who need a sufficient money base to provide contributions for their own support or in order to help others. Isn't it the pits that no one has devised a system that can help the poor without also helping those rich people we envy so much? That's just not fair, and none of our controls ever succeed in making it fair.

As to the poor in other countries, the vast majority are truly and permanently unfortunate because they live in countries with disastrous economic systems, that is, every system other than capitalism. I want our country to remain rich and powerful, and I want the people in other countries to become the same. Once those people taste the fruits of economic freedom, we will all benefit from the wealth they create, and they will be far less likely to want to kill us.

It Can't Happen Here?

There are many who think we can make unlimited adjustments to a successful system without any repercussions. They believe that corrupt dictatorships can flourish only somewhere else and that widespread poverty occurs only in other countries.

Like Hell it can't happen here! Just as individuals can go "from rags to riches to rags in three generations," our entire nation can do the same. Success is not hereditary. Republicans can list the corrupt Democrats who got into office and abused their power, and Democrats can make a similar list of Republicans. Sometimes, we used the system to vote or impeach them out of office, and sometimes we endured the abuses, but it does happen here, and it can get much worse. The only barriers between us and the development of an abusive government are the written documents establishing our system and our vigilance in defending those pieces of paper.

Likewise, you can point to the super-rich like Bill Gates and Warren Buffett and maintain that our country's economy is bulletproof, but widespread poverty can also happen here. The only barriers between us and poverty are our free enterprise economic system and our vigilance in defending it. There are far more similarities than differences between the *potential* of the United States and the former Soviet Union. Both countries have or had intelligent people, a large territory, and ample natural resources. The main differences between the two countries were the form of government, the economic system, and the results. Those were also the main differences between capitalistic (consumer-oriented) West Berlin and government-controlled (bureaucrat-oriented) East Berlin, where even the people and their language were the same on both sides of the infamous wall.

I am not talking about pure laissez-faire free enterprise. Some people in every walk of life truly are evil, and the automatic controls of competition go only so far, so we need laws, police, and prosecutors for both business and government criminals. However, free enterprise has proven that it can create wealth for all of us, and we need to let it continue to reward those who use the system to create the wealth we enjoy.

No, the wealth is not divided immediately or equally, but everyone gets a chance for a big share and everyone does get a share. That is much better than allowing the Controllers to kill the system just so we can pretend to divide the poverty equally. That's right; socialism only pretends to be fair. It is a failure even in the restatement of its intention of spreading the poverty evenly because there are always leaders who find ways to profit from the desperate situation that the masses are forced to endure under the corrupt system. As George Orwell observed, some people in totalitarian states are "more equal than others."

You may say that most of us are doing quite well here in spite of the fact that the official definition of poverty has been manipulated and contrived to indicate otherwise. Why would "they" do that? Simple! Since poverty has been defined so that it appears there is a poverty "crisis," there is an "obvious" need for a government solution, the "best" of all solutions. To the contrary, Neal Boortz recently quoted some statistics showing that the average poor person in the U.S. has an income equal to the average average person in Europe and that we spend as much on waveriders here as the gross national product of North Korea. My point is that things can get much worse, and we can have a real poverty crisis if we continue to meddle with the Constitution and the free enterprise system that combined to cause it all to happen. We need to follow the sound advice of the old Southernism and remember to "Dance with who brung you."

Part II

Big Government vs. Freedom

Revolutions

Every four years, we go somewhat crazy in America at election time. Tempers flare as each side accuses the other side of lying and worse. We have arguments, demonstrations, riots, fistfights, arrests, injuries, and even some homicides. Sounds pretty bad, doesn't it? Well, it is downright ugly until compared with the alternatives. What we do is to have regularly scheduled revolutions, and all revolutions are ugly. The good news is that in this country, we are not dominated for decades by a dictator, the bloodshed during our election process is minimal, and at some point a winner and a loser have been chosen and all of the emotions have been spent. At that time, most of us accept the reality of the SOB that won and settle down to live peacefully until time for our next revolution four years later.

What we do not need is exactly what we have now—a law limiting political speech. We have not only passed such a law, but it has been approved by our Supreme Court Justices who have forgotten or ignored their oaths to protect our Constitution. The law, called the Bipartisan Campaign Reform Act of 2002, states that it is too messy for you to decide what you want to say about candidates for political office. Therefore, there is now a lid on your freedom to express your beliefs and emotions. Before you buy an ad to express your political thoughts, you now need to retain an attorney to guide you through the maze of regulations. If you think our elections are messy now, just keep that lid on the pressure cooker, watch the heat rise, and try not to be near the epicenter when the inevitable explosion results. Believe me, an explosion is inevitable from this reduction in status of another right to a mere privilege that can be licensed and controlled by the Imperial Government of the United States of America.

However, what we do need is to enforce the constitutional limitations on the functions of our government. Both Republicans and Democrats have noticed the increasing divisiveness in our country, and both sides blame the other for it. The true cause of this real problem is that more and more of the things that people want are available only from the government, and anything that I get from that source means that there are fewer resources available to meet your needs. Consequently, we end up fighting in the political arena over those limited resources instead of competing in the marketplace for our respective choices from a long list of options provided by the marketplace. If we continue to reduce the limitations on government, our "revolutions" will continue to get nastier and at some point could become a real revolution with some serious shedding of blood.

Rights vs. Privileges

> *"Human rights are not a privilege conferred by government. They are every human being's entitlement by virtue of his humanity. The right to life does not depend, and must not be contingent, on the pleasure of anyone else, not even a parent or sovereign.... You must weep that your own government, at present, seems blind to this truth."*
>
> —MOTHER TERESA

On 23 January 2004, President Bush signed into law a bill to protect the right of Amish teenagers to pursue opportunities in woodworking, supervised by their parents and without the intrusion of the Federal Government. There is something wrong here. What made it necessary for the Amish to get a law passed just so that they could raise their children? Unless there were allegations and proof of some form of child abuse, by what right did an unknown government Controller decide that he knew best how to raise these children and was denying this group of parents the right to teach their children their approach to woodworking?

The problem is based in a contrived distinction between rights and privileges, and the unknown Controller who first developed that distinction had a stroke of evil genius. The Constitution creates a serious problem for Controllers as it is very specific about rights, which are either granted to the government or prohibited to the people. Otherwise, they are retained by the states or the people. Privileges are not mentioned in the Constitution, and no distinction is made between rights and privileges.

Nevertheless, the concept of privileges somehow took root, and we now hear constantly that certain activities we would like to engage in are not rights; they are only privileges. In addition to Amish parents whose right to raise their children had somehow been reduced to a mere privilege, other examples are legion. Over a recent two-week period, I heard an Alabama judge and a number of participants n talk shows say that the various activities being discussed at the time were mere privileges and not rights. Why would they and so many others support such a distinction and ignore the Creator-given rights our Constitution guaranteed? The question answers itself. It is to circumvent the Constitution and impose unlawful control, because "government officials are much wiser than you or I." If something can successfully be called a privilege, it can be licensed and controlled in spite of the clarity of the Ninth Amendment: "The enumeration in the Constitution, of certain rights, shall not be construed to deny or disparage others retained by the people." For example, there is a law in Georgia taxing the "privilege" of selling property. That is, we have allowed our right to own property to be reduced to a government-controlled privilege when we attempt to sell some of that property. If that is not a disparagement of a right retained by the people, I obviously do not know what the word "disparage" means.

My right to earn a living as a real estate broker has become a highly regulated and licensed privilege by this artificially contrived distinction without any constitutional amendment allowing the Controllers to disparage and reduce my rights. Writing this book is one of the few business activities available to me that still retains its full status as a right.

For a more controversial example, there is no constitutional prohibition against individuals owning guns. To the contrary, the authors of that document restrained the power of our government repeatedly, using the words "no" and "not" 46 times in the first seven articles and the first ten amendments, and all powers not given to the federal government were expressly denied to it. Since our government was not given the power to deny the private ownership of guns, and until we pass a constitutional amendment to the contrary, the government simply does not have that power, regardless of how we and our representatives have voted or for how long. Gun ownership is a right, and there is no such thing as a privilege, at least not under our form of government. However, we have allowed our right to bear arms to become a privilege whenever we want to carry one somewhere, and our right to own modern guns is limited to whatever someone else decides is "reasonable" or what they think we should "need" within the context of limited activities such as hunting.

As an aside, why is it that major suspects in crime investigations are called "suspects" whereas preliminary and minor suspects are called "persons of interest"? Is there any real difference in the contents being described by these different labels? Could it possibly be that all suspects have rights that make life more difficult for Controllers when trying to investigate crimes? Is it just easier for the police to avoid dealing with those rights by changing the verbiage in such a way that disparages those rights? How long does it take for the police to finally state that a certain suspect is a suspect and no longer just a person of interest, and at what point will all suspects carry the label of just a person of interest until the investigation is complete and it is time to get an arrest warrant? Believe me, Controllers are constantly looking for loopholes in the Constitution, and they are far more adept at finding them than the best criminals are at finding loopholes in other laws that they want to break. As we go to press, I just heard a news report saying that a "person of interest" in a crime has posted bail to get out of police custody (i.e., jail). Well, I guess that is okay. He might be guilty, and there is no need to call him a suspect with rights just because our Founders risked their lives committing treason against King George III to provide us all with legal red tape. It is so much less troublesome just to change this person's label than to deal with his rights.

There is no valid reason to defend the fallacious distinctions between rights vs. privileges and suspect vs. person of interest because no right has a lifetime unconditional guarantee. Every right carries a long list of responsibilities with it, and it is clear that anyone can lose the rights guaranteed by the Constitution under certain circumstances. For example, my right to swing my fist stops when I get too close to your nose, and anyone can lose his rights to liberty, the pursuit of happiness, and even to life if he murders someone. Likewise, the freedom to move freely around the country is a right that can be lost by doing so in a way that harms others. So how did the Controllers get away with disparaging your right to freedom of movement and convince you that this right to freedom of movement by the currently available means of transportation includes walking and a horse-drawn wagon but does not include an automobile? Why did you let the use of an automobile become a privilege that can be denied? Why does it not have the status of a right just because technology has replaced buggies with automobiles? As I said, the unknown Controller who first developed the fictitious distinction between rights and privileges had a stroke of evil genius.

Since we have allowed such a contrived distinction to exist, we now have to contend with those who get to decide which activity is which. Since we seem to be conceding that all power is owned by the government, it can decide just what activities it will let us engage in and even whittle down those few rights that were specifically guaranteed in the Bill of Rights. Today, almost all of us accept the premise that government in most instances has all of the power to decide what activities it will allow us and what prerequisites, forms, and fees will be required for the "privilege" to do so.

"The state has the right to regulate licenses of all kinds," asserts Bill O'Reilly. So, now all we have is the opportunity to apply for the licenses and to pay whatever they demand for these privileges. I recently bought a car in Georgia and was forced to register the title in Alabama to obtain a license to drive it here. Since the Controllers in Georgia have devised a different set of rules from those devised by the Controllers in Alabama, it took me three trips to the courthouse, two letters, numerous telephone calls, and about nine hours of my life to establish my "privilege" to drive that car. One problem was that a document typed in Georgia needed to be handwritten in Alabama. Read that again. The Alabama Controllers insisted that the document be handwritten (so it would be less legible?) instead of typed and therefore easy to read.

Everyone has a different set of unpleasant experiences with government "red tape," but everyone has to deal with it. After multiplying my nine hours by millions of American citizens, you will have to explain to me how the ends (law and order) justify the means (control) that steal such significant portions of our lives. I am just too dense to grasp why that time could not be much better spent playing golf or creating and producing goods and services, also known as wealth. We, our grandchildren, and the poor of today and tomorrow need that wealth that the Controllers are destroying every day with zero accountability.

> *"Between depriving a man of one hour from his life and depriving him of his life there exists only a difference of degree. You have done violence to him, consumed his energy."*
>
> —FRANK HERBERT

As Neal Boortz has said, Americans wave the flag and enjoy a day off on the Fourth of July, but most of us do not realize that we are not truly free and do not even want to be free. How many American products of our government monopoly schools want the freedom and the responsibility to save for our own retirements, choose the schools for our own children, arrange for our own healthcare, etc.? About the only freedom we want is freedom from responsibility. We want security and are willing to give up freedom to the Controllers to get it. We even send our periodic payments to the Socialism Security Ponzi Scheme willingly, just to avoid the freedom to save for our retirements and the responsibility that comes with it.

When will you desire freedom enough to demand with your votes and lawsuits that our leaders revert to the premise upon which this country was founded? This was a limited government in which the people decide what privileges we will let the government exercise and what licenses we will require of our government officials, not the other way around. When will you demand with your votes and lawsuits that all powers not given to the federal government or prohibited to the people remain with the states or the people as their rights and not as mere government-controlled privileges? When will you get the guts to take responsibility for your life and get back to the activities that create wealth?

When will you give a damn?

Labels vs. Contents

> *"The beginning of wisdom is to call things by their right names."*
>
> —CHINESE PROVERB

Why did I title my book as I did instead of bestowing on it something with more zip such as, *How to Marry Rich in Two Days*? Well, even if the other title were available, it certainly would not fit the contents of my book. My thoughts will not help anyone marry rich, win the lottery, get a good job, or acquire emotional or spiritual riches. This book addresses different aspects of wealth, namely how our Constitution and Adam Smith's observations on free enterprise have made it possible for us to create wealth and how we always experience a disastrous destruction of wealth whenever we let the right-wing and left-wing control freaks take over our government.

But, does it matter that the label matches the contents? And, which is more important, the label or the contents? If the label on my book were misleading about its contents, would that be a lie, and if so, so what? Well, I am one of those old-timers who have the quaint beliefs that labels are important and that they should match the contents.

One of the subtle problems resulting from mislabeling occurs when people start to believe that the false label accurately describes something. For example, we now hear people question why we have an electoral college since we have a democracy. The truth is that we have an electoral college because our Founders wanted to prevent us from having a democracy. We have gotten so used to calling our republic a democracy that we are constantly having difficulties making reality fit fallacious theories.

So, what do you think? If a corporation advertises a mixture of sugar and fat as a health food, do you care? If Republicans and Democrats join together to create a government chain letter and label it Social Security, is the label more important than the contents? If our elected officials deliberately remove all funds from the Social Security Trust Fund, is it a fund or is it fraud? If representatives and senators entitle a law "The Jobs and Tax Relief Act of Whatever Year You Chose" and fill it with welfare provisions for non-taxpayers, is that a lie, and if so, is that of any significance? If newspersons disguise an editorial and present it as news in a publication or television program, is that important? If legislators led by McCain and Feingold entitle a bill the "Bipartisan Campaign Reform Act of 2002," does it matter that a more nearly correct title would be "An Act to Rescind Freedom of Political Speech during Certain Periods for All but a

Privileged Few without Going to the Trouble to Amend the Constitution"?

Just try to be consistent with your answers. I happen to believe that there should be truth in advertising both for corporations and for government officials. I believe that character counts for both Republican and Democratic elected officials and especially for my fellow Libertarians. I believe that labels should not lie about the contents of books, food, and laws. And yes, in this case, I believe that "there ought to be a law" in those instances where fraud is being committed, because fraud hurts other people. Activities that hurt others are correctly considered criminal and are valid concerns for government. The checks and balances of competition need some support in this area from the criminal prosecutors.

Corporations never profess to care about us, but they produce valuable goods and services and pay us money when we work for them. That is, they create wealth and provide us with the capacity to enjoy some of it. Government says that it cares about us, but it places unreasonable controls over us, and it confiscates our money and squanders it. That is, it takes away the freedom we think we have and reduces our share of the wealth being created. So, why is it that so many people hate corporations and love government? How can so many people notice every dishonest person and every bad policy associated with corporations and fail to notice the same problems when they are much worse but it is "only" government that is involved? The government's "I CARE" label must be more important than its destructive contents to these people, but it is not to anyone who stops to think about the issue.

By the way, if you had purchased your share of our current government on eBay, what rating would you have given the seller after the transaction? What rating would you have given for honesty? For performance of the product sold to you? For value received at the huge price you paid? Does the label "Land of the Free" still match reality?

A Duck by Any Other Name…

"If it looks like a duck, quacks like a duck, swims like a duck, and waddles like a duck, it's a duck."

—UNKNOWN BUT USED BY THE IRS TO BLOCK ATTEMPTS OF TAXPAYERS TO FIND LOOPHOLES WHERE NONE EXIST

When discussing the various forms of totalitarian states, we once again have problems with the labels "Liberal" and "Conservative." In spite of all of the cheap shots in the media and movies referring to Nazis, fascists, dictators, shahs, and czarists as right-wingers, I consider myself to be a right-winger on economic issues and resent my label being attributed to some of the most despicable individuals and organizations in history like Hitler and Mussolini. At the same time, I consider myself to be liberal on many human rights issues and also resent my part-time label as a left-winger being attributed at times to Sandinistas, communists, and socialists including Stalin and Castro.

It just does not matter whether a totalitarian government is dominated by Controllers of the right, the left, or a church; some of them are worse than others, but none of them can be characterized as warm and fuzzy. Some Controllers have named their government and economic systems communism, socialism, fascism, and various religious states such as the Islamic Republic of Iran. You can call it family values, the New Deal, the Great Society, fairness, caring, or any other name you want. To various degrees, they are all versions of the same totalitarian concept that has failed to cause their citizens to be free, happy, or wealthy regardless of whatever name it has been called.

The leaders of these groups are chosen or choose themselves in different ways, and some adopt especially evil projects like trying to eradicate all intelligentsia, mental defectives, Jews, Slavs, Gypsies, "witches," homosexuals, Tutsis, Christians, Muslims, atheists, etc. But they all abuse their power, and major distinctions get hard to find between these various types of Controllers. The battles between the various groups are primarily turf wars with each group wanting to be the one to profit from the power, control, extortion, and, in the most extreme versions, torture and murder. With all of them, the peasants belong to the state while the Persuaders want the state to belong to the people.

> *"If Stalin is on the left, and Mussolini on the right, whom do you feel closer to?"*
>
> —JON CARRIEL

"You cannot make a silk purse out of a sow's ear." A bad idea by any name is still a bad idea, and totalitarianism is a bad idea. So how much force and control should we allow our government to exercise? Almost everyone agrees that some people are criminal and that we have to give the government some powers of control over us. However, the debate is endless as to just how many of us are evil, how best to respond to those who are, and just how much control should the government have.

Controllers say that most of us are stupid and/or evil and need to be guided and controlled by government. Since the employees of government are drawn from the same pool of "stupid and evil" people as the rest of us, it has never been explained to my satisfaction exactly how they become worthy of controlling the rest of us to the extent currently advocated by our local Republican and Democratic proponents of "reasonable" totalitarianism, the Controllers.

However, if you are a Controller, you have a clear choice for president whenever she runs, Hillary Clinton. Following (or leading?) the political philosophy of her husband, she proposes to control the people of this country until we finally get it right.

> *"When personal freedom's being abused, you have to move to limit it."*
>
> —BILL CLINTON

For example, she noticed that the incredible innovations in the medical field have outpaced the ability of the public to pay for them. Since there are problems, and Controllers like Senator Clinton believe that government force and control is the only answer to any problem, she took a shot at socializing the entire medical industry. With enough support from the products of government monopoly schools, she will also get the opportunity to socialize all other businesses so that we can find out if our current problems will cease to exist under the "benevolent" control of a super-government. If she succeeds, the plan will be something like this:

- Something is desirable, but it costs more money than individuals want to pay for it.
- We will force everyone to send money to the government.
- The government will hire people to collect and mismanage the money. They will dissipate a substantial portion of the fund and will not be creating wealth while spending their time doing this.
- From the remaining pool of money, the government will buy the something and deliver it to the individuals wanting it.

That is, some believe that something we cannot afford will magically become affordable by first throwing away some of our money. Or, is it much worse than stupidity? Is it that a huge number of people have found out that they can use the ballot box to steal what they want from others so they don't care how much is wasted in the process?

What is Hillary's appeal? One of her major appeals is that she has convinced many voters that "she cares." I submit that she cares enough to buy our votes with our own money, promising to make our country closer to the "ideal" socialistic state like Cuba attempts to be. But was the controlling dictator Batista any better or worse for Cuba that the controlling communist Castro? Was the Shah any better or worse for Iran than the Allatolah? Were the Sandinistas any better or worse than the Contras in Nicaragua? No, there is absolutely no substantive difference in any of these different brands of despotism.

And will the controlling Senator Clinton be any worse for our country if she should become president than her opposition whenever she runs? Who knows? I am going to vote against her every chance I get, but voting for her Republican opposition is somewhat like saying that I prefer to have one hand cut off rather than to have both of my eyes poked out. Republican President Richard Nixon and Republican Governor Jeb Bush instituted price controls (but only because there was a "crisis," and every Controller knows that Government is the only answer to a crisis). Republican President Bush the Younger, in an apparent attempt to out-pander even the most socialistic of Democrats, expanded the cost of our already overblown government faster than Democrat President Bill Clinton. The current Republican Party has some potential candidates at all levels who are only slightly less controlling than Senator Clinton in fiscal matters, and they can get serious about having the government control your sex life and your religious life.

In the 2004 election, both the Democrat and the Republican candidate for president sought the support of Senator John McCain, who co-authored the bill to limit freedom of speech in the political area (Bipartisan Campaign Reform Act of 2002). The theory is that rich people can use their money to dominate an election, so the Controllers of both parties tried to put a lid on that ability. Then, when heated allegations started flying, both of these candidates denounced the exercise of free speech by "ordinary citizens" (sometimes now called 527 Organizations). Both of these presidential candidates stated in effect that you are too stupid to listen to all sides and make an intelligent decision.

So, just how were "we, the people" supposed to choose a president in 2004 who would honor the pledge that he would be required to make to defend the Constitution of the United States? How were we supposed to choose a president in 2004 whom we could reasonably expect to appoint judges and Supreme Court Justices who would honor the pledge they too would be required to make to defend the Constitution of the

United States? Both candidates for president had already proved themselves totally unworthy by refusing during the campaigns to denounce the McCain-Feingold Bill to turn our right to free speech into a mere privilege without any amendment to the Constitution. They both had failed to honor their pledges to defend this constitutional right, which at last glance had still not been completely erased from the First, Ninth, and Tenth Amendments.

How did the prohibition of certain campaign spending (a form of political speech) work during the presidential election of 2004? Anyone wanting to use any of the media to state his positions to large numbers of potential voters first had to hire a lawyer to guide him through the maze of exceptions to his freedom of speech, and only then were Democrats and Republicans both able to spend vast sums of money from small to large contributors using various organizations. However, the large number of small- to medium-sized donations made by numerous people financing the ads of the Swift Boat Vets against Senator Kerry apparently had far more impact on the outcome than the huge donations from the super-wealthy George Soros to finance the ads by MoveOn.org against President Bush. After the voters had listened to both sides under conditions of disparaged, reduced, modified, and damaged free speech, more than 50% concluded that President Bush was the better choice for Commander-in-Chief. In time, we will find out whether his policies will be effective in defending our country, but we already know that he will not honor his oath to defend the Constitution; he even signed one of the bills attacking it.

If anyone had a complaint about money driving the result of an election, it should be Libertarians, as we made such a weak presentation of our message that we could not get many donations from the super-rich or anyone else. Nevertheless, I for one still believe in the freedom of speech that is mandated in our Constitution. Until you can show me where this freedom was legally reduced to a mere privilege, I will continue to disagree vehemently with the McCain-Feingold Law, which rescinds that freedom without a constitutional amendment. I will also continue to disagree vehemently with any other law attempting to limit our rights that are under siege by those who have learned that most of these rights can be destroyed by the simple method of applying a new label. Once we accept that they are only privileges, we will lose them because the Founders of our country did not anticipate and negate such a diabolical attack on the rights that they had sacrificed so much to secure.

So, even though none of our Democrats or Republicans has become as tyrannical as the despots in many of the other countries in the world, we still have a question to face. Just what brand of totalitarian control are you willing to endure, the Democratic version or the Republican version? George Wallace said, "There's not a dime's worth of difference between the Republicans and the Democrats," and William Shakespeare suggested, "A pox on both your houses." I do not know anything about poxes, curses, or voodoo, but I do understand cause and effect. If you continue to support the big government of controlling and wasteful Republicans and Democrats, you and yours might as well be poxed, cursed, and voodooed. Effects always follow causes, and big government always leads directly to poverty for all as soon as the government gets big enough. Ours is well on the way, so when are you going to reject both of these parties and stand up to defend the freedoms that were handed to you? When are you going to stop being afraid of the responsibility that freedom places on you? When are you going to stop the Controllers of both major parties from destroying the system that would increase the wealth of your grandchildren? If Controllers stay in power, it is your fault, because you put them there, but you can remove them at any election you choose, and you can sue in a federal court the very next time they violate the Constitution.

Not a Democracy

Just what form of government do we have? Well, if I were a Republican, I would be tempted to go to the federal courthouse every second November, right after the polls close and sue to have the elections of all Democrats reversed, because it says very clearly in Article IV of the Constitution, "The United States shall guarantee to every state in this Union a republican form of government..."

> *"The trouble with most folks isn't so much their ignorance, as knowing so many things that ain't so."*
>
> —JOSH BILLINGS

> *"The merit of our Constitution was not that it promotes democracy, but checks it."*
>
> —HORATIO SEYMOUR

> *"Hold on, my friends, to the Constitution and to the Republic for which it stands."*
>
> —DANIEL WEBSTER

As you know, a group of traitors in the American colonies started a rebellion in 1776 that we celebrate every year. Well, instead of going back to work the next day after some barbecue and fireworks, they were busy for the next six years defending their lives, fortunes, and sacred honor against King George III's army and navy. The ones who were still alive at the end of the conflict did something no other rebellious faction has ever done so successfully. Always before and since, changes in government amounted basically to one group of criminals replacing another group of criminals. For some examples from recent history, communist thugs replaced the Czar's thugs in Russia, religious tyranny replaced the Shah's tyranny in Iran, and torturers of the right-wing Contras replaced left-wing Sandinista torturers in Nicaragua. The list goes on forever.

But these successful American rebels did not replace King George III with King George Washington even though many of them wanted to. After another six years in 1788, they had written and adopted a constitution to re-organize the new country with a dramatic experiment in government.

So, just what form of government did these successful rebels form to replace the tyranny of King George III? Everywhere you turn, you hear about our wonderful democracy, how many times we have fought wars to defend it, and how we need to promote democratic principles in other areas of the world. However, the government of this country was never intended to be a "mob-ruled" democracy. For some reason, we have an electoral college that creates the probability every time we have a strong third-party candidate that the winner will have less than 50% of the popular vote, such as in 1992 when Ross Perot was strong and Bill Clinton beat Bush the Elder with only a 43.3% plurality. Our electoral college has also resulted in the election of three presidents (in 1876, 1888, and 2000) who did not even obtain a plurality of the popular vote. (A different scenario occurred in 1824, when the House of Representatives rather than the electoral college selected a winner who had not received a plurality.) And with or without the phrase, "under God," we never pledge allegiance to the flag and to the *democracy* for which it stands.

The Founders of this country were exceptionally well versed in the various forms of government and consciously intended this one to be a constitutional republic, somewhat similar to the form of government in the republic of Rome from 509 B.C.E. until it was terminated in 27 B.C.E. when Augustus appointed himself emperor.

Basically, a democracy allows every citizen to vote on every issue, and a republic has representatives to vote for everyone. However, there are many different versions of republics, and the word is not to be confused with the Republican Party or with the totalitarian governments in existence today that call themselves republics. I do not speak any of the Chinese dialects and do not know the Chinese name for the country in Asia that we refer to as the People's Republic of China. However, I do know that *that* government is not a republic of the people in the sense that this government was intended to be. The adult population in the U.S. has a much greater degree of control over our representatives than has ever been the case in that so-called republic.

Another difference between various republics is that the Founders of ours devised an incredibly complex system to divide power between the states and the federal government and between the various branches of the federal government. Their methods to reduce concentrations of power were even designed to prevent a majority of the people from accomplishing its desires without first overcoming a long list of constraints. For example, the people elected the members of the House of Representatives, but the state legislatures elected senators until the 17th Amendment was ratified in 1913, 125 years after the Constitution was ratified. The Founders knew that they had to make it difficult for any official or any group to be guilty of the abuses that would *always* result from an unrestrained exercise of power.

I recently read a printout of a speech entitled "Suppose We Had a Real Democracy in the United States." It was given in January 2004 by a well-educated member of the ACLU and the Open Society Institute. He made a very good case that we do not have a real democracy and proposed a number of changes that we should make in our society to achieve that goal. Our Founders, however, did not do a sloppy job of creating a democracy; they consciously and deliberately did an incredible job of creating a constitutional republic. Democracy, as originated in Athens, had been considered by the Founders and rejected for a number of reasons in addition to the logistical problems caused by having all citizens vote on all issues. According to Edmund Randolph, Virginia delegate at the Constitutional Convention, the delegates had found that the origins of the evils in the country prior to the Constitution had been found "in the turbulence and follies of democracy," and the object of the Founders of our country was to avoid those evils by forming a republic.

As an extreme example of the problems inherent with democracies, a vote of 51–49 under such a form of government could result in the execution of all left-handed people. In our history, and acting somewhat like the democracy we were not intended to be, a majority of unchecked voters in many states legalized two school systems that were separate and unequal, until the judges finally did their duty and issued orders, the president and other officials in the Executive Branch enforced those orders, and the mobs were forced to relinquish powers that they had gotten quite used to exercising in violation of previously unenforced constitutional constraints.

As a commonplace example of the democracy our country is becoming instead of the republic that our Founders created, a vote of 51–49 currently results all the time in the confiscation of the earnings and accumulations of money from those who have it in order to give it to those who want it. This "Robin Hood" form of armed robbery is allowed in democracies regardless of the reasons why the more successful and the less successful reached the levels they did. Due to the restrictions and divisions of authority between the various branches of our government, the Executive Branch is totally powerless in this area, and it will do no good to try to get our legislators to change this system because they have to obey the mob or be replaced by someone who will.

However, just like they did with segregation, at some point a smart lawyer will present the right case, and our Judicial Branch will do its job. They will remind us with a court order that we are not governed, directly or indirectly, by mob consensus but by our Constitution, and our Constitution does not permit mandatory income redistribution unless and until it is amended. Someday, the judges will stop us from pointing the government's guns at others and saying, "We recognize the fact that we all have charitable feelings; this is the list of charities that our representatives have chosen to support as developed through the political process of compromises and trade-offs; and this is your share, so pay up or else." Until the attorneys make the judges take notice and the pendulum swings back, you can wish that all of your contributions could go to the ABC Foundation or the XYZ religious institution. Just don't insist on it unless you are prepared for an extended visit to a federal prison.

As Fisher Ames stated soon after our Constitution was adopted, "A democracy differs more from a republic than a democracy differs from despotism." He felt that a democracy oppresses the chief owners of property, whom he believed to be the truest lovers of their country.

How can I maintain that oppressing the chief owners of property by mandatory income redistribution is prohibited under our Constitution, however well-meaning that action may be? The authors of that document restrained the power of our government repeatedly, using the words "no" and "not" 46 times in the first seven articles and the first ten amendments. All powers not given to the government were expressly denied to it. Since our government was not given the power to redistribute wealth, and until we pass a constitutional amendment to the contrary, it simply does not have that power, regardless of how we and our representatives have voted or for how long.

In our republic, "we, the people" have a huge amount of power, even the power to change our Constitution, but until we do so, the Constitution is the supreme law of our land, and our judges are empowered to overrule any majority-rule decisions that are contrary to that supreme law. That is, under certain circumstances, the judges have a sworn duty to thwart the will of the people.

> *"The government of the absolute majority...when not effectively checked, is the most tyrannical and oppressive that can be devised."*
>
> —JOHN C. CALHOUN

Don't feel bad if you thought we had a democracy until now. Unfortunately, very few graduates of our government monopoly schools know what our government is supposed to be or why. I am one of these graduates, and I had the benefit of government monopoly schools that were far superior to the average today. However, I was over sixty years old and doing research for this book before I knew why we pledge allegiance to the "flag and to the republic for which it stands."

Another problem in our republic is that some of our judges have forgotten the limits of their powers. Now, don't get me wrong; judges have a tough job, and every time they make a ruling, they make someone unhappy. But while they are empowered to rule on the laws and to overrule laws that violate the Constitution, there are some judges who rule according to whatever they believe the laws should be and whatever they believe the Constitution should have said. That is, they change the laws without going through the deliberately laborious legislative procedure, and they change the Constitution without going through the even more laborious amendment procedure that was also deliberately instituted by our Founders.

In the written decisions of these out-of-control judges, they usurp the functions of government that were given to the Legislative Branch and denied to the Judicial and Executive Branches. They either go through incredible mental gyrations to justify their positions or simply cite the precedent of another opinion by another judge who has already done so. After a few precedents have been embellished by a few more precedents, the original Constitution of the United States cannot be recognized when the next case comes up for a decision. They need to put their casebooks aside every now and then and read the Constitution to see what it really does say instead of just what other judges have said about it.

This reminds me of the story of the monk, Brother Antonius, who had spent his entire life in medieval Europe copying scriptures onto parchment. Old and bent over, he told his friend Brother Sebastius one day that he was going down to the cellar to check the original just to make sure that they had not made any mistakes while copying from copies. After quite some time had passed, Brother Sebastius got worried and went down to check on his friend. There he found Antonius wailing, tearing out what little hair he had left, and beating his head against a post. Sebastius asked him, "What is wrong, my friend?" Antonius looked up and said, "The word is *celebrate*."

I have read the doublespeak in some of the cases in constitutional law and understand fully why it has gotten to the point that commentators from all points of the political spectrum use phrases like "out-of-control pinheads" when referring to judicial decisions in which their ox is gored. In fact, these judges can cause as much damage if not checked as the damage that can be caused by unchecked, out-of-control, pinhead voters. The U.S. Supreme Court, for example, can decide which cases it will review, and if it says that it has jurisdiction, no one can overrule that assumption of power. Once it hears a case, it deliberates (and negotiates?) in secrecy. We never know if Justice A has agreed to support Justice B on a case involving environmental issues in exchange for Justice B's support on a case involving religious issues. We just have to live with the consequences of a nine-member legislative body with superpowers. When it issues a 5-4 decision, five powerful people have told more than three hundred million people what the law was or what the new law has become, but it often is even worse than that. Sometimes, there are four liberal judges and four conservative judges who cancel each other out, and Justice Sandra Day O'Connor tells all of us just how high to jump. That degree of "legislative" power in one person is dangerous, and Congress needs to restore balance between the three branches of our government by revising the enabling legislation that establishes and governs the judicial system, but right now I need to go see how the Alabama Crimson Tide is faring in the football game. Ho, hum.

I do not have a solution to this problem of certain judges making a hostile takeover of our Constitution and of the legislative functions of government. Once enough of our final arbiters of the law become completely lawless and pass from the bench any laws they consider desirable, our government will cease to be a constitutional republic that derives its powers from the consent of the governed. Instead, we will descend into a combination of legal anarchy and judicial dictatorship as each judge writes his or her own set of laws until the Supreme Court decides which ones it chooses to reverse.

But hopefully, our Founders have already created the solution for this hostile takeover, and none of us will have to look for it. When voting for the president, informed voters recognize the power of judges and give serious consideration to the power of all presidents to affect the future by their judicial appointments. Then, after the elections and depending on the outcomes, Democrats in the Senate try to block some of the nominations to the bench by Republican presidents or vice versa. The side wanting prompt approval of their judicial appointments accuses the other side of foul play and dirty politics, and those charges sometimes might be justified. However, it is also another example of the incredibly complex system of checks and balances in our successful republic that is definitely not a mob-ruled democracy. Nevertheless, it sure would be refreshing for a president and the Senate someday to appoint and confirm a judge based on the appointee's allegiance to and thorough knowledge of our Constitution instead of whether he or she has a conservative or liberal bias.

So just what did our Founders intend our government to be? Benjamin Franklin's answer to that question from one lady was, "A Republic, madam, if you can keep it." Well, Mr. Francis Scott Key, to answer the question you asked in your song, yes, the Star Spangled Banner does yet wave. But, Mr. Franklin, I am not as optimistic that we will be able to keep the republic for which it stands. Most of us do not have a clue as to what an incredibly complicated and wonderful form of limited government you and your associates gave us.

Pop Quiz:

1. Why are decisions by voters in a democracy more divisive and dangerous than decisions by those same people "voting" with their money in a free market society? Answer: Majority decisions in a democracy affect everyone, whereas individual decisions in the marketplace affect very few people other than the buyer, the seller, and the tax collector who have all agreed to the transaction. For example, in a free market, some parents can send their children to a school that emphasizes math and literature, while others can send theirs to a different school that emphasizes art and music. Some can choose politically correct schools and others can choose schools with a preferred religious orientation. Therefore, as many issues as possible need to be removed from the political arena and returned to the private sector where they belong.
2. What prevents a majority from being a mob? Answer: The limitations contained in the Constitution of the United States that make our government a republic and prevent it from being a democracy.
3. What is the difference between a rich country and a poor one? Answer: The Constitution of the United States combined with free enterprise.

Elastic Clause

Congress has the power: "To make all Laws which shall be necessary and proper for carrying into Execution the foregoing Powers, and all other Powers vested by this Constitution in the Government of the United States, or in any Department or Officer thereof." (Article 1, Section 8, Clause 18)

Does this mean that a majority of "we, the people" can get our representatives in Congress to pass a law mandating the execution of all left-handed people? Of course not. When a mob becomes the majority, it is a large and powerful group, but it is still just a mob. The laws passed by our representatives have to be "necessary and proper," and they must be passed for the purpose of executing powers that have been vested in the U.S. Government by the Constitution.

For those reasons, laws attempting to legitimize "Robin Hood" redistribution of income and wealth under the elastic clause will fail in time under the proper challenge in court. We just need to copy a page from the ACLU playbook and present the case. The powers of Congress are elastic, not infinite. The fact that the Constitution remains the supreme law of our land until amended eventually brings us back to sanity, keeps us free, and makes us wealthy.

Functions of Government

> *"...That to secure these rights, Governments are instituted among Men, deriving their just powers from the consent of the governed..."*
>
> —DECLARATION OF INDEPENDENCE

> *"The powers not delegated to the United States by the Constitution, nor prohibited by it to the States, are reserved to the States respectively, or to the people."*
>
> —TENTH AMENDMENT TO THE CONSTITUTION OF THE UNITED STATES

The key point in these quotations is the assertion that governments get powers only by the consent of those to be governed and only to the extent of that consent. But, what do you think? Should we accept the tendency of increasing government control over every aspect of our lives? Is that a good thing? Will that promote increasing prosperity for your grandchildren? Do you belong to the government or does it belong to you? Are you a Controller or a Persuader?

> *"There shall be no limitations on the powers of the federal government. It is quite all right for the U.S. Government to usurp from the States and/or from the people any powers it chooses whenever the Controllers of the country should decide that the ends justify the means."*
>
> —TENTH AMENDMENT TO THE CONSTITUTION AS INTERPRETED BY SOME OF OUR JUDGES

I am outraged. The people who wrote the Constitution gave us this country at great personal sacrifice, and we have modified their plan almost completely out of existence. If some feel that any provision or amendment should be abolished, we need to follow the established procedure and debate the issue fully. We should never just ignore it and accomplish its quiet de facto demise.

Many revisionist judges and commentators say that our Constitution is a living, evolving document. That sounds good, but the contents behind that label have a meaning that is exactly the opposite of what the label states. A free translation of the contents proposed by these revisionists is that the Constitution is old, dead, and can be interpreted to meet the ideology of any particular judge on any given day. It is totally irrelevant to them that the framers of our Constitution provided the manner in which to allow it to evolve. The provisions for amendments are deliberately difficult because they did not want a mob-ruled democracy. They had a healthy concern about the abuses that a democracy can produce and formed a republic with provisions to protect an infinite number of minority groups.

President John F. Kennedy once made an incredibly dramatic speech, saying in part, "Ask not what your country can do for you. Ask what you can do for your country." With an excellent delivery in his highly cultured Bostonian accent, he inspired people all over the country and even in other countries. Unfortunately, President Kennedy was destructively wrong in that famous "Ask not" speech, and Bertrand Russell was correct when he said, "Governments exist for the sake of individuals, not individuals for the sake of governments." President Kennedy should have said, "Ask not what your country can do for you, and ask not what you can do for your country. Ask your country to protect you from foreign and domestic criminals and then to stay out of your life and bank account. Work hard at your business, be individually productive and prosperous, and the world will slowly and surely become a better place."

But my revision of President Kennedy's speech just does not have the same dramatic effect as the original. His sounded so fantastic! And that is the worst part of it. His speech was a dramatic sound bite, almost short enough to be put on a bumper sticker, and delivered so well that it got the attention of millions of people all over the world. His speech led a huge number of impressionable listeners down the path to destruction as they became more willing to accept the subjugation of the individual by the group. A generation of Controllers was cultivated by that one speech, and their influence on additional generations continues to bear its rotten fruit today.

There is no need for me to ask what I can do for my country, because I am doing it right now with this book. I am advising the citizens of my country to get back to basics and to get back to business. If you feel somewhat guilty about the wealth we have due to our "luck," you can best respond by defending the system that made us so "lucky" and helping others around the world to establish the same "lucky" system.

I repeat, the basics are covered very well in our Constitution, and there is a procedure for amending it whenever necessary. In the meantime, as the Ashleigh Brilliant book title says, "Be a Good Neighbor, and Leave Me Alone."

Don't Ignore It; Amend It or Defend It

> *"I do solemnly swear (or affirm) that I will support and defend the Constitution of the United States against all enemies, foreign and domestic; that I will bear true faith and allegiance to the same; that I take this obligation freely, without ay mental reservation or purpose of evasion; and that I will well and faithfully discharge the duties of the office on which I am about to enter: So help me God."*

With slight modifications for the president, all federal officers, elected and military, swear the above oath, promising to perform their respective duties and to support the Constitution. But just how many federal officers know what the Constitution says and support it? A free translation of the oaths as sworn by most of these officers would be something like this, "I know that I have to swear this oath to get this job, and I am going through the motions with no idea of what the Constitution says or any of the implications of my oath to defend it."

Even worse, how many people taking the oath believe that they can create a new and better form of government than the one they are swearing to defend? Hillary Clinton once said, "God bless the America we are trying to create." Well, Mrs. Clinton, with all due disrespect, I have a news flash for you: America has already been created with a constitutional mandate of limited government, and it was making excellent progress toward the unreachable goal of Utopia long before your brand of Controllers started "caring" enough to try to change our government into something that is far more totalitarian. The Founders who have already created our government were far wiser than you will ever be, and you need to obey the oath you took when you left the co-presidency and became a senator. With leaders like you, our Congress has passed innumerable laws that ignore the Constitution completely, and the results have just created more problems leading to more laws and more problems, ad infinitum.

Wow! Just what was that tirade all about? A few decades ago, I too swore to support and defend the Constitution, and now that I know more about what that oath means, it is about time that I start defending it. Wearing a military uniform and preparing to shoot bullets and artillery shells at enemies of the country whenever called is just not the same as defending our form of government. Sufficient military force can defend a country from foreign enemies, but it takes persuasion, votes, and lawsuits to defend our Constitution.

One way to defend our form of limited government is to expose the actions of those within it who are attacking it every day. Although Senator Clinton is leading one of the serious attacks on our Constitution, she is far from being alone in her party, and the Republican leaders won't honor their oaths to defend it either. You almost never hear any Republican or Democrat leader say that his position on a given issue is to do nothing because the Constitution prohibits the federal government from doing otherwise. They are too afraid to take the correct stand because almost all of the voters received a pathetic education in economics and government from our government monopoly schools and a thorough indoctrination from the mainstream media dominated by Controllers.

As this book goes to press, one of the Republican attacks on the Constitution is well underway in the tragic situation of Terri Schiavo. Giving further evidence to support the maxim that hard facts make bad law, Republican congressmen and the Republican president responded to a narrow but vocal portion of their constituency with a law allowing the Feds to overrule the state of Florida and decide how best to react to Mrs. Schiavo's plight. The Democrats in Congress modified the bill only to a limited extent before passage.

A few in Congress objected that Florida was not established as a subservient division of the Imperial Federal Government, but hotter heads prevailed. I predicted that Republican judges would find precedents in their rap sheets (they prefer to call them case law or legal precedents) that would justify the Schiavo Law. I also predicted that Democratic judges would find the opposite conclusion fully documented in their rap sheets. I am happy to report that my prediction in these areas seems to be false, at least this time.

I also predicted that no federal judge would honor his or her oath to defend the Constitution. None of them would even read the document to see if the original version, as currently amended, authorizes the intervention of federal government into this situation. The judges would assume the action of Congress and the president to be within their scope of authority and would base their rulings in the case on other legal points. Their main way to defend the Constitution is with words, and I believed that they would remain silent on the issue of constitutionality. I concluded that the best medical treatment available today for our Constitution is to pull the plug and remove all forms of life support, because this "living" document appeared to be terminal and was only being maintained in a persistent vegetative state.

I am happy to report that, at least in the case of 11th Federal Circuit Court of Appeals Judge Stanley Birch, Jr., I was wrong. He stated in his opinion, "In resolving the Schiavo controversy, it is my judgment that, despite sincere and altruistic motivation, the Legislative and Executive branches of our government have acted in a manner demonstrably at odds with our Founding Fathers' blueprint for the governance of a free people—our Constitution." Also, "But when the fervor of political passions moves the Executive and the Legislative branches to act in ways inimical to basic constitutional principles, it is the duty of the judiciary to intervene."

If we somehow could get the media to report the reasoning behind Judge Birch's ruling, and if we could get judges like him on the U. S. Supreme Court, our constitutional republic might actually survive. Just don't get your hopes too high. Judges who defend the Constitution and fail to support one party line or the other have to wait a long time for promotions.

I do not agree with those who say that our Founders did a sloppy job of creating a democracy or that they should have created a socialist society. To the contrary, they did an excellent job of controlling the inevitable excesses and failures of democracies and socialism by creating a constitutional republic with checks, balances, and respect for property rights. They also did an excellent job of dividing jurisdiction for various issues between the national and state governments. It ain't broke, and we would be far better off if we voters would prevent our "leaders" from trying to fix it. That is, before correcting any perceived problem with our legal system, we need to perform the required deliberation to amend our Constitution unless adequate authority for the correction already exists.

In addition to numerous misguided legislators on both sides of the aisle who pander to misguided voters, our judges have violated their oaths by misusing their powers to steal additional powers in areas denied to them. They are constantly making changes to the laws, a power that was given only to the Legislative Branch. They have built interpretation on top of interpretation to the point that it is impossible to recognize the original Constitution by studying only the current rulings. In far too many cases, our judges have ruled according to what they want the law to say instead of what it really says. We have inherited the English common law system of evolving court precedents to apply specific fact situations to the common laws we have adopted and to our own legislation, which expands and modifies those laws. However, our Constitution places very specific limitations on the extent to which our legislation and court precedents will be allowed to evolve before a constitutional amendment is required.

And with presidents of both major parties in the White House, our Executive Branch has provided "leadership" in controlling the symptoms of every problem imaginable with the only test being whether their activities will impress the mob and buy some more votes instead of whether their activities support and defend the Constitution.

In 1517, Martin Luther nailed his Ninety-Five Theses to the door of the church in Wittenberg, Germany, alleging various abuses by the Pope of the Catholic Church. One of Luther's primary charges was that the Pope at the time had been using his power to make money for himself. A few centuries later, I am mailing this multi-page printed complaint to the headquarters of the Republican and Democratic Parties. With all due respect (that means that I am about to make another disrespectful statement), whatever that Pope in 1517 had acquired by abuse of his power was chump change compared to what our system is stealing from us today. But far worse, if that Pope truly was guilty as charged of abuses to Christian theology, they pale in comparison to what you have allowed Republicans and Democrats to do to the Constitution of the United States. Your apathy has allowed and encouraged our leaders to abandon the very foundation of this country and the basis of its wealth.

Our Founders were Persuaders who established a limited government with an incredibly complex set of checks and balances to limit abuses by any governmental official and even by any currently existing majority of the population. They had valid reasons for the form of government they established. Unfortunately, what they wrote is a far cry from what the Controllers have changed it into today. We have allowed innumerable changes to the basic structure of our form of government and have ignored all of the violations of oaths by our federal officers who swore to protect our Constitution. Now, our government resembles a Socialist party platform, and most of us even call it a democracy. To repeat: If something about our situation has changed that requires changes to our Constitution, amend it. Don't ignore it!

What Should We Get Government to Do?

Nothing!

Excuse me?

Okay, it is too extreme to say that we should allow government to do nothing. It is just as stupid to allow anarchy as it is to look to government to solve all of our problems. I know, saying that two ideas are stupid is political incorrectness twice. Let me return to my natural state of polite diplomacy and just say that the proponents of both extremes have their heads so far up their asses that they don't have a clue about what is going on in the real world. We desperately need to stop to look at what we are doing. With the mainstream media in the lead, we ignore the mandates of our Constitution and evaluate the foreign and domestic plans of each candidate for office against the "ideal" of having the government make friends with everyone abroad at any cost and supply everyone's needs at home, again at any cost.

I know that many in the media are graduates of government monopoly schools, but so am I. There is such a thing as experience, and it can be more than just gaining the ability to ignore mistakes as we repeat them over and over. All anyone has to do is to live awhile to notice that in foreign relations there is evil in the world and that appeasing that evil never works, whether it is called "peaceful coexistence," "détente," "global test," or anything else. And in the domestic area, there is evidence everywhere you turn that limited government and free enterprise work better and cost less than government planning.

But you still hear demands led by our media for our candidates to have detailed plans for government to take care of us. There were even numerous commentators bemoaning how sad it was for the American people to lose our faith in government as a result of the President Nixon scandal. In other words, they think that it would be a good thing for us to have blind faith in our government.

That is crazy. We should not have blind faith in any of our institutions, and our Founders were well aware of what a disastrous course of action that would be. A healthy skepticism about our government was the best thing that resulted from the Nixon debacle. It is sad to realize how short our memories are and how quickly that skepticism faded.

> *"Power tends to corrupt, and absolute power corrupts absolutely."*
>
> —LORD ACTON

Even the Controllers must surely agree that there is a tendency for everyone today to assume automatically that the government should meet our every need. It is just that the Controllers contend that such a response is a good one.

Proponents of big government maintain that there are only two options: get government to solve all problems or callously allow the problems to continue unaddressed. The truth is that there are more than two options to address most problems. You can reject the response, "There ought to be a law," choose one of the other possible responses, and be more caring by being more effective. So when should we seek government solutions for a problem? That is right, our Constitution states that we have the right to choose what powers to give to the government and not the other way around.

- We should give our government direct responsibility for certain problems, such as defending us against foreign and domestic criminals.
- Until we can become mature enough to use the Libertarian system of relying primarily on voluntary fees with very few mandatory taxes to raise money for government functions, we should give our governments *indirect* responsibility for some problems, such as collecting taxes for garbage disposal and education, and then getting other entities to deliver the product by hiring a garbage disposal company and issuing education vouchers.
- We should keep our governments completely out of many issues, such as redistributing income equally among all workers and nonworkers and thereby destroying the incentives and benefits of free enterprise. Also, we should prohibit our governments from making sure that all speech is politically correct and thereby destroying free speech with all of its benefits.

I support the authors of our Constitution, who mandated a limited form of government, but I hasten to emphasize that the limitations they imposed do not extend to our military defense other than as determined from time to time by the president and Congress.

Acceptable Controls

Anarchy allows strong evil people to run rampant, so government must be given the power to control certain behaviors to avoid that situation. The problem is just where to draw the line, and everyone has a different opinion. As I have already stated, every control carries with it a huge list of costs, and each person must decide which controls are worth the expense. Since I prefer for my country to be wealthy instead of wasting the human and other resources we have, I vote for the absolute minimum of controls, far less than are currently reducing our ability to produce wealth.

Until humans stop behaving the way humans have always behaved, we obviously need armed forces, police, and various investigative agencies to protect us from foreign and domestic criminals. But it is not that simple. Before apprehending and punishing the criminals, we need to decide just what constitutes a crime. Should it be a crime to say something that is racially or sexually offensive? Should all homosexual acts be crimes? Should it be a crime to wear a cross, star of David, or head scarf to school?

Should it be an international crime for one country to attack another country? To prepare to attack another country? To defend an attack by another country? To preempt a potential attack by another country?

Domestically, the test should be whether the actions of a person threaten the life, liberty, or property of another citizen. If not, leave him or her alone. Internationally, we need to take aggressive steps to stop any actions of a country that threaten our lives, liberty, or property, and we do not need anyone's (e.g., the United Nations) permission to defend ourselves.

Should we use force in trying to control the actions of a dictator who is torturing and killing his Caucasian subjects in Germany? His Arab subjects in Iraq? His Oriental subjects in Cambodia? His Negro subjects in Uganda? Those are harder questions to answer, and the best I can come up with is a definite maybe. Sometimes the costs are justified by the benefits, and many times they are not. One hopes that there will be more than one desired benefit from a decision to fight and that we will think carefully before making such an extreme decision. With hindsight, it seems to have been an excellent decision for the U.S. Army to suffer so many casualties and to cause so much collateral damage from 1861 to 1865 in order to maintain the Union and to free the slaves and their millions of descendants in this country.

Was it also a good decision for the U.S. armed forces to suffer so many casualties and cause so much collateral damage during our attempt to make numerous changes in Iraq by invading it? I have my opinions, as does almost everyone else, but new facts are being discovered every day, and we may need a few decades of hindsight to get a truly clear picture. (Translation: I have chosen to dance around the issue of Iraq because I have bigger fish to fry, namely the divisive and impoverishing concept that the best government is a big government.)

Welfare

> *"The poor will always be with us."*
>
> —JESUS OF NAZARETH

Before jumping into this bed of snakes, I need to put in my earplugs because all of the liberal Controllers in the audience are going to start attacking my motives, character, lack of empathy, etc. At least, they will not be as bad as the conservative

Controllers will be when I disagree with them in other parts of the book, because most of the liberal variety of Controllers do not approve of the private ownership of assault weapons. Okay, let's try to make some sense out of this welfare nightmare.

Almost everyone agrees that our current welfare system is far from perfect, and many attempts have been made at welfare reform. What we need is not a reform but a total shift in paradigms. If Controllers really wanted to show their concern for the problems of the poor and were willing to stop being control freaks, they would terminate all of the hugely expensive and counterproductive government programs instead of adding more. That's right, many government programs are counterproductive. They are wrong, wrong, wrong, and they should be terminated in favor of a system that would work.

Welfare comes primarily in the category of an area that would be best served by government indirectly and not directly. *Maybe* we should get the government to provide a *brief* safety net for emergencies. But, the most effective way for us to show compassion and to ensure that adequate funds will be available for the needy would be for the government to supplement the natural tendency of Americans to be charitable by providing tax credits or enhancing the tax deductions for charitable contributions. Then, charitable individuals would make contributions to the charities that earn their approval, and these charities in turn would be able to disburse assistance of various types to those they deem worthy. Unlike our current system where money is disbursed to both the needy and the lazy without thought, we need to revert to the original system where the charitable organizations must first earn the approval of charitable individuals, and then the needy must meet the criteria of the charities. There is certainly no hope that our court system will soon declare any form of legislated welfare to be unconstitutional, so any changes to the current system will have to be passed by Congress at our insistence. That is, if you are not afraid of freedom.

But what about those charities and applicants deemed unworthy? They would not get the money, and that is not politically correct, but so what? There is a finite amount of money and compassion, and when less is wasted, more can be useful. I am a lot more interested in results than in aimless action, and the truly unfortunate poor would be the ones to benefit the most. It is an unpopular fact that charities with money tend to do a better job than government of helping the needy and refusing to be enablers for the lazy and greedy. Charities do not own printing presses and have to get the most benefit they can from the money they have. Therefore, they watch their expenditures a lot more carefully than government employees who will get promotions if they can expand their empires with more employees to waste more money.

An exception should be made in the case of minor children who are being abused or neglected by their parents. Children have long been recognized as wards of the state, and there are far too many times when the police powers of government are needed to provide protection and meet their other needs. Our governments should be given direct responsibility for children who do not have caring parents, and if government resources were not spread as thinly as they are, these needy children would get far better care than they get today.

Yes, I am sometimes a Controller when it comes to children, and it is often a very tough call to decide when to let their parents raise them as they see fit and when to step in to protect them with the big guns of government. However, at the other end of the age spectrum, I am not at all proud to admit that I am almost old enough to be a member of the so-called "greatest generation" that has morphed into the "gimmie" generation of welfare program promoters under the leadership of organizations such as the AARP (the Association of Those Persons Who Failed to Provide Adequately for Their Own Retirement and Want to Advance the Quality of That Retirement at the Expense of Their Neighbor's Children and Grandchildren Who Are Still Working).

Welfare vs. Freedom

> *"I have little interest in streamlining government or in making it more efficient, for I mean to reduce its size. I do not undertake to promote welfare, for I propose to extend freedom. My aim is not to pass laws, but to repeal them. It is not to inaugurate new programs, but to cancel old ones that do violence to the Constitution or that have failed their purpose, or that impose on the people an unwarranted financial burden. I will not attempt to discover whether legislation is 'needed' before I have first determined whether it is constitutionally permissible. And if I should later be attacked for neglecting my constituents' 'interests,' I shall reply that I was informed that their main interest is liberty and that in that cause I am doing the very best I can."*
>
> —BARRY GOLDWATER

How many of you readers, the proud products of government monopoly school indoctrination, agree with Senator Goldwater's position? You and I were taught that government is the answer to every problem, so how heartless do you have to be to agree with such a cold and uncaring position statement? We are getting the government we deserve, the problems we deserve, and the unhappiness we deserve because we have abandoned our Constitution in favor of the seemingly easy fix, "Let the government do it." For president, we elected the "Great Society" Lyndon Johnson with his "War on Poverty" over the "cold and heartless" Barry Goldwater. Did the controls of Johnson's programs make our society great? Did his programs win the war on poverty?

Oh, since not, I guess we just need to waste more money on the proposed solution that did not work, has never worked, and never will work. We still have not become a completely socialist or fascist state, so I guess we just need more controls so we can reach the ideal. I guess there is no need for you to promote the free enterprise system and a limited government. Regardless of the results, it must be much more caring to be a Controller who ignores the systems that have proven that they do work, that they do improve society, and that they do make steady reductions in poverty than to be a mere Persuader who abides by the Constitution.

Controllers say the government should take care of welfare for the unfortunates who did nothing to cause their situations. Controllers also give us a false dilemma, saying that there are only two options. If you do not feel government is the best answer for the unfortunates, you are a cad. So, to demonstrate their compassion, the Controllers do not pull out their own checkbooks. Instead, they resort to force, making others with money write checks for the benefit of the unfortunates. The Controllers in their infinite wisdom use the police power of the state to enforce their demands that each person write a check as computed by a specified formula. These collections are managed by the agencies as specified by the Controllers and given to those persons designated as deserving by them. If someone should want to satisfy his charitable impulses by giving to different agencies for the benefit of different recipients, he will need very deep pockets, because he will first be forced to support the programs dictated by the Controllers.

A Message to the Poor

I am not sure just who wrote the official definition of poverty in the United States or whether the political motivation for a larger government may have influenced that person's decision on where to draw the line between the poor and the "lucky." I do know that there is a lot of money in poverty and that a huge number of bureaucrats have a vested interest in maintaining and expanding a permanent class of poor people to provide the fuel to run their industry. Without an abundant supply of poverty, these "public servants" would be unable to justify their jobs and expand their empires. It is certainly not in their best interests to help those of you who are truly poor ever to become self-sufficient. However, it is undisputed that our government has become a vast vacuum cleaner sucking up a huge percentage of the resources available to help those of you who are poor by whatever standards you choose to measure the situation. If we Persuaders are successful in reducing the size and functions of government back to what was originally intended and in convincing everyone to put much more reliance on voluntary welfare for those of you in need, what will happen to you?

But first, I need to ask you some things. How are you doing? Is your financial situation improving, staying the same, or getting worse? Is your income increasing fast enough to stay even with the rate of inflation caused by our out-of-control, raging 'roid-monster government? Do you have adequate resources for medical care and prescription (government controlled) drugs? Are you optimistic about your future? The people promoting an expansion of the current system claim to care about your plight. Do you feel that the government bureaucrats really care for you and your situation? Are these bureaucrats more caring than the employees and volunteer workers at the charitable institutions you have encountered? Do you find that our current system of government welfare helps you emotionally, or do you suffer from an increasing poverty of spirit? Is the current system working for you? Is it empowering you to improve your condition, or is it sapping your spirit and holding you and your descendants in perpetual dependency? Do you feel any resentment about the resources that could be helping you but that are being dissipated by a government bureaucracy and by those poor people who were just lazy or made stupid choices instead of being truly unfortunate? Do you feel that you probably could be better helped by a different system without as many of those deficiencies?

Persuaders propose to scrap the current system and replace it with one that we believe will be much more beneficial to the giver, the receiver, and society at large. One example of the creativity and effectiveness of a non-government charitable organization is the program currently underway by Rotary International, an international service organization with approximately 1,200,000 members in approximately 31,000 clubs worldwide. In 1985, Rotary decided to eradicate polio from the Earth and established the PolioPlus program with a twenty-year deadline of 2005. It raised money and volunteers from within its membership and elsewhere, bought vaccine, hired medical personnel, kept records, and made incredible progress. In 2003, there were only 617 confirmed cases of polio in only 6 countries due to this program, and one hopes that Rotary has helped to create a polio-free world and has started working on another goal by the time you read this.

Another example of the effectiveness of voluntary charities is Habitat for Humanity. This organization gives people a hand up along with a hand out. Each recipient of one of its houses is required to invest part of the labor and part of the money into his or her own house. Recipients are also required to assist in the building of houses for others. In the process of providing affordable houses, this organization builds character, respect, and a sense of community. So that it can use its limited resources to make a real difference in the lives of those with situations of true misfortune, it refuses to reward those guilty of bad behavior by giving handouts indiscriminately or equally to just anyone.

I maintain that the poor will be helped far more effectively by these and other existing and potential private charities than by maintaining the government dole system in perpetuity. What say you?

Transition Period

What will happen to poor people if we change from a mandatory welfare system to a system of voluntary welfare supported directly by the normal generosity of the American people and indirectly by tax benefits to donors? Before making any substantive change in our system and regardless of its eventual benefits, we must recognize that many of the poor rely heavily on various forms of government assistance and that they have become dependent on these "entitlements" over many generations. Unfortunately, if government does not do something, no one will, because there are not enough other funds available. Hell, I guess not! After we let the government grab it all, of course there is nothing left. That is just arguing in a circle.

There is no constitutional provision that directs the federal government to drain all of the available money for welfare out of the system. To the contrary, the Tenth Amendment to the Constitution prohibits the government from doing just that—not that anyone in power has noticed recently. The politically appointed dictators for life on the Supreme Court are certainly not taking judicial notice of the unconstitutional takings and misuse of private property.

So, until such time as a new system is in place, we must recognize that our existing system has drained a huge percentage of the available resources for assisting the poor (and everything else) into the government pool. Until changes have become established, we really are limited to the two choices offered by the Controllers of ignoring the plight of the poor or helping them through government intervention.

The absolutely necessary paradigm shift to revise our failing welfare system must incorporate a transition period. Surely we can get Congress not to make any major change in this area as immediate and traumatic as The Tax Reform Act of 1986. The law prior to that major change had used tax benefits to create artificial values for real estate investments, and the replacement in 1986 was basically a good one, but there was no transition period for the market to make an orderly adjustment. Without any provision for a transition period, a more accurate label for that law would have been something like, "A Law to Wreak Financial Havoc on Owners, Lenders, and Brokers of Investment Real Estate." The day that law was passed, the value of every apartment house, office building, shopping center, and other real estate investment in the entire country dropped by about 25% to 30%. (Do not forget that the free enterprise marketplace reacts immediately to everything affecting the value of anything, and it does this without the intervention of any government bureaucrat.)

Then the owners of investment properties, the real estate brokers selling these properties, and the lenders holding mortgages on them had to absorb the losses or go bankrupt. Many went bankrupt, including almost all of the Savings and Loan Associations, which were already barely hanging on. They had already been weakened by the effects of numerous prior changes in the laws and regulations pertaining to that industry that had been written by well-meaning but highly disruptive Controllers.

As bad as the highly publicized abuses were by some officers and directors of some S&Ls, almost all of the S&Ls would have been able to survive those abuses. However, almost none of them survived the failure of Congress in 1986 to include a transition period for the drastic changes they had made to the tax laws. Some of the small percentage of S&L directors who were crooked went to jail while the well-intentioned fools in the Senate and the House of Representatives voted themselves another raise and a few more perks.

So, I would demand a more gradual transition for welfare recipients than befell me in 1986 as a broker of investment real estate. Without a transition period, any major change in welfare would be a disaster for far too many and should not even be considered. However, with a transition period, everyone and especially the poor, will benefit from a change to a voluntary system to be run by existing and newly formed charitable institutions.

Corporate Welfare

> *"Government 'help' to business is just as disastrous as government persecution...the only way a government can be of service to national prosperity is by keeping its hands off."*
>
> —AYN RAND

Individuals wanting to justify their government welfare checks point out that corporations have their hands in the till too, and they have a valid point. It is totally wrong for taxpayers to allow businesses to get various forms of government assistance. That is corporate welfare, and it is wrong.

We have been forced to pay for farmers not to grow crops. We have been forced to maintain obsolete military bases. We have been forced to pay for research into numerous areas for the benefit of specific businesses. We have been forced to pay all of the expenses of salaries, travel, office space, theft, consultants, kickbacks, etc., for the agencies mismanaging all of these programs. All of this is corporate welfare, and all of it is wrong, but the worst is that the government employees involved in controlling these programs are not in the real world creating wealth.

I am a real estate broker and a member of the National Association of Realtors®, so let me give you an example from my field. According to reports, there is currently a housing affordability crisis in some of our large cities, and many hardworking schoolteachers, policemen, etc., cannot afford adequate housing. To respond, our association is cooperating with some of the Controller/Socialist/Big Government politicians such as Boston's Mayor Thomas M. Menino to promote a plan. This plan will get government (the Controllers' only solution to any problem) to provide below-market interest rates to certain homebuyers under certain circumstances. The buyers will agree to certain limits on their resale prices.

First, notice the use of the word "crisis." This is the word used today to mean that we have a problem that is so big that we deserve and need a government solution (the "best" of all options).

> *"The whole aim of practical politics is to keep the populace alarmed (and hence clamorous to be led to safety) by menacing it with an endless series of hobgoblins..."*
>
> —H. L. MENCKEN

A careful analysis will reveal that the areas of the country most affected by this housing affordability problem also have a large number of government "assistance" programs instituted in the past to address other "crises." This is no coincidence. The aggravated affordability problems in these geographical areas are the inevitable results of the past expansion of government into problem areas that it should regulate for criminal activity and otherwise leave alone.

Next, you will notice that part of the "solution" is a price control. All experience to the contrary, Controllers still believe that they can negate the law of supply and demand by passing a law of their own. They are wrong! A limit on prices reduces production. That in turn reduces supply. That in turn raises prices, the exact opposite of what the price control was supposed to do. Idealistic Controllers would be just as ineffective and cause much less human misery if they would just concentrate on repealing the law of gravity.

So, how does all this affect you? If we Realtors® are stupid enough to buy this plan to address a real housing affordability problem, and if you are apathetic enough to let us get away with it, there will be some benefits in the short run. A few real estate brokers will make a few commissions selling some houses to some buyers who would not otherwise have been able to buy, and taxes will be paid to governments on these transactions.

Then the costs will start to mount. It costs money for government to supplement the market interest rate and to mismanage their programs, and we all have to pay these costs through taxes and inflation. Eventually these government costs affect everything we buy, and there is an affordability "crisis" for everything.

> *"A 1909 survey in Washington found that people were spending just under 18 percent of their incomes for housing...How could there have been affordable housing back in the bad old days, before there was so much compassion, social justice and a Department of Housing and Urban Development? This was back when people built, sold and rented housing for the sake of—you should excuse the expression—profit."*
>
> —THOMAS SOWELL

We absolutely do not need and cannot afford the government "assistance" constantly being promoted by leaders of both major political parties as cures for the "crisis" of the day. These leaders acquire and maintain their political positions by appearing to be caring and compassionate, supporting laws that sound good at first but that are counterproductive for the economy of the nation. The leaders who have led us into affordability problems are not qualified to provide anyone with solutions for those problems.

What we don't need to do is to copy those mistakes in every field of endeavor with each new "crisis" until everyone has insurmountable affordability problems on every product made. Repetition of bad policies will not solve the real problems we face; it will only make our situation worse. Quit letting politicians buy your votes with your own money. You may want that money someday to buy some real estate, and I would like to earn the commission.

A Message to Government Workers

I have made some very harsh statements about bureaucrats but only because we have forced bureaucrats to undertake functions for which they are not qualified, just as I would be severely criticized if I attempted brain surgery, but the main difference between a bureaucrat and an entrepreneur is not within the person but within the system. A cursory comparison of the U.S. and the former U.S.S.R. quickly demonstrates how free enterprise and socialism provide different incentives to workers and get different results. Likewise, the incentives offered to government workers are different from those offered in the private sector, and the results are also different. I am not an anarchist and recognize that both types of jobs are necessary. However, we have evolved into a society with too many government jobs that have drained too many resources and human talents from the private sector.

> *"The soft-minded man always fears change. He feels security in the status quo, and he has an almost morbid fear of the new. For him, the greatest pain is the pain of a new idea."*
>
> —MARTIN LUTHER KING, JR.

If we Persuaders are successful in reducing the size and functions of government back to what was originally intended by the Founders, what will happen to you government workers with all of the changes I am proposing? I have been standing up here with a meat ax proposing to chop out huge parts of our out-of-control government. (Well, actually right now, I am unarmed and sitting in front of a computer, but I do propose a major reduction in the current size of our government.) The question remains: what will happen to your monthly paychecks?

First, tell me. Are you rich? Since you are on a government salary, my guess is that you are not rich but that you are doing okay because almost all Americans are in far better shape than most others in the world. However, you may have an independent source of income or you may be just barely getting by. Prices are so high these days that most of you government workers and most of us in the private sector are not really rich. If we were all doing better, there would be far fewer bankruptcies and far fewer ads for credit cards, home equity loans, debt consolidation, and counseling services for solving the problem of excessive personal debt.

You have heard plenty of stories about "what it used to cost," but why are prices so high? Back in the good old days, things were far from perfect, and salaries and wages were far lower than they are today. However, it generally did not require two wage earners in one household to keep the bills current.

There are a number of reasons why it takes so many more pieces of paper today to buy the wealth of a soft drink, automobile, house, etc., but one of the main reasons is the increased cost of maintaining governments that have expanded from under 20% of our economy to a current total of approximately 40%. It is simply enormously expensive to control all of the people in this country with laws and regulations. With so many people in government controlling the rest of us and so much time spent by all of us filling out forms and otherwise complying with the controls, there is just not enough time being spent producing wealth. There's got to be a better way, and there is. There is no need to reinvent the wheel. All we have to do is to follow the Persuaders with their free enterprise system in commerce and in almost every other facet of our lives.

So, back to the question. What will happen to you government workers when we stop passing laws and stop trying to control the symptoms of every problem? First, I would hope for a more gradual transition for you than befell me as a broker of investment properties as a result of the Income Tax Law of 1986. A hiring freeze plus natural attrition should be sufficient to whittle the size of government gradually back to what it should be. That is, nothing would happen to you except that you might have to relocate to a different government agency if you were employed by one that was being completely eliminated, such as the disastrous Department of Education.

Then, when many of the present government jobs no longer exist, a larger percentage of the population can be employed in the private sector and create wealth instead of being a drain on it. As the general level of wealth is increased by adding more efforts to the total, and by preventing government from dissipating it, much of that wealth will come to your descendants. At that time, once we have slashed our largest expense—our 'roid monster government—we will probably no longer need two wage earners in one household to stay ahead of the bill collectors.

For those who cannot conceive of operating a country without a huge number of secure government jobs, you need to remember that all of the money for the employees in both the private and government sectors comes from the free enterprise system, and the only question is—just what are we getting for our money, more wealth or stifling controls? Also notice that many existing jobs in the private sector will become available again as some couples decide to stop working two full jobs between them. There might even be enough jobs opening up for those currently engaged in debt counseling and who will also be seeking other employment.

A Message to Private Charities

Do you think you could help more people with a larger budget? The answer to that question is obvious. However, the next question is how to get that larger budget, and the answer to that may not be as obvious. In addition to increasing your promotions efforts to attract more of the currently available funds, you can have an influence on the amount of those available funds. You have probably noticed that you do not get many contributions from destitute people, so you need to support the free enterprise system, which increases the general level of wealth. That way, all of the ducks can quack proudly when the pond rises.

Also, you need to support the principles of limited government mandated by our Constitution to prevent those available funds from being squandered. That is, government should receive little or zero funds for charitable works because it does such a poor job in this area, and government should reduce its controlling functions because that reduces wealth for everyone. The principles are simple, but you need to support them in order to receive the money you need for your charitable causes. Of course, it would not hurt you any if we were all able to obtain a tax credit or larger tax deduction for charitable contributions. That would make it even easier for those desiring to help you.

Just be sure you do not overlook the fact that the number of poor people needing help will decrease as a robust free enterprise economy creates more jobs, but your need for employees will increase as your budget increases and your charitable works expand into other areas. Don't worry: there will be plenty of qualified applicants to interview when the government programs are gradually phased out, and workers, money, and goodwill can flow freely in your direction.

Controls Cause Poverty of Spirit

> *"People are marvelous in their generosity if the just know the cause is there."*
>
> —WILL ROGERS

How would you feel if your country were taken over by a totalitarian government of the left, right, or church and this new regime said that, based on your income, you would be required to pay a specified amount into a fund? This fund would be mismanaged by numerous departments of the totalitarian regime to provide a few benefits to those deemed worthy. The needy would be designated by a group of Controllers and Socialists interested in buying your vote (and the votes of others) with your own money. You could refuse to pay into this fund only if you were willing to pay the price: a lengthy prison term, interest and penalties, plus a forcible confiscation of the required money anyway. Each $1,000 that you contributed to other charitable programs of your choice would reduce the amount demanded by the Controllers by a maximum of $396. In addition, you would continue to pay all of the sales taxes, property taxes, license fees, state taxes, inflation, and all other taxes for other necessary and unnecessary controls imposed on you.

How charitable would you continue to feel? How much would you be tempted to say that you have made the minimum payment due on the Controllers' charitable credit card bill and stop there? How likely is it that you would tend to close your eyes to the natural uncaring inefficiencies of bureaucracies and just let them "take care" of the poor? How motivated would you be to seek solutions for the underlying causes of the poverty around you instead of just letting government deal with whatever symptoms of the problem it decides to address? Would such a plan of forced contributions into a mismanaged fund encourage you just to make your required payments and then to turn your back on the disadvantaged, retreat into your gated community, and adopt the NIMBY (not in my backyard) attitude?

You may be a saint, but controls cause a poverty of spirit among far too many of us ordinary humans, and our current system needs to revert back to its roots of fewer controls by a limited government.

Responsibility

> *"Failure is a choice. Poverty is a mental disease."*
>
> —NEAL BOORTZ

First, we should avoid destructive behaviors in our own lives. Then, we should not try to force others to avoid the same destructive behaviors but encourage them to do so. Then, short of behaviors that hurt others, we should let everyone make his or her own choices. Finally, we should see that everyone reaps what they sow. Freedom is not a license to act irresponsibly without any consequences.

> *"One evening, when I was yet in my nurse's arms, I wanted to touch the tea urn, which was boiling merrily…My nurse would have taken me away from the urn, but my mother said 'Let him touch it.' So I touched it—and that was my first lesson in the meaning of liberty."*
>
> —JOHN RUSKIN

The Controllers say that we have to mandate helmets for motorcycle riders, prohibit drug use, etc., because we have to pay for any resulting problems. Why? Tell me one reason why we have to pick up the tab for the stupidity of others? Sure, we should help the innocent victims and especially the innocent and helpless children, but why do we insist on rewarding the irresponsibility of adults while punishing their responsibility? This is just another illustration of how fallacious the entire control system of government is. By rewarding irresponsibility, we are filling the country with irresponsible people.

The Controllers will insist that there are only two options: ignore the victims or get government to pay. So what are we going to do? Take the case of the motorcycle rider who chooses to leave his helmet in the bar and later gets a serious head injury. First, we could remove enough controls from his insurance company so that it could have the option to charge more premiums for riding drunk and without a helmet or, under the legal doctrines of contributory negligence and assumption of risk, it could be allowed to pay nothing for head injuries resulting from such activity. Then, the injured rider (I do not agree with those who would call him a victim) would have to pay for his injuries or resort to family or charities for assistance. Don't show your compassion by pointing the government's gun at my head and forcing me to pay for his folly. I have enough folly of my own to deal with.

Independents

What in the Hell is an independent voter? Am I an independent because I am not a Republican or a Democrat? Since in issues of national defense, I am a hawk and my Libertarian Party is currently dominated by doves, I voted in the 2004 elections for the lesser evil as I perceived it between the two major parties. Does that make me an independent?

All "independents" seem to agree with me that both major parties in the U.S. are at least partially undesirable, but what do "independent" thinkers and voters stand for? Do independents have any consistent belief systems? Do they have allegiance to a minor political party? When they vote for the "best candidate" instead of the nominee of a chosen political party, how do they judge one candidate to be better than the others? Do they vote for the candidate who will support that one key issue that is the most important to them? For the one with the most sex appeal? For the last one they heard on TV stating empty platitudes that sounded good? Do they vote at all? Do they really stand for anything or just find fault with everything and hold themselves above all the lesser beings on the planet?

We all know that anarchists overreact to the problems that are caused by all governments and advocate that we have no governments at all. We also know approximately what Republicans and Democrats stand for. The Republicans are for big government and stifling government controls. The Democrats are for huge government and even more government controls, although the areas that the Democrats want to control are somewhat different from those of the Republicans. Most Americans are either Republicans or Democrats and rarely promote individual responsibility or question whether government might be the worst available solution for any given problem or need. We ignore the mandates for limited government in our Constitution and only disagree over just what would be the best government program to solve the current "crisis." The leaders of both major parties know that "we, the people" measure compassion and effectiveness by the amount of government expenditures and not by results, so both groups brag about how much of your money they have spent on whatever issue is being discussed. Both groups will do what they perceive to be the best way to defend the country militarily even though some approaches are as ridiculous as asking our enemies in the UN for approval before proceeding. The leaders of both parties follow the dictates of uninformed voters, and neither group will honor their oaths of office to defend the concepts of limited government mandated by our Constitution.

We know that fascists, communists, leaders of church states, dictators, kings, and czars believe in riches and power for the leadership while the masses suffer poverty and controls. Socialists want to make sure that no one makes more money than anyone else, and you can find many "reasonably" modified socialists among Republicans and Democrats. To the extent that they are successful, they only ensure riches and power for the leadership while the masses suffer the same poverty and control as in any other totalitarian state.

In the United States, we talk all the time about our wonderful freedom, and we have allowed ourselves to have more freedom than the people of any other country to date. But oh, how we fear that freedom! We accept and defend a mismanaged government Social Non-Security chain letter because we are so afraid of taking the responsibility to make free choices for our own retirements. We allow government to dictate our children's schools and to decide what "privileges" government will allow us to exercise in guns, travel, speech, and an infinite number of other areas. The various controls we allow the Democrats and Republicans to impose on all of us make a clear statement of just how afraid we are of actually having freedom and the responsibility it entails. And we damn sure are afraid to let others in our country have some freedom too, because we "know" they will not act responsibly. Only government officials have achieved perfection.

If you are masochistic enough to read this entire book, you will have a good idea of what Libertarians stand for. Some have incorrectly defined us as believers in the concept that people should have complete freedom of thought and action and should not be subject to the authority of the state. However, that is the definition of anarchists, and we are neither anarchists nor the other extreme, totalitarians. Although the word "libertine" sounds like it is very close to "Libertarian," the differences are immense because Libertarians emphasize maximum individual responsibility along with our desire for the maximum possible freedom. We support the Constitution and believe that it dictates maximum individual responsibility along with severely limited government, minimal controls, maximum freedom, and the resulting maximum wealth. We want the power of all of our human institutions to be checked and balanced by competition and a division of all power, and we support Adam Smith's concepts of economic checks and balances through competition.

Nevertheless, we Libertarians are humans, and we have differences among us on how to apply our general principles to each individual fact situation. We are often forced to compromise and vote for candidates of other parties when we disagree with our own party on major issues. Since I am not a "yellow dog" supporter of the Libertarians or any other political party, I guess some people would call me an independent. Well, I have been called worse.

Eminent Domain

> *"...nor shall private property be taken for public use, without just compensation."*
>
> —FIFTH AMENDMENT TO THE CONSTITUTION OF THE UNITED STATES

For quite some time, we have permitted our governments to have the power of eminent domain. This power has been used countless times for public roads, parks, buildings, etc. Property would be taken for a public use and adequate compensation would be guaranteed to the owner who was forced to relinquish it.

Now, there is a trend toward using eminent domain to take property away from one private owner to convey it to another private owner, and the only "public use" justification is that such action will produce higher taxes to support more public programs. Such an action is being taken today in Alabaster, Alabama, about thirty miles from my home. The city of Alabaster is taking homes away from individuals so that they can be conveyed to a developer as part of a shopping center to be anchored by Wal-Mart.

If higher taxes are allowed to constitute the justification for the taking of private property for the "public good," your home is in some degree of danger of being taken because shopping centers produce more sales and property taxes than homes. If government officials want it, they think that they are entitled to it. Has there been any money passed under the table to speed the immoral taking of private property for the benefit of another private owner? I don't know, but the temptation is surely there. Once again, a limited government would have a limited number of things to sell to those willing to buy, and the FBI would have more time available to address other problems.

Those houses being taken in Alabaster are not yours, and in fact, there are only so many shopping centers that the marketplace will support, so your home is probably not in much danger. However, this is just one more example of how you are allowing government to reduce your rights to the status of mere privileges that it can limit, license, and control. Once again, your apathy is allowing the Controllers to ruin your country and your children's potential inheritance. Your individual rights are being subordinated to group rights just because the takers say that they have good intentions. All they want is to produce some tax revenue for beneficial public projects. Your privilege (once considered to be a right) to private property is considered of little consequence when compared to all of the good they promise to accomplish. You only need to agree that intentions are more important than results and go back to couch potato land.

Freedom of Religion

In religion, we have hit the ball hard and touched all of the bases, but we can't seem to find home plate with a Seeing Eye dog. The Controllers used to believe that government needed to control everybody's religion and enforce a single doctrine to prevent chaos, such as the Church of England. After terrible religious wars, torture, and other persecution, it was eventually recognized that freedom of religion would stop the wars and persecution, and people could enjoy peace using that approach.

Now the Controllers in Iran have reinstated a national religion, and conditions there are as horrible as they were under the Shah. In this country, some Controllers (the conservatives/right-wingers this time) want to have government employees such as schoolteachers promote a specific religion while other Controllers (liberals/left-wingers) want to enforce freedom *from* religion being expressed in any public place by anyone at any time. One group maintains that our national motto amounts to the establishment of a religion by Congress. If "In God We Trust" is ever removed from the scene, I suggest it be replaced with the motto, "In Government We Distrust." The Founders agreed with that statement, and I certainly do not like the sentiment of some: "In Politicians and Bureaucrats We Trust."

This religion issue is just not that hard a problem to solve. It has already been addressed in our Declaration of Independence and Constitution by our Founders. Some of them were Deists, some were Christians, and the religious beliefs of some were unknown. They all agreed that it was a bad idea to force any specific religion on others, but none of them were afraid that the ACLU would sue them if they mentioned a general belief in

God in their public and private communications. History tells us that they expressed such a general belief in God in the Declaration of Independence, just as did Patrick Henry immediately before being hanged as a traitor. There is no valid reason for our monopoly school systems to stop studying the complete statements of our Founders because those brave and intelligent men never crossed over the line to establish any official state religion.

Just remember: any individual can make references to God, but no one in their official capacity as a government official can promote a *specific* state religion. "For God's sake," let's move on.

The Root of All Evil

According to different versions of the saying, some have claimed that money or the love of money is the root of all evil. There is no doubt that a desire for money is a motivating force, but some are motivated to create value to acquire that money, and some are motivated to steal to acquire it.

Among those who steal to acquire money, don't forget those whose modus operandi is the immoral use of the ballot box to get the government to steal for them. Under the guise of making the high achievers pay their "fair" share, the non-achievers and low achievers use the government to confiscate money for their benefit. Convenience store robbers, while maintaining that they did not do it, are at least generally honest enough to say that stealing is simply stealing. They usually get a very small audience to their occasional protestations that their thefts are somehow morally right.

Media Bias

> *"Do you swear to tell the truth, the whole truth, and nothing but the truth, so help you God?"*

The media does not seem to have much trouble telling the truth and nothing but the truth, but it seems to be impossible for them to tell the whole truth. If we are in a war or an occupation following the formal hostilities, they will tell the good news or the bad news, but only one side. Each television network, newspaper, or radio station will tell us about instances of guns that were used in violence, or they will tell us about guns that were used in self-defense against violence. It is rare for one company to give examples of both, i.e., the whole truth.

Most people today can be pressed to admit that there must be a few examples where a gun was used as a positive force in self-defense. They might even concede that there is bound to be a small tradeoff of occasional good gun use against the examples of guns being used in violent crimes. However, how many of us really know whether the positive outweighs the negative? We just have a feeling that the negative must greatly outweigh the positive.

Why do we feel that way? Media bias. For some reason, the mainstream media has implemented a pattern of selective reporting to show a preponderance of negative uses of guns with almost no reports on examples of the positive. Where are the stories about the use of guns to protect the innocent from the criminals, the 2003 report on guns by the Center for Disease Control in Atlanta, the results of the test in England comparing handgun deaths prior to and after starting that nation's experiment with gun control, the benefits that millions of Jews, Slavs, and Gypsies in Nazi Europe could have received from private ownership of guns, and the story about Nikita Khrushchev's realization that it would be extremely difficult and maybe impossible for the Soviet Union to occupy the United States since we did have substantial private ownership of guns? Why does the NRA have political clout from the approval of so many non-crazy Americans?

Also, where are the stories about the people who got rich creating something of value, the underlying causes of the violent and destructive use of guns and other instruments, how the profit motive has motivated drug companies to develop drugs that have raised our life expectancy, what will happen to rich and poor people in the future if drug companies can no longer afford the risk of developing new drugs, examples of government controls creating poverty, etc.?

In a recent Peter Jennings report about price controls on drugs in Canada, it was stated that the price was controlled on a specific drug in Canada and that it therefore costs less there than it does in the United States. It was implied that all it took was government action (price control) to obtain a major benefit (lower prices) with the only offset being the reduction of excessive profits to the drug companies. However, other vital parts of the story were omitted, and the false position was supported (I believe deliberately so) that price controls are good. My opinion is that it was a deliberate editing of a "news" story to present an editorial opinion—and a fallacious one at that.

For example, there was no mention of the costs in the United States of our "litigation lottery" system in which every company has to price its products at a level sufficient to cover the costs of future lawsuits. But the most damaging omission is the fact (not just my opinion) that the law of supply and demand cannot be rescinded by humans. Any price gain for the public in Canada will have to be covered by higher prices to the public in the United States and/or it will result in the reduction of research and development of new drugs for all.

There is no wonder that many people think big government is the only answer. The way the facts are presented by the graduates of government monopoly schools to other graduates of government monopoly schools, what other conclusion can be reached? This situation, however, is rapidly changing, and it is changing in our partially free society without any government intervention. The huge and powerful *New York Times* has recently admitted that it has been guilty of media bias, and the implications are enormous. Also, some astute businessmen, motivated substantially but not totally by the chance of profit, have started competing news sources and are being very successful by presenting what a sizable portion of the public wants, another side of the picture. Even ordinary citizens have punctured holes in fallacious stories simply by using the Internet to communicate with each other as in the fabricated story presented by CBS about President Bush's supposed failure to report as ordered when he was in the National Guard.

These dents in media bias and selective reporting are not just news; they are history, and they have the potential to change the future. Unfortunately, they are not getting near as much attention today as a sensational murder on the West Coast. Even after the admission of media bias, the mainstream media continues selective reporting to emphasize those portions of the whole truth that support its agenda, but competition has entered the picture, and other media are now reporting portions of the truth that support their respective agendas.

A news report is just as much a product and producing them is just as much a business as if it were a breakfast cereal. As with any product, Adam Smith taught us that you cannot trust any individual producer, but you can trust the free enterprise system to a large extent if there is sufficient competition. Some companies in any field are worse than others, and some consumers make poorer decisions than others. Some consumers will choose slanted news reports, and some will pass over nutritious cereal to buy sugar bombs. If there are enough people choosing the slanted news and sugar bombs, the free enterprise system will deliver, because it is consumer driven and is not driven by our anointed bureaucrats or by our "corrupt" corporations. Competition is an extremely efficient force in news reporting, just as in every other business and every other facet of human endeavor, even education. Once the people have gotten all facets of the truth about the current events of the day, we will be able to debate the relative merits of the various options available and have a chance to reach the correct conclusions about them. That is an incredible change from just a few years ago.

"The (whole) truth shall set you free."

Freedom of Speech

> *"Congress shall make no law...abridging the freedom of speech, or of the press..."*
>
> —FIRST AMENDMENT TO THE U.S. CONSTITUTION

> *"I may disapprove of what you say, but I will defend to the death your right to say it."*
>
> —VOLTAIRE

How many times do we hear the phrase "freedom of speech" misused? Put simply, and contrary to some incredibly destructive decisions by the Supreme Court, our Constitution mandates that you can say just about anything you want to, and the government cannot impose a criminal sanction of a fine, jail term, expulsion from a government monopoly school, or other punishment on you for doing so.

But what if you are a performer and your customers refuse to buy your songs or attend your performances because you said something that offended them? What if you state an opinion and are attacked relentlessly by commentators and guests on radio and TV talk shows who disagree with you? Have they breached this freedom? Sorry, they have not. Responses of these types are examples of the exercise of our freedom of speech and do not constitute any violation of it. All you can demand is a "Get Out of Jail Free" card and the freedom to respond to others with detailed explanations of how they are such buttheaded ignoramuses for defending their ridiculous positions while disagreeing with your statements of the unimpeachable truth. They have the right to their opinions too, as stupid as you may think them to be.

Nonviolent reactions by individuals are not prohibited whether they are favorable or unfavorable, and speech is therefore not completely free. It is just not supposed to be criminal. I do not expect Controllers to stop stating their beliefs just to keep from offending me, and likewise, I am not losing any sleep worrying about my statements offending them. I do not expect to go to jail for writing the opinions in this book, but I do expect a mixture of favorable and unfavorable reactions to it.

> *"If you are operational, you will suffer casualties."*
>
> —U.S. ARMY

The issue gets more complicated if you say something your boss considers offensive and fires you or demands your resignation, and it really gets complicated if your boss is a governmental agency (i.e., the taxpayers), such as a government school. In addition to the prohibition against criminal prosecution contained in the First Amendment, there are numerous state and federal laws that attempt to weigh the rights of employers to control their business investments vs. the rights of individuals to be free of undue constraints by powerful organizations. These laws vary so much over our country that they will have to be the subject of someone else's book.

In addition to those who want to be able to say anything without any consequences whatsoever, there is the other end of the spectrum. Since some speech is truly offensive to some people, Controllers want the government to do something about it. Offensive speech is actually the only type that needs to be protected. Never mind the fact that the First, Ninth, and Tenth Amendments prohibit the government from getting involved. Never mind the fact that people have the right to be offensive and others have the right to react favorably or unfavorably. Controllers maintain that the ends justify the means, that government is the answer to any problem, and that something must be done by government in every area, including the prevention of offensive speech.

Once again, our out-of-control judges have gotten into the picture. The camel got its nose into the tent with a Supreme Court ruling that some speech is criminal behavior, such as shouting "fire" in a crowded theater. With that as a precedent, other rulings were made that other types of speech could be deemed criminal. These rulings automatically became precedents too, and the camel will come all the way inside whenever we relax. There is a serious risk that any speech can now be deemed criminal at the whim of any federal judge in spite of the Bill of Rights. Just take a look at the political correctness guidelines at any government college and you will see examples of government speech control with government-imposed punishments for violations.

Much worse, we have recently received a ruling from our Supreme Court on the Bipartisan Campaign Reform Act of 2002 that prohibits certain people (but not all) from making political statements during specified periods of an election campaign. The majority of the justices failed to fulfill their oaths to support the Constitution and to recognize that the First Amendment prohibits Congress from passing any law that abridges freedom of speech. Instead, they decided to rule that this law is okay since it states noble intentions and has a nice label. They upheld the law in spite of glaring conflicts between the contents of the statute and the piece of paper called our Constitution that we used to respect and they swore to defend.

Tuna Fish Sandwiches

Have you ever noticed how long it takes to make a tuna fish sandwich if all you do is keep putting peanut butter and jelly on bread? Controllers never seem to notice how long it takes to make everyone on Earth wealthy by applying the principles of socialism to the world economies.

Drug dealers say that if you take their drugs, you will feel better, and they deliver. Those who take their drugs do feel better for a while. Then, when problems result from the drugs, the pushers offer more of the same, and the problems get worse until the user quits or dies.

Controllers' economic proposals are similar. They say that if we accept more government programs, we will feel better, and they also deliver. If we accept their proposals, we do get some short-term benefits and feel better for a while. But when the repercussions of controlling "solutions" make our problems worse, they have nothing to offer us but more of the same, and our problems will just keep getting worse as we spiral downward with their programs on our backs. Eventually, our businesses will die, and our workers will be laid off if we do not quit. Right now would be an excellent time to quit, but we are hooked, and there is no twelve-step program available to cure our dependency on the government control pushers and our addiction to government controls. At some point, the situation will get serious enough that we will be forced to answer the question of just how high a price we are prepared for our grandchildren to pay for our being control freaks.

Voting with Feet

Why is it that so many people are immigrating legally and illegally to the United States? It used to be that this was the "land of opportunity," and maybe that is still the reason. At least some of these immigrants are risking their lives to come here, even knowing that the first jobs they will have to accept are those that are being rejected by some of our citizens who prefer perpetual welfare over an entry-level job.

However, a lot of intelligent people are now wondering if we have become the land of suckers. Are these immigrants still coming over, under, around, and through our borders for the chance to be rewarded for work and creativity, or are some of them now coming to take advantage of our foolish giveaway programs? Knowing that some of them are truly coming to work, why is it a good idea for us to continue our foolish giveaway programs for our citizens while importing laborers from somewhere else along with those other imports who just want the handouts too?

So far, they are still coming, so we still have something to be proud of. When we have to build an American version of the Berlin Wall to keep them from leaving, we will know that we have adjusted our system all the way to total disaster and destruction. But Controllers will not object so long as their motives remain pure.

> *"The road to Hell is paved with good intentions."*
>
> —UNKNOWN

The USA Patriot Act of 2003

> *"Those who would give up essential Liberty to purchase a little temporary safety deserve neither Liberty nor safety."*
>
> —BENJAMIN FRANKLIN

> *"19 terrorists in 6 weeks have been able to command 300 million North Americans to do away with the entirety of their civil liberties that took 700 years to advance from the Magna Carta onward. The terrorists have already won the political and ideological war with one terrorist act. It is mindboggling that we are that weak as a society."*
>
> —ROCCO GALATI

Remember that labels are not more important than contents and that politicians of all parties and ideologies like to have inspiring titles for their proposed laws. Unfortunately, there is no "truth in advertising" law that applies to legislators. Many groups, as different as the American Civil Liberties Union and the National Rifle Association, are very alarmed at the contents of the law with the imposing name, "The USA Patriot Act." The various attacks by Islamic militants on U.S. interests were designed to cause a number of changes to our system, and many people fear that with this act we have given victory to our enemies.

For example, the USA Patriot Act gave the FBI the power to access library records, student records, and the most private medical records of any American citizen, without a warrant and without probable cause. Even telling anyone what the FBI had done was made a violation of that law so that you would never know if your constitutional rights had been violated by another illegal power grab by the Controllers.

We have limited the number of acts of violence by the terrorists, but many fear that we have also reduced the individual liberties that make our nation the envy of the world. There is little doubt that we have enhanced the opinion that government is the solution to all problems regardless of the cost in money and freedoms. "The operation was a success, but the patient died."

If this law is as bad as many fear, we do have hope. At great sacrifice, our Founders gave us a new form of government, and it was carefully planned to minimize the potential abuses of any form of government. We have three branches in our government that are designed to act as checks and balances against each other. Since our country was established as a republic and was never intended to be a "mob-ruled" democracy, we have a Constitution and a judicial system.

Will our judges protect the system as defined by our Constitution, or will they write new law according to how they think it should be? Will they invalidate any unconstitutional provisions in the Patriot Act, or will they develop new precedents to justify them, based in part on past faulty precedents? Will they protect our system or issue a ruling according to their personal political ideologies like they did with the challenge to the Bipartisan Campaign Reform Act of 2002?

The answers are largely up to us. Just how apathetic will we be when it comes to ensuring that we continue to enjoy the government that was handed to us by the Founders? As we go to press, the Supreme Court is striking down some of the worst provisions in the law, so there is some reason for hope.

Sex Crimes?

Whereas most of today's so-called left-wingers or liberals are the Controllers on so many issues, it is the so-called right-wingers or conservatives who are generally the Controllers on the issue of homosexuals and who consider homosexuality to be a sex crime. Particularly when discussing same-sex marriage, the Controllers resort to historical traditions, God's laws, and the fictitious distinction between rights and privileges that someone conjured up to subvert the Bill of Rights. Many say that same-sex unions are contrary to God's law prohibiting homosexuality as expressed in Leviticus 18:22 and 20:13.

I say—so what? That is, just what does any particular religious belief have to do with the secular laws of this country? It also states in Leviticus 19:28 that it is a sin to put tattoos on your body, and no one is lynching any tattoo artists or lobbying our representatives to incorporate a sanction into our overblown criminal code for having a tattoo. There are a host of additional religious offenses that are not addressed by our secular laws, such as the demand that women remain silent in church and prohibitions against eating pork, shellfish, and turtle soup.

Not that it has any bearing on our country's legal system, but I believe in God, and I also believe that He has infinite powers and was able to create an entire universe. It appears to me that He probably would not need a lot of human help in punishing those who break His laws. He should be able to do that quite adequately on His timetable and in His manner. Besides, there are a lot of differing religious beliefs, and it is impossible to govern a country trying to follow all of them. That is why our Founders in the First Amendment prohibited Congress from making any law that would establish a religion or prohibit anyone from freely exercising a religion of his or her choice. Although the Declaration of Independence maintains that all people are endowed by their Creator with certain unalienable rights, it does not support Antonin Scalia's assertion that "government derives its authority from God." To the contrary, the Declaration of Independence maintains that governments derive "their just powers from the consent of the governed."

> *"Our civil rights have no dependence on our religious opinions, any more than our opinions in physics or geometry."*
>
> —THOMAS JEFFERSON

In discussions of the value of proposed legislation, it is totally immaterial whether or not anyone believes in God or whether anyone's religious beliefs are consistent with the statements in Leviticus about homosexuality. As John Stuart Mill observed, "the only purpose for which power can be rightfully exercised over any member of a civilized community, against his will, is to prevent harm to others. His own good, either physical or moral, is not sufficient warrant."

It is likewise immaterial whether anyone agrees with Galileo that there is no conflict between a belief or disbelief in God and the scientific knowledge that the Earth is not the center of the universe. Furthermore, it is immaterial whether anyone agrees with Darwin that there is no conflict between a belief or disbelief in God and the scientific knowledge that evolution is either a law of nature or a part of God's plan.

If we humans should decide to punish those who steal, kill, etc., this decision should be based solely on our desire for some measure of peace on Earth, regardless of whether some of us believe that our laws coincide at times with those of the Creator. It is simply outside the scope of authority granted to our government to decide whether homosexuality is a sin or if it just the behavior of one of the infinite varieties of humans created by God or evolved through nature.

Those issues are also far beyond the scope of intellect possessed by the author. (Don't you hate it when someone refers to himself in the third person like I just did? Well, if that is the worst that I have offended you in this book, you really need to wake up and start taking notes. There will be some serious exams before the end of your life, and your descendants need you to make some damn good grades.)

The operative question in governing our country is just who will be hurt by letting same-sex partners formalize their existing agreements? I do not see how that will threaten my life, liberty, or property. Does it threaten yours, and if so, how? Or, are you just a control freak who is willing to expend the country's resources regulating yet another activity? Incidentally, many real estate managers consider the best possible tenant for an apartment to be a committed homosexual couple. They generally earn good incomes, pay their bills, take care of the property, do not make much noise, do not move often once they feel safe in one location, and do not have any children to drain their available funds or create any damage, so there should be no reason for a landlord to discriminate against them.

However, the issue of homosexual couples as adoptive parents of minors does require more thought. Protecting the rights of minors is an issue that absolutely must be controlled by government. At times, children simply need the police power of the state to protect them. In fact, there would be fewer children falling through the cracks of the system responsible for their protection if less of the nation's resources were dissipated on government attempts to control other activities best left to God and other institutions.

There is little that can be done in many cases, such as when a child is born into a traditional marriage and later becomes the child of a parent in a same-sex union due to divorce and a change in lifestyle of the caretaker. However, delightful movie comedies to the contrary, I still question the wisdom of allowing the adoption of a child by a same-sex partnership. Every child seems to need the nurturing of both a loving adult male and a loving adult female. There are already far too many children in families that do not meet those criteria because of a lack of love between the adult male and the adult female, and I am not yet convinced that it is beneficial to voluntarily add another group of children to the list unless the only available option is foster care. Experts on the subject have written about the gaps in development in boys who have been under-fathered and over-mothered. They have also written about the same problem in reverse for girls, but I do not claim to be an expert in the field and am only suggesting that careful study be undertaken before entrusting helpless children to anyone.

Pedophilia, rape, and abuse of power for sex (heterosexual or homosexual) harm others and are rightly considered to be criminal acts. In such cases there truly "ought to be a law." If we are unable to prevent such harmful acts with persuasion, we can and should enforce controls and penalties. We can and should control each individual's ability to repeat these crimes by restraining him/her (usually him) behind bars. The time spent enforcing these controls will be costly, and there will be less wealth to share as a result. However, this is a necessary expense to protect ourselves from harm.

I consider promiscuity (both heterosexual or homosexual) to be immoral, but on this point, I maintain that we should be Persuaders and not Controllers. We can explain the emotional and health problems that occur from such behaviors and attempt to convince others which choices are harmful. Then, we can make sure that each individual has to be responsible for the choices he or she makes that result in problems.

I believe that most homosexuals are not harming others and, short of behaviors that actually harm others, they are not committing what we should classify as a crime simply by being what they are. Maybe a certain percentage of the population has genes or other factors that caused them at birth to have a sexual nature different from mine. Maybe they made a conscious decision as to lifestyle, or maybe they chose their lifestyle at the same time that I chose to be a right-handed male heterosexual with blue eyes and gray hair—that is, never. (I damn sure never chose the gray hair—or wrinkles either, for that matter.)

Maybe a majority of American voters believes it is a sin to act on homosexual impulses, and maybe not. The key point is that for the purpose of governing this country, the issue is immaterial. Government controls should always be reserved to punish those who commit acts that truly harm others and, ideally, to deter others from doing likewise. Government absolutely should not be used to satisfy the compulsion of some to criminalize behaviors that they consider to be stupid, sinful, or immoral just for the supposed benefits of controlling symptoms of problems.

I am a Persuader as to the acts I consider to be immoral and even see some type of formalized union of same-sex couples as a positive force in reducing both the immoral and the truly criminal acts. If we would stop spending so much time trying to exert government control on homosexual behavior between consenting adults, more of those behaviors would mature into stable relationships, and even the militant homosexuals would have less reason to be so militant in response to the totally unreasonable attitude presently being directed toward them. My only request of homosexuals in the area of same-sex unions is for them to call these unions something other than "marriage," as that term has a long history as a male-female union for the purpose of giving birth to children and raising them in a nurturing family environment.

And, yes, whereas I never became a homosexual or made a conscious choice to be a heterosexual, I did make a series of choices that led me to become an opinionated son-of-a-bitch. It is a very good thing for me that I lived most of my life during the brief period in American history after our various governments had ceased imposing criminal sanctions for controversial speech and before they started a trend toward instituting the despicable practice again. Right now, the Controllers are using labels of political correctness, election reform, patriotism, and hate speech to make successful attacks on our freedom of speech. If the current trend continues, they will be putting people like me into dungeons in another generation or two.

Abortion, Etc.

The Right Wing of Controllers International wants to deny all or almost all abortions. The Left-Wingers want to make abortions available to all, at public expense, and for any reason or no reason at all. People who were not aborted generally express a preference for their own lives over what some would call a premature death and others call a termination of the potential for life. When presented with a state law addressing this extremely difficult conflict of desires and rights, the Supreme Court twisted itself into knots to find a justification for assuming jurisdiction in spite of the numerous prohibitions of power in the Constitution that had told these justices very clearly that it was none of their damn business. After usurping jurisdiction, the judges were also somehow able to determine that the Constitution had said something on the subject so that they were able to rule in favor of one side over the other. By a strange coincidence, they ruled that the U.S. Constitution had mandated for the state law to be exactly what the majority of the federal justices happened to think it should be. Consequently, they usurped the authority of the state legislature that had written the law in question and passed a federal law from the bench.

They even went so far as to "find" in our Constitution the authorization for the Supreme Court to legislate the details of what was and was not permissible during each of the three trimesters of pregnancy. That discovery is as ludicrous as their current ability to find authorization in our Constitution for them to rely on a domestic consensus of opinion and the laws of other countries when preempting the laws of some of our sovereign states and ruling on the proposed execution of certain minors for committing certain state crimes.

Possibly the most degrading and embarrassing period of our nation's judicial history occurred during the height of the legal battle of free speech vs. pornography. Back in the 1970s, it was common knowledge that judges throughout our entire judicial system were spending countless hours studying such magazines as *Hustler* and *Screw* and movies such as *Deep Throat* and *Debbie Does Dallas* to see which ones could pass the "socially redeeming value" test. The judicial activism of our august Supreme Court justices had somehow discovered that the Constitution permitted them to rewrite state laws and that the standard of socially redeeming value was required by our Constitution for controversial salacious materials to be protected by the First Amendment. I hope the politically appointed "Your Honors" got enough voyeuristic pleasure from the exercise to compensate for the damage they caused to the Constitution that we have to endure every day. We on the other side of the bench are constantly dealing with the repercussions of the fact that they had usurped state legislative powers while rushing to their absurd conclusions. All the garbage they wrote in their decisions back then will have to be honored as legal precedents until we struggle through the process of amending the Constitution. It would really make life easier if our judges would just read the document every decade or so.

The new law pertaining to abortion is either better or worse than what the state legislature had written, but the way it was created is a recipe for disaster. The nine political appointees comprising the Supreme Court had no more authority to create this law than the government of France—only the backing of the rest of our government, which has more willingness than the French to use military force to enforce edicts. The worst aspect is there is no effective check or balance to remove or amend it. Our Constitution had established an extremely limited federal government, leaving most issues, including abortion, to the states. The Constitution had also given all powers to pass any federal legislation only to Congress and not to the courts. Our Supreme Court got power hungry and changed all of that, so we now have too great a concentration of power at the federal level and specifically within the federal court system.

One of the most disturbing aspects of Roe v. Wade is that it is a highly visible example of how the Supreme Court has developed since the War of Secession into a federal agency acting in concert with Congress to expand the federal government at the expense of the people and the states. After that war, the people (well, at least the victors) recognized there was a need to protect the former slaves at the federal level and followed the dictates of the Constitution to do so. They passed the Fourteenth Amendment for the necessary authority and in that amendment gave Congress the "power to enforce this article by appropriate legislation." That is, the new power of Congress and the civil rights legislation that followed had been duly authorized by an amendment to our Constitution and not just by passing the desired laws and expecting the Supreme Court to cooperate by calling the Constitution a "living document" that could be ignored.

Now, the Supreme Court does not recognize any requirement to wait for constitutional amendments and congressional legislation. It simply refers to prior Supreme Court rulings, using them as precedents regardless of how erroneous they may be. Unfortunately, it rarely refers to the Constitution to correct the errors of the past and to get back on track, and the list of cases the justices cite as precedents simply amounts to their rap sheet of other times they have been guilty of the illegal use of authority. It seems they enjoyed the legally granted power they exercised over the Southern states in issues of slavery and civil rights and decided to expand illegally into all the states and into many other issues.

Another example is Alabama's Supreme Court Judge Roy Moore and the religious/historical monument to the Ten Commandments that he put in Alabama's Supreme Court Building. Regardless of whether the State of Alabama should have allowed such a display, just what jurisdiction did the federal courts have over the issue? Why do we concede that the federal courts have authority in any area they choose? The First Amendment does deny Congress the right to meddle in religious matters, but it is silent on what the various branches of the Alabama government choose to do, and the combined Ninth and Tenth Amendments expressly tell the federal government to mind its own business.

> *"The enumeration in the Constitution, of certain rights, shall not be construed to deny or disparage others retained by the people. The powers not delegated to the United States by the Constitution, nor prohibited by it to the States, are reserved to the States respectively, or to the people."*

Our State Constitution is not very embarrassing—but only because very few people know what it says. If I ever had to swear an oath to defend it, I would need to delay my response for a year or two just to find out what such an oath would mean. Those few who give a damn know that it is a total disgrace, but that is no more justification for the federal government to get involved than it would be for the government of Haiti to do so. Remember that the states were in existence before they joined together to become the United States, and the only powers the U.S. Government has are those limited powers given to it by the states and the people, either in the original document or by amendments to it. The U.S. Supreme Court has gotten so used to legislating solutions for state issues that they no longer even consider whether there is an enabling provision or amendment to the Constitution allowing them to enter into state concerns. They need to stop their illegal meddling in the affairs of states and start paying attention to unconstitutional activities at the federal level, such as the "McCain-Feingold Act to Restrict Free Speech without a Constitutional Amendment Authorizing Such Governmental Activity."

We, the people, may choose to be Controllers. We also may be so afraid that someone with serious money will dominate political speech that we are willing to address only the symptoms and thus eliminate free speech for all of us. If so, we will pass a constitutional amendment saying so. Until that time, the judges need to start honoring their oaths to defend the Constitution instead of going along with whatever Congress wants except when they find it necessary to defend their court precedents and their own personal and political biases.

Am I a fool to disagree with the propaganda of our government monopoly schools that all true wisdom lies with government, especially the federal government or possibly even the United Nations? More importantly, since I consider it contemptible for the well-informed people on our U.S. Supreme Court to refuse to obey their oaths of office, does that place me in contempt of court? Who knows? It all depends on what powers they want to usurp today. We, the people now have to hope (or pray as the case may be) that our favorite group wins the next election. Knowing that all winners will take unconstitutional (aka, illegal) actions, we can only hope that we like most of the results, because almost no one in Washington will ever consider the constitutionality of any power grab by a fellow Washingtonian.

Some judicial appointees to the U.S. District Courts (trial level) happen to have excellent abilities to adjudicate, but the only operative prerequisites for the job are that they have law degrees and political pull, but just not in that order. It is common knowledge that the judges of the twelve U.S. Courts of Appeal and the U.S. Supreme Court will vote *in closed session* to protect the sacred precedents of their respective courts or their conservative or liberal bias, and almost all presidents and senators have simply yielded to the judges' power grab as a fait accompli. No one has insisted on a Sunshine Law forcing the deliberations to be conducted in public, and the primary response of presidents and senators now is to try to pack the appellate benches with judges who agree with their own respective biases rather than trying to find judges who will obey their oaths to support the Constitution.

With a few exceptions for gross misconduct, federal judges are guaranteed appointments for life, and that is one of the few parts of the Constitution that they will defend. For those judges who take office knowing that they will never honor their oaths to defend other parts of those words written on paper, I guess our only solution is to let them serve their lifetime appointments from inside jail cells in one of our numerous penitentiaries, since they have been guilty of an extremely serious form of perjury. Maybe some jail time will help to convince them their powers are limited, documents are not "alive," and our Constitution was not written on Silly Putty.

But—back to the issue of abortion. Long after the ruling of Roe v. Wade, both sides remain militant in their positions, and both continue to ignore the Constitution while seeking ways either to maintain the status quo or to change it. Unfortunately, both sides seem to forget there is a real problem in any society where the desires and needs of pregnant women are so often in conflict with the desires and needs of their unborn babies (or clumps of tissue with the potential of life). There is another facet of this problem in our society where there are so many babies who survive their mothers' pregnancies but are unwanted, abused, and neglected. So many of these children run away from horrible torment in their homes only to suffer short lives of worse torment as prostitutes and thieves on the streets.

It is outside the scope of this book for a detailed analysis of the underlying problems that result in the symptoms of a huge number of abortions being performed simultaneous with a huge number of unwanted babies being born into and outside of marriage. (That means that I have no clue as to the solutions to these underlying problems or even as to what the underlying problems are.)

Adam Smith told us in 1776 that the best way for everyone to prosper financially is to use free enterprise competition to control the facts that most people are greedy and that there is a finite amount of everything in the world. Our country's Founders told us in 1788 what powers to give our government and what limits to place on it so that it will be a positive force and not a negative one. All we have to do for our grandchildren to be wealthy is to get back to what they said. However, Mr. Smith and our Founders did not give us much guidance in the much more complicated area of the care and nurturing of our off-spring. It seems that human lives must be subject to the laws of supply and demand just like soybeans and pork bellies. An increasing supply of people in the world without a commensurate increase in demand seems to have resulted in a decreasing value for each person.

Who is studying the underlying causes of the symptoms of the problem? Why are there so many unwanted babies? I do not know. Are the underlying causes of the symptoms valid concerns that someone should address? Absolutely! Evidence suggests there is a strong correlation between low incomes and unwanted children. Further study should be made to determine if less emphasis on control and more freedom to create wealth would result in fewer abortions and unwanted children.

"War" on Drugs

> *"There are not enough jails, not enough policemen, not enough courts to enforce a law not supported by the people."*
>
> —HUBERT H. HUMPHREY

"Give 'em hell, Harry" Truman once said, "I never give them hell. I just tell the truth and they think it's hell." Today's version is that we tell a lie and hope everyone is too dense to realize that we are not waging any war on drugs—and it is not even close to being Hell on Earth for most of the pushers. Once again there is a gap between the label and the contents. Since our leaders say we have declared "war," we tend to conclude that we must be truly committed to a cause and that we have the will to win. If you still believe that, you are sadly mistaken.

We are not committed and have only four choices:

1. Surrender.
2. Get committed and fight to win.
3. Continue what we are doing.
4. Retreat and try another approach.

What we are doing now is untenable. It is just another Vietnam. We never acquired the will to win that war, and we finally suffered enough losses to admit temporary defeat, stop fighting, and retreat to fight Communism another way. The decision of the British to stop resisting us in our War for Independence is another example of a retreat to fight another way, but an example of a defeat was their decision a few years later after losing the War of 1812 to cease all attempts to force us to become a colony again.

In addition to the serious question of whether the enforcement approach of Controllers can ever truly win any war, look at our experience with Prohibition. In the "war" led by the Controllers to prohibit the sale and consumption of alcohol, we never had the will to win and simply created a situation that made the selling of alcohol extremely profitable for Al Capone and others like him. Illegal alcohol is much more expensive than legal alcohol, and huge profits went to those criminals who were the most ruthless in providing it.

The current efforts of Controllers to prohibit drugs other than alcohol exhibit the same failure of will to win and are creating a fertile environment for the same type of people to accumulate huge fortunes. I do not believe that controlling the symptoms is the answer to solving the underlying problem of drug use. Even if it were, I do not see us ever acquiring the will to win and therefore suggest that the only conclusion left is to concede temporary defeat and retreat to fight another way.

Remember that a retreat is not necessarily the same as surrender. Drugs create serious problems that we cannot afford to ignore. They have the power to destroy lives, families, and even countries, and we absolutely must do something about the problem. A decision to decriminalize the sale or use of a dangerous substance is not the same as saying that it is okay, and I have no idea how we got into the trap of thinking that if something is not criminal, it must be okay. The fact that we have somehow let government make our value judgments is crazy and sick.

Remember the positions our government has taken that you are furious about. I am especially angry about the Socialism Security Ponzi Fraud by which my government started stealing from my children before they were born and forced all of us into a mandatory chain letter. You may have similar anger but over completely different issues. The politicians are constantly buying votes from an unlimited number of "special interest groups," and they make no attempt to control the costs you have to pay for anything they decide to do. The Federal Department of Cost Control does not even exist. Our government officials do not occupy the moral high ground as they pass laws on us while ignoring the Constitution that attempts in vain to control them, and you need to set your moral values without referring to their laws.

We need to remember that the private use of tobacco is not criminal, but more and more of us have realized that tobacco is a very dangerous and destructive substance. Following the pattern of noncriminal tobacco and decriminalized alcohol—and until our society is mature enough for a predominately Libertarian voluntary fee system—we can tax drug sales for revenue and stop spending billions of dollars on finding, arresting, trying, and incarcerating those who sell or use drugs. The combination of more money coming in and less going out will be substantial.

But the secondary benefits of decriminalizing drug sales and use may be even more substantial. Since the decriminalized drugs will cost less, those drug users who do not have substantial incomes will commit fewer crimes to support their habits, and we will save the money currently being spent to replace the property that a significant percentage of drug users steal in order to obtain the huge amounts of money required to buy illegal drugs. Also, since the number of these secondary crimes of theft will decrease, we can also spend less money on finding, arresting, trying, and incarcerating those who would otherwise be committing them.

If we decriminalize drug sales and use, we will not be able to continue feeding the feelings of moral superiority we get by punishing the "pushers" and "junkies," but the most cost-effective way to get people off drugs is through treatment and twelve-step addiction programs. If we stop punishing them at great expense, we can help them and our society. Eventually, we can educate and persuade others of the dangers of drug use, just as we are now making progress educating and persuading others of the dangers of cigarettes and alcohol. The controls we now try to impose on drugs are certainly not working, and we need to consider another option. I suggest education and persuasion. While we are at it, we could also take a hard look at the controls that some want to place on guns and other symptoms of real problems in our society.

> *"I am convinced that we can do to guns what we've done to drugs: create a multi-billion dollar underground market over which we have absolutely no control."*
>
> —GEORGE L. ROMAN

Government Monopoly Schools

> *"One of these days they are going to remove so much of the 'hooey' and the thousands of things the schools have become clogged up with, and we will find that we can educate our broods for about one-tenth of the price and learn 'em something that they might actually use after they escape."*
>
> —WILL ROGERS

I have some questions for you. Would you let a politician or bureaucrat tell you whether to subscribe to any religion? Would you also let him tell you which religion was acceptable? Would you let a politician or bureaucrat tell you what political party you had to support? Would you let him tell you what type and brand of breakfast food to eat? Would you let him tell you what news source to read, watch, or listen to?

Of course you would not! Those are absolutely ridiculous questions. We are afraid of freedom, but we are not that afraid. In each case, we would demand the right to examine the alternatives and decide for ourselves what is best for us.

But now—would you let a bureaucrat tell you what school is best for your child? Uh oh! Would you? Did you? The wealthy can pay taxes to support the government monopoly schools and still have enough money to send their children to any private school in the country. The middle class can often move into a decent school district somewhere in the suburbs. Everyone else has to accept the school designated by the bureaucrats as all they can get for their children. Many of these schools are marginal or worse, but very few complaints are voiced. Those forced to send their children to the bad ones are stuck with the current version of the separate and unequal education of the segregation era. Even the "good" public schools are the result of voting and compromises, and your individual choices are limited.

Everyone seems to agree that education is vitally important for our children and our society. Many Persuaders will cross the line with me and agree that we should use government force to pool our resources to provide the best education possible for our children. However, after we have used the tax system to raise money for education, what is the absolute best we can do? Should we give the government a monopoly over the delivery of the product, or should we somehow allow competition from the marketplace to create and deliver innovative and high-quality methods of education?

Government did not create electricity, the telephone, the automobile, the airplane, computers, or the high-speed dental drill. Our children are far more important than any of these innovations, but we relegate them to an antiquated government monopoly system. Once again, the Controllers consider government to be the only solution for every problem when it should be the solution only for those problems for which it is suited. By using a voucher system to provide funds for the education of each individual child, we would encourage competition and reap the benefits of the free market system. Since even the poorest children would have their vouchers available to buy the best services available, entrepreneurs would have the incentive to produce. Some providers would start developing innovations using the Internet, television, videos, and other techniques that we cannot possibly predict. It is certain that the chance of innovations will be slim-to-none under our current government monopoly system. We have tried this system for centuries and have ample proof that the results are severely limited.

Even the United Nations gives the correct lip service to one aspect of education, saying in their Universal Declaration of Human Rights, "Parents have a prior right to choose the kind of education that shall be given to their children." We in this country certainly do not try to reach that goal and willingly accept whatever is delivered at whatever cost government can get away with. For far too many of our children, and especially the poor, it is a shabby product at an astronomical cost.

Why can we understand that a business monopoly is detrimental and, simultaneously, cannot understand that a government monopoly in our school system is even more detrimental? Why do we use competition to limit the greed and stupidity of businessmen but protect any greedy or stupid bureaucrats in our schools with a monopoly? Surely our children are much more important than a new gadget on a car? The evidence is abundant, but our eyes are closed. We have been indoctrinated to the point that we are able to attribute every flaw in the current system to something other than the system itself.

> *"Don't confuse me with the facts; my mind is made up."*
>
> —UNKNOWN

Why are the Controllers more concerned about the teachers' unions than they are about the education of our children? It is not like all schools will disappear along with all of the job opportunities for qualified teachers and administrators just because we decide to terminate a government monopoly.

A 1914 educational report in the State of Maryland showed ample funds but disturbing illiteracy figures, inadequate buildings, frequent truancy, badly trained teachers, poorly educated and politically appointed supervisors, and deficient accountability. So, what was the state's answer to the problem? What else? If any government operation is performing poorly, the only solution ever considered is for more control through more government, and of course, financed by more taxes.

I do not know how the Maryland school system is performing today as a result of their "solution," but everyone knows that something is seriously wrong with public education in most areas of our country. It is time to try a different solution, but instead, what are we doing? We recently created a national Department of Education and keep increasing its budget with hopes that a faulty system will somehow produce excellent results if we just waste enough money on it.

Having a Federal Department of Education is worse than stupid; it is crazy. It sucks time, money, and energy out of our economy and produces nothing. That department is an unnecessary drag on our economy. We need to abolish it and send the money (as vouchers) directly to the children, whose educations require more than lip service in order to improve. Okay, you disagree—so name one single accomplishment that the Department of Education has made. Incidentally, accomplishments should be measured by students' performance in real life, not by amount of dollars spent.

For example, we could accomplish something by sending \$240,000 in education vouchers to parents of school children. Do you really think it was better for us to pay millions of dollars for the services of the bureaucrats at the disaster known as the Department of Education? Did they use their extensive and expensive talents during President George W. Bush's first term to send $240,000 to TV commentator Armstrong Williams to provide an excellent education to hundreds of children? Well, not exactly! The money was really paid to Mr. Williams to promote (i.e., propagandize with taxpayer money) the "No Child Left Behind" program on his show and to interview Education Secretary Rod Paige for TV and radio spots that aired during the show in 2004. The money sent to him was part of a $1 million deal with the Ketchum public relations firm that also produced "video news releases" designed to look like news stories. By the way, those millions of dollars in salaries and office expenses for bureaucrats never reached any schoolteacher either, and the Bush administration also used taxpayer money for "news releases" to promote its Medicare prescription drug plan.

But what if we adopt a voucher system and some of the new entrepreneurial educators turn out to be crooks who just take the money, deliver a poor product, and get rich from their ill-gotten gains? That is a valid concern, as it absolutely will happen in some cases, just as surely as there are some government employees who are currently delivering a poor educational product while embezzling substantial sums from the system to get rich. Since there are some crooks in every area of human endeavor (even in our sacred government), a valid function of government is to assist the natural controls of competition to enforce reasonable rules of fair play. There would be ample space in our prisons for educational scammers and other "white collar" criminals if we would just stop pretending to fight a "war" on drugs.

But what if some parents use the education funds to send their children to religious schools? So what? As Neal Boortz recently said, children sent to religious schools will be indoctrinated toward acceptance of certain religious beliefs, but children sent to government monopoly schools are already being indoctrinated toward acceptance of certain attitudes about government. Right now, children are being taught ideas that result from political voting and compromises, and it is common folklore that a camel is a horse designed by a committee using the same system of back-scratching and payoffs. Under a voucher system, the parents of each child will determine what they consider the best for that child, and any mistakes made will not affect every child in an entire government monopoly school district.

We certainly see ample evidence that students educated by the government monopoly schools have been taught that this country is a democracy instead of a republic and that the solution to every problem is more government. I went to government monopoly schools that were better than most, and that is what I was taught. I had no clue about the negative effects of too much government until I read *Atlas Shrugged* and other books by Ayn Rand, which I strongly recommend to the reader. Ms. Rand was born in Russia and lived there, through the Revolution, until age 21, at which point she moved to the United States. Her perspective on Controllers vs. Persuaders is based on real-life experiences in two countries that were at opposite ends of the spectrum until we both changed. Unfortunately, the changes in our country were for the worse, and the changes for the better in the former Soviet Union are shaky at best.

Other products of the government monopoly school systems have gotten jobs in the media, where they constantly reinforce the government monopoly school indoctrination through a careful editing of the facts to be presented in most of the daily "news" programs and publications. This is known as selective reporting and media bias, but it is not completely the fault of the individuals in the media. It is the logical consequence of the system we allow, and it is our fault that we allow it. We can change it, but we are products of the same schools, and other things just seem to be more important. Besides, why should we ever challenge the assertion that more government is the best solution to every problem? That is what everyone says, and it is so easy.

Q: "What is worse, ignorance or apathy?"
A: "I don't know, and I don't care."

The main thing we need to fear about the voucher system is that government control will accompany the government money, and all of the potential benefits will be lost. The main reason to change the present system is that government controls are choking the educational process. We will have to ensure that free enterprise with minimal controls is allowed to create a better product and that government controls are not allowed to destroy the new system.

Legal Loopholes

We hear all the time about a known criminal being set free because of a technicality. Just what are these legal loopholes, and why do our judges allow known criminals back on the streets to harm us? Are these judges out of control? There is little doubt that some judges are out of control and are legislating from the bench according to their view of what the law should be instead of ruling on what it is. However, there are very good reasons that we require these judges to set criminals free on "mere technicalities."

In the movie *The Star Chamber*, Michael Douglas played the part of a judge who became distressed at the number of guilty persons he was legally required to release due to various technicalities. Consequently, he became one of nine judges who decided to do something about the problem. They reviewed cases and hired assassins to kill the guilty who otherwise would have gotten away. When Michael Douglas' character discovered that two of those he had set up for assassination were actually innocent, he became upset and turned states' witness against the other judges to stop them from taking the law into their hands any longer.

The movie dramatized the points that no one should act as judge, jury, and executioner and that some of the accused who at first appear to be guilty are truly innocent. The movie failed, however, to address an even more important point that the right-wing faction of Controllers seem to be unable to grasp. After we give the police departments and prosecutors the power to take our freedom away under certain circumstances, just what will make them adhere to the rules? The most effective way we have found so far to prevent unreasonable searches, torture chambers, and dungeons is to set free all of the innocent and all of the guilty who would otherwise be convicted only because government officials abused their power. These "loopholes" are put into our legal system deliberately because of the propensity of government to abuse power and the need to protect all of us against such abuse.

The Founders of our country intentionally made everything difficult for government to do (or rather, to get away with). To pass a law, a proposed bill has to be passed by two houses of Congress and signed by the president, all three of which are elected according to different rules. Congress can overrule a presidential veto, but it takes the votes of more than a simple majority of both houses to do so. Then, for any new law that does get passed to be actually enforced, it has to pass the test of constitutionality in the court system. The process doesn't end there, either. We, the people, can force the passage of a constitutional amendment to overrule the judges.

So, there is no surprise that the penalty imposed on the government is extremely stiff for taking a citizen's freedom away without following the rules we citizens impose on our government. If you know a better way to protect our rights, feel free to lobby for changes in the law. Meanwhile, stop accepting the verdict of the prosecutors and some of the media that U.S. citizen Jose Padilla is obviously guilty and therefore not entitled to a trial. As John Donne said, "Ask not for whom the bell tolls; it tolls for thee."

> *"To declare that in the administration of criminal law the end justifies the means—to declare that the Government may commit crimes in order to secure conviction of a private criminal—would bring terrible retribution."*
>
> —JUSTICE LOUIS D. BRANDEIS

Test question: Was it good or bad that we, the people, lost some of our faith in government due to the impeachment of President Nixon for his abuses of power? Clue: Our Founders firmly believed that unchecked power should not be given to any person, to any private institution, to a central government, or even to any branch of a central government. They were not big supporters of the concept of blind faith in human nature, and they did not create a mob-ruled democracy. They created a republic.

National Disasters

If your house is destroyed by a storm, fire, earthquake, etc., our current system is such that you need to hope or pray that 1) You paid your insurance premiums, or 2) There was a large number of other houses destroyed by the same disaster. If enough voters are involved, the problem will get the attention of the politicians in both parties in Washington, and checks will flow. It is just too bad for you if the disaster is extensive and you were responsible enough to pay your insurance premiums. The unintended result of the actions of the well-meaning Controllers is that responsible behavior will be penalized and irresponsible behavior will be rewarded anytime enough votes are involved.

The reverse occurs when there are only a few voters affected by the disaster. If it is just your house that gets destroyed, you should have gotten insurance, and those who are irresponsible will reap the consequences. "Misery loves company," but politicians love misery only if it has enough company.

Nonviolent Responses

James Douglass has said that the best possible response to evil is a well-organized and assertive nonviolent resistance; the next best is a well-organized and well-executed violent response;

and the worst possible response is passive acquiescence and appeasement.

I submit that a poorly executed, tentative, or unfinished resistance of any kind should also be listed among the worst possible responses, and to the contrary of what Mr. Douglass has stated, I submit the hypothesis that a "good cop, bad cop" approach may be the best of all responses. That is, the most effective resistance to evil might be to speak firmly and every now and then to swing a big stick.

There are far too many evil people, foreign and domestic, who will consider you to be a "paper tiger" and take advantage of what they perceive as your weakness if you keep talking softly and never swing the big stick. Every now and then in today's world, you seem to have to remind someone that if he continues to live by the sword, he can die by the cruise missile. Or, as some of my relatives have said, "You sometimes have to hit a mule with a fence post to get his attention." For example:

- The Jews did not make any significant resistance, violent or otherwise, to the Nazis and were almost exterminated in Europe.
- There was only a small percentage of honorable Germans who made a poorly organized resistance to the evil programs of Hitler's gangster government. They lost their lives and gained nothing.
- A better organized and supported resistance in Denmark blocked Hitler from accomplishing many of his goals there, and many of the resisters survived.
- An even better organized and supported nonviolent resistance led by Mahatma Gandhi forced England to abandon its claims on India at a time when "the sun never set on the British Empire." Bloodshed on both sides was kept to a minimum.
- President Kennedy was guilty of a poorly executed and tentative military response to Fidel Castro when he withdrew

the planned air support of the attack at the Bay of Pigs. Men died and nothing was accomplished.

- If there had been only a few supporters of Rosa Parks in 1955, those supporters would have lost their jobs, and the Montgomery, Alabama, bus boycott would have failed. It took many months for a united front to make a substantial change, again with minimal bloodshed.
- When the U.S.–led coalition left Iraq after the Gulf War of 1991 without removing Saddam Hussein, his evil regime flourished like kudzu. (For you non-Southerners, kudzu is a vine imported from Japan to feed livestock and stop erosion. It will grow on rocks, in gullies, and over slowly moving wagons.)
- Everyone knew that Mr. Hussein had possessed and used weapons of mass destruction during his control of Iraq. After the Gulf War of 1991, he relocated those weapons, postponed any plans for developing more such weapons, allowed UN inspectors into the country, and made at least a show of cooperation primarily during the times that the U.S. was making the most serious threats of using military force again.
- President Lincoln's Emancipation Proclamation did not attempt to free the slaves in the Union states but only in the Confederate states, where it was ignored as the edict of a foreign government. It was only after the U.S. Army suffered a huge number of casualties and caused immense human suffering and other collateral damage that the slaves were set free in the South and soon thereafter in the North.
- However, the slaves were not truly set free until after Martin Luther King, Jr.'s successful nonviolent resistance to the form of slavery we called segregation, discrimination, and separate but equal. Even then, some of the anti-segregation forces, such as the Black Panthers, were violent, and some believe that this violence expedited the success of Dr. King's nonviolent approach.

We certainly need to strive for the goal of being able to achieve win-win solutions by reason alone, or by reason supported by well-organized and assertive but nonviolent resistance to evil. We are, however, at best in a transition period and still a long way from that goal today. Until the anti-war proponents can establish effective nonviolent ways to combat evil in the world, I will not support anyone for commander-in-chief, vice commander-in-chief, senator, or representative who hampers our ability and resolve to use force here and abroad to protect my family. This applies specifically to those members of my own Libertarian Party who believe in living and letting live while evil people are trying to kill us and our way of life—certainly not the same as living and letting *us* live. The idealists who rely totally on negotiations and appeasement with tyrants within the United Nations and elsewhere have their heads firmly buried in the sand while my family is at risk, and I will vote against them every chance I get. I will do this even though it means that I will have to vote for socialistic Democrat and Republican Controllers who have changed the old campaign slogan, "A Chicken in Every Pot" and now promise us "A Regulation in Every Pot," one campaign promise they enthusiastically deliver. However, as bad as they are, our domestic control freaks are not even close to being as expensive as the imported brands—at least not yet.

There is one lesson that we should have learned from the Vietnam War concerning the use of miliary force. Regardless of whether you tend to seek peace primarily through military strength or through nonviolent means, wars undeniably result in suffering and death. There are many issues worth killing and dying for, including the ones that prompted our Founders to start a war in 1776. However, wars should be entered into only with valid reasons, clear objectives, sufficient public support, and the will to win. We sent our young men into harm's way in Vietnam with the maximum of political constraints, the minimum of public support, and the vaguest of goals. They had no chance of accomplishing whatever their mission was, and we should have learned by comparing the results of World War II with those of the Korean Conflict that you have to commit to get all the way into a war or stay completely out of it. In total, approximately 58,000 American men and women paid the ultimate price in Vietnam as pawns in this prime example of a poorly executed and tentative military response to a perceived problem. They lost everything, and we gained absolutely nothing.

United Nations

Let's start with basics and try to be realistic. The UN is run by humans; it has some value; and it has some limitations, just like the U.S. Government, the Red Cross, IBM, and your church. But we are discussing what roles various governments should play in our lives, and I do mean our lives. The debate is about life-and-death issues, and there are some truly evil tyrants in the world who do not magically become honorable people just by becoming members of an international group with a name that sounds good.

Just how much control should we give to the government of the United States, and just how much control should we give to the wannabe government of the United Nations? Remember the lessons we should have learned in American history about power grabs by a central government. The American states were formed first, and they delegated very limited power to the federal government when they formed it a few years later. After a little more than two hundred years, the federal government has turned the tables and now has the power to do anything it wants, and the power of the states and the people has become very limited. With the UN, the countries were formed first, and they likewise delegated very limited powers to that world organization when they formed it. I hate to think what will happen to Americans if that organization should acquire the power to do anything it wants. Just how many areas will the United Nations government enter with or without our consent? I consider an idealistic view of this international body to be a serious threat to the liberties and financial security of my family.

Even when labels match the contents at first, it is absolutely essential to maintain constant vigilance because the contents can be changed whenever we drop our guard. There are some areas in which I deny that the State (Nation) of Alabama has ever relinquished its powers to the United States (Nations) of America, and I certainly do not want to relinquish the sovereignty of the U.S. to the United Nations (States) of the World. It is a bad idea for the U.S. ever to relinquish to the UN the sole right to wage war, even though it was a good idea for the states to relinquish that power to the U.S. Even though we were successful in giving our presidents the power of commander-in-chief of our national forces and the power to federalize all of our state National Guard forces whenever the situation dictates such an action, it is a bad idea for the UN secretary general to become the commander-in-chief of anything or for him to gain the power to internationalize U.S. military forces. Over time, the word "State" has been reduced in status to the word "state," meaning a subservient part of a nation, and I do not want the meaning of the word "Nation" or "Country" ever to be changed to refer to a subservient part of the UN. I certainly do not want any Americans to die trying to force Ireland or China back into the United Nations if they should ever try to secede.

On the positive side, the United Nations has provided a forum to discuss numerous international issues, and it has made some attempts at improving the human condition, setting a number of long-range goals in their Universal Declaration of Human Rights. This declaration was adopted by the General Assembly in 1948, shortly after the end of yet another major breach of world peace, World War II. Sadly, many of their goals have been highly questionable from the beginning, and most of their best goals have not been reached. Remember that your right to swing your fist stops when it gets too close to my nose, and consider the following questionable goals of the UN as stated in the Universal Declaration of Human Rights:

1. Someone other than the employee is supposed to provide everyone protection against unemployment.
2. Regardless of the value of the employee, someone is supposed to provide favorable remuneration and a standard of living adequate for the health and well-being of the person and of his or her family, including food, clothing, housing, and medical care and necessary social services.
3. Someone other than the individual worker is supposed to insure him against the risks of unemployment, sickness, disability, widowhood, old age, etc.
4. Someone (I guess the various member governments) shall indoctrinate the students by directing education "to the full development of the human personality..."

The United Nations is an excellent forum for the Persuaders of the world to meet and discuss ways to define and achieve real peace. The UN has a wonderful label and the potential to promote peaceful intercourse among nations. In fact, it would be difficult to find a nation in or out of the UN that will say that it does not believe in peace. But, don't forget that contents are more important than labels. The only nations that are actually united are those that agree from time to time on any specific issue, and many nations desire peace only so long as they are free to define the word to meet their own agendas. For example, Hitler's definition of the word was for everyone else peacefully to allow him to do anything he wanted. Some religious fundamentalists consider it peaceful to force everyone to believe in God or Allah as they define Him and for everyone to follow His laws as they interpret them.

Glenn Beck said that the letters "UN" are not an abbreviation but a prefix for such words as un-able, etc. That is really the good news. Remember that this quasi-government wants to become a real government when it grows up. It has serious aspirations of attaining real powers to control your life, and there are some Americans who think that is a great idea. Your forebears pledged and many of them lost their lives and their fortunes, but not their sacred honor, to get free from King George III of England, and many leaders represented in the UN, like Kim Chong-il of North Korea, make King George III look like a Cub Scout leader. So, don't automatically worry every time that the United States rejects a treaty or other proposal promoted by this international body so well represented by corrupt dictators and thugs, and do not let the Controllers of the world reach their goal of our submission to it.

Your grandchildren will become destitute if the UN ever becomes a real grownup government with the power to control their lives. Under the pretense of getting you to pay your fair share to help the poor unfortunates of the world, they will tax you into poverty, but the poor unfortunates will never see much of the money. The dictators of the world will get most of that. It was child's play for Saddam Hussein to convert the "Oil for Food" program into a program of "Oil for Palaces and Maybe a Little Bribery and Terrorism," and there are plenty of other dictators with bank accounts in Switzerland who are rubbing their hands over the possibility that the foolish people in the United States will turn over our assets to the UN.

And just why are there so many poor people in other parts of the world anyway? We are not the only country with intelligent people and abundant natural resources. The difference is that they have controlling governments, and the idealists of both major parties in this country want our government to be more like theirs. Well, I would prefer for my grandchildren to be different. I want something a lot better for me and mine than the poverty and despair that controlling totalitarian governments of all types inevitably cause.

Global Test Question #1

After reading the following statement, explain just how the UN supports individual freedom and opposes slavery to the state.

> *"Everyone has duties to the community in which alone the free and full development of his personality is possible."*
>
> —UNITED NATIONS UNIVERSAL DECLARATION OF HUMAN RIGHTS, ARTICLE 29

Global Test Question #2

Include all five permanent members, and name a total of nine of the following fifteen Member Nations of the Security Council of the United Nations that you trust with your security:

- China, Permanent Member
- France, Permanent Member
- Russian Federation, Permanent Member
- United Kingdom, Permanent Member
- United States, Permanent Member

- Angola
- Bulgaria
- Cameroon
- Chile
- Germany
- Guinea
- Mexico
- Pakistan
- Spain
- Syrian Arab Republic

To assist you in this test question, you may want to know that each Council member has one vote. Decisions on procedural matters are made by an affirmative vote of at least nine of the 15 members. Decisions on substantive matters require nine votes, including the concurring votes of all five permanent members. This is the rule of "great Power unanimity," often referred to as the "veto" power.

Under the Charter, all Members of the United Nations agree to accept and carry out the decisions of the Security Council.

Whereas other organs of the United Nations make recommendations to governments, the Council alone has the power to make decisions that Member States are obligated under the Charter to carry out.

Global Test Question #3

From the following list of countries represented on the International Court of Justice in 2003, list more than one that you are willing to give the power to pass judgment on you:

- Brazil
- China
- Egypt
- France
- Germany
- Japan
- Jordan
- Netherlands
- Madagascar
- Russian Federation
- Sierra Leone
- Slovakia
- United Kingdom
- United States
- Venezuela

Global Test Question #4

Giving full consideration to Communist China, Cuba, Iran, Iraq, North Korea, Syria, and Vietnam, name 96 (a majority) of the following 191 Member States of the United Nations that you are willing to let vote on issues pertaining to the well-being of your children and grandchildren:

Member	*Date of Admission*
Afghanistan	19 Nov. 1946
Albania	14 Dec. 1955
Algeria	8 Oct. 1962
Andorra	28 July 1993
Angola	Dec. 1976
Antigua and Barbuda	11 Nov. 1981
Argentina	24 Oct. 1945

Armenia	2 Mar. 1992
Australia	1 Nov. 1945
Austria	14 Dec. 1955
Azerbaijan	2 Mar. 1992
Bahamas	18 Sep. 1973
Bahrain	21 Sep. 1971
Bangladesh	17 Sep. 1974
Barbados	9 Dec. 1966
Belarus	24 Oct. 1945
Belgium	27 Dec. 1945
Belize	25 Sep. 1981
Benin	20 Sep. 1960
Bhutan	21 Sep. 1971

How are you doing? That was the first twenty countries, so you should have close to ten check marks by now.

Bolivia	14 Nov. 1945
Bosnia and Herzegovina	22 May 1992
Botswana	17 Oct. 1966
Brazil	24 Oct. 1945
Brunei Darussalam	21 Sep. 1984
Bulgaria	14 Dec. 1955
Burkina Faso	20 Sep. 1960
Burundi	18 Sep. 1962
Cambodia	14 Dec. 1955
Cameroon	20 Sep. 1960
Canada	9 Nov. 1945
Cape Verde	16 Sep. 1975
Central African Republic	20 Sep. 1960
Chad	20 Sep. 1960
Chile	24 Oct. 1945
China	24 Oct. 1945
Colombia	5 Nov. 1945
Comoros	12 Nov. 1975
Congo	20 Sep. 1960
Costa Rica	2 Nov. 1945
Côte d'Ivoire	20 Sep. 1960
Croatia	22 May 1992

Cuba	24 Oct. 1945
Cyprus	20 Sep. 1960
Czech Republic	19 Jan. 1993
Democratic People's Republic of Korea	17 Sep. 1991
Democratic Republic of the Congo	20 Sep. 1960
Denmark	24 Oct. 1945
Djibouti	20 Sep. 1977
Dominica	18 Dec. 1978

Okay, that was the first fifty, so you should now have about twenty-five check marks.

Dominican Republic	24 Oct. 1945
Ecuador	21 Dec. 1945
Egypt	24 Oct. 1945
El Salvador	24 Oct. 1945
Equatorial Guinea	12 Nov. 1968
Eritrea	28 May 1993
Estonia	17 Sep. 1991
Ethiopia	13 Nov. 1945
Fiji	13 Oct. 1970
Finland	14 Dec. 1955
France	24 Oct. 1945
Gabon	20 Sep. 1960
Gambia	21 Sep. 1965
Georgia	31 July 1992
Germany	18 Sep. 1973
Ghana	8 Mar. 1957
Greece	25 Oct. 1945
Grenada	17 Sep. 1974
Guatemala	21 Nov. 1945
Guinea	12 Dec. 1958
Guinea-Bissau	17 Sep. 1974
Guyana	20 Sep. 1966
Haiti	24 Oct. 1945
Honduras	17 Dec. 1945
Hungary	14 Dec. 1955

Iceland	19 Nov. 1946
India	30 Oct. 1945
Indonesia	28 Sep. 1950
Iran (Islamic Republic of)	24 Oct. 1945
Iraq	21 Dec. 1945
Ireland	14 Dec. 1955
Israel	11 May 1949
Italy	14 Dec. 1955
Jamaica	18 Sep. 1962
Japan	18 Dec. 1956
Jordan	14 Dec. 1955
Kazakhstan	2 Mar. 1992
Kenya	16 Dec. 1963
Kiribati	14 Sept. 1999
Kuwait	14 May 1963
Kyrgyzstan	2 Mar. 1992
Lao People's Democratic Republic	14 Dec. 1955
Latvia	17 Sep. 1991
Lebanon	24 Oct. 1945
Lesotho	17 Oct. 1966
Liberia	2 Nov. 1945
Libyan Arab Jamahiriya	14 Dec. 1955
Liechtenstein	18 Sep. 1990
Lithuania	17 Sep. 1991
Luxembourg	24 Oct. 1945
Madagascar	20 Sep. 1960
Malawi	1 Dec. 1964
Malaysia	17 Sep. 1957
Maldives	21 Sep. 1965
Mali	28 Sep. 1960
Malta	1 Dec. 1964
Marshall Islands	17 Sep. 1991
Mauritania	27 Oct. 1961
Mauritius	24 Apr. 1968
Mexico	7 Nov. 1945
Micronesia (Federated States of)	17 Sep. 1991

Monaco	28 May 1993
Mongolia	27 Oct. 1961
Morocco	12 Nov. 1956
Mozambique	16 Sep. 1975
Myanmar	19 Apr. 1948
Namibia	23 Apr. 1990
Nauru	14 Sept. 1999
Nepal	14 Dec. 1955
Netherlands	10 Dec. 1945
New Zealand	24 Oct. 1945
Nicaragua	24 Oct. 1945
Niger	20 Sep. 1960
Nigeria	7 Oct. 1960
Norway	27 Nov. 1945
Oman	7 Oct. 1971
Pakistan	30 Sep. 1947
Palau	15 Dec. 1994
Panama	13 Nov. 1945
Papua New Guinea	10 Oct. 1975
Paraguay	24 Oct. 1945
Peru	31 Oct. 1945
Philippines	24 Oct. 1945
Poland	24 Oct. 1945
Portugal	14 Dec. 1955
Qatar	21 Sep. 1971
Republic of Korea	17 Sep. 1991
Republic of Moldova	2 Mar. 1992
Romania	14 Dec. 1955
Russian Federation	24 Oct. 1945
Rwanda	18 Sep. 1962
Saint Kitts and Nevis	23 Sep. 1983
Saint Lucia	18 Sep. 1979
Saint Vincent and the Grenadines	16 Sep. 1980
Samoa	15 Dec. 1976
San Marino	2 Mar. 1992
Sao Tome and Principe	16 Sep. 1975
Saudi Arabia	24 Oct. 1945

Senegal	28 Sep. 1960
Serbia and Montenegro	1 Nov. 2000
Seychelles	21 Sep. 1976
Sierra Leone	27 Sep. 1961
Singapore	21 Sep. 1965
Slovakia	19 Jan. 1993
Slovenia	22 May 1992
Solomon Islands	19 Sep. 1978
Somalia	20 Sep. 1960
South Africa	7 Nov. 1945
Spain	14 Dec. 1955
Sri Lanka	14 Dec. 1955
Sudan	12 Nov. 1956
Suriname	4 Dec. 1975
Swaziland	24 Sep. 1968
Sweden	19 Nov. 1946
Switzerland	10 Sep. 2002
Syrian Arab Republic	24 Oct. 1945
Tajikistan	2 Mar. 1992
Thailand	16 Dec. 1946
The former Yugoslav Republic of Macedonia	8 Apr. 1993
Timor-Leste	27 Sep. 2002
Togo	20 Sep. 1960
Tonga	14 Sep. 1999
Trinidad and Tobago	18 Sep. 1962
Tunisia	12 Nov. 1956
Turkey	24 Oct. 1945
Turkmenistan	2 Mar. 1992
Tuvalu	5 Sept. 2000
Uganda	25 Oct. 1962
Ukraine	24 Oct. 1945
United Arab Emirates	9 Dec. 1971
United Kingdom of Great Britain and Northern Ireland	24 Oct. 1945
United Republic of Tanzania	14 Dec. 1961
United States of America	24 Oct. 1945
Uruguay	18 Dec. 1945

Uzbekistan	2 Mar. 1992
Vanuatu	15 Sep. 1981
Venezuela	15 Nov. 1945
Vietnam	20 Sep. 1977
Yemen	30 Sep. 1947
Zambia	1 Dec. 1964
Zimbabwe	25 Aug. 1980

Global Test Questions #5–#7

#5. List more than one-half of the preceding 191 Member States of the United Nations whose governments derive their powers from the consent of their people.

#6. List more than one-half of the preceding 191 Member States of the United Nations that will conduct a free election of major government officials within the next five years.

#7. Name one brutal dictatorship represented in the United Nations that is likely to ever vote to depose another brutal dictatorship.

After recognizing the corrupt nature of so many foreign governments represented in the UN, I was unable to pass my version of Senator John Kerry's "global test." As a result, I also fail to worry about whether most of the member nations in the UN disagree with our government on anything. Despite numerous statements of good intentions by the UN, there has been substantial lack of progress in human rights, and the worst examples cannot be attributed to the so-called "ugly American." Only the absolute worst control freaks in the United States can compare to how some Controllers in other parts of the world deal with the symptoms of their problems.

For example, in dealing with the "problem" of female sexuality, as of 2003 approximately two million girls, usually aged four to twelve, are subjected to female genital mutilation somewhere in the world every year, with some or all of their genitalia being cut away, generally under very painful and unsanitary conditions. According to UNICEF/UNFPA, 98% of girls in Djibouti and Somalia are mutilated. Egypt, Ethiopia, Kenya, Nigeria, Somalia, and the Sudan account for 75% of all cases.

Another example is the fact that as of the writing of this book, more than nine million black Africans have been slaughtered since 1960 through genocide, politicide, and mass murder. The Democratic Republic of the Congo leads the way with 2,095,000 deaths, closely followed by the Sudan with two million, Nigeria and Mozambique with a million each, Ethiopia with 855,000, Rwanda with 823,000, and Uganda with 555,000.

Instead of worrying about what members of the UN think about us, my reaction is just the opposite. The more that tyrants from other countries object to any of our official positions, and the lower our approval record is in the UN, the more likely it is that I will agree with and support the positions we have taken. My sympathy for the people oppressed by those governments is matched only by my contempt for the governments that oppress them and criticize us. The despots can run their mouths and strut around the UN buildings in their fancy stolen clothes, but their subjects are destitute, and they just do not occupy the moral high ground.

Individuals vs. Groups

> *"There is no room in this country for hyphenated Americanism. The one absolutely certain way of bringing this nation to ruin, of preventing all possibility of its continuing to be a nation of all, would be to permit it to become a tangle of squabbling nationalities."*
>
> —THEODORE ROOSEVELT

> *"I have a dream that my four children will one day live in a nation where they will not be judged by the color of their skin but by the content of their character."*
>
> —MARTIN LUTHER KING, JR.

There is not much that can be added to these statements by President Roosevelt and Dr. King. They are right, and we are wrong. We are so concerned about groups and so much against individualism that we are no longer a melting pot. We are just "a tangle of squabbling nationalities," basing our judgments on the color of a person's skin, and we are on the path toward national ruin.

I am not going to lose any sleep over it, but as long as various groups feel compelled to state their group identities, I wish that Native Americans could come up with another term for themselves, as there are numerous African Americans and Caucasians who consider themselves to be native Alabamians since they were born in Alabama. Likewise, they also consider themselves to be native Americans because they were born in America.

In fact, I also wish that African Americans would come up with another term for themselves to distinguish between those African Americans who are of Negro descent and those who are of Caucasian or other descent. But that would still leave us with the problem of what to call those of mixed descent.

Pop Test on Ethnic Groups: What should we call a native Texan whose ancestry is part Hispanic, part Irish, part Arab, part Jew, part Native American, part African American of Caucasian descent, part African American of Negro descent, part Chinese, part Polynesian, and part Neanderthal (just checking to see if you are still awake)? His name is John Doe, and he is a Methodist, a male homosexual, an addicted gambler, 68 years old, weighs 450 pounds, and is a divorcee with two children. He lost two legs and part of his hearing and eyesight while fighting in Vietnam.

Here's a novel idea. Why don't we call him John, Mr. Doe, or an American? And while we are at it, would it dishonor Dr.

King's memory to judge this person by the content of his character and not by his collection of group memberships and heritages?

Mandatory Volunteerism

How about that title for doublespeak? I guess it means that we are supposed to consent voluntarily to government controls. Whatever it means, you can include me out.

> *"We must organize all labor, no matter how dirty and arduous it may be, so that every (citizen) may regard himself as part of that great army of free labor.... The generation that is now fifteen years old...must arrange all their tasks of education in such a way that every day, and in every city, the young people shall engage in the practical solution of the problems of common labor, even the smallest, most simple kind."*
>
> —VLADIMIR LENIN

> *"I am here because I want to redefine the meaning of citizenship in America.... If you're asked in school 'What does it mean to be a good citizen?' I want the answer to be, 'Well, to be a good citizen, you have to obey the law, you've got to go to work or be in school, you've got to pay your taxes and—oh, yes, you have to serve..."*
>
> —BILL CLINTON AT VOLUNTEERISM SUMMIT

Part III

Training Your Best Friends to Become Controllers

If I have failed to convince you that it is far better to be a Persuader than to be a Controller, not all is lost. This section will assist you in helping others to see the light and to follow your lead. If at first you don't succeed, you should probably face reality and quit, but let's give it a try.

Government

> *"The Conventions of a number of the States, having at the time of their adopting the Constitution, expressed a desire, in order to prevent misconstruction or abuse of its powers, that further declaratory and restrictive clauses should be added..."*
>
> —PREAMBLE TO THE BILL OF RIGHTS

> *"The government consists of a gang of men exactly like you and me. They have, taking one with another, no special talent for the business of government; they have only a talent for getting and holding office. Their principal device to that end is to search out groups who pant and pine for something they can't get and to promise to give it to them. Nine times out of ten that promise is worth nothing. The tenth time is made good by looting A to satisfy B. In other words, government is a broker in pillage, and every election is sort of an advance auction sale of stolen goods."*
>
> —H. L. MENCKEN

Contrary to the opinions of the Founders of our country, Mr. Mencken, and others, you must explain to your friends that the only perfect human institution in the world is Government (with a capital "G" to show proper reverence). You must explain to them that the authors of our Declaration of Independence were twice wrong when they stated the opinion that all people "are endowed by their Creator with certain unalienable Rights." Those so-called rights are really just privileges, and they were not given to us by any creator. They came from, and can be regulated or even be taken away by, the only perfect institution that has ever existed, our Almighty Government.

It is absolutely amazing how ordinary people with ordinary character flaws are transformed when they become a part of Government with the power to enforce certain of our behaviors. You need to provide your friends with as many examples of this as possible. Just to get you started: Evil people who are not Government employees often start voluntary chain letters with criminal intent and have to be put in prison at Government expense. But when enlightened public servants, working for the Government with only the best of intentions, start a chain letter and force us all to join it, it is hailed by all as Social Security. You have to agree that "Social Security" is a nicer label than the "National Mandatory Chain Letter" and that labels are much more important than contents.

Also, when greedy corporate CEOs and CFOs put fraudulent entries into their company's records, we all agree they should be punished with prison sentences and fines, and many believe that the resulting retribution is not sufficient for the damage done, especially by those at the top. To avoid the humiliation of even the minor punishments they do receive, they should have experienced the magical transformation that would have occurred if only they had become a part of Government. The "CEO" and "CFO" of the Government have discovered that there is absolutely nothing wrong with the absence of funds in the Social Security Trust Fund, the fund to which we were perfectly entitled to force everyone to contribute.

Since only Government is perfect, and we are Americans who have rights without any responsibilities:

1. Government should provide us jobs, and ideally, all people would become enlightened enough to work for the Government.
2. Government should provide us healthcare.
3. Government should provide us prescription drugs.
4. Government should provide us a comfortable retirement.
5. Government should provide our education and indoctrination.
6. Government should provide welfare to all.
7. Government should insure us against all uninsured natural disasters, especially those that affect a large number of voters.
8. Government should license, regulate, and control all activities.
9. Government can make us wealthy.
10. Only Government workers should own guns.
11. Government should talk about protecting us from foreign and domestic criminals, but it should not take any action that might offend anyone or have any costs.
12. Government should end all wars in time for the big game, mindless sitcom, pornographic movie, or un-reality show.
13. Government should control our every endeavor.

United Nations

Of course, the ideal Government would have to be the United Nations, and the UN Charter certainly ranks higher on the scale than our feeble Declaration of Independence or Constitution. The very name, "United Nations," just sounds so good. How inspiring to have such a wonderful label for this warm community of nations—united, peaceful, and happy. It is too bad that it still does not have the power or the will to enforce its rules, but that will come in time.

Just be sure that your friends never learn exactly what types of governments are represented in this friendly group. They should never learn that each of the countries in this warm and peaceful "global village" has its own priorities and that relatively few of the governments represented there get their powers from the consent of the governed. They probably already know that many of the world's leaders do not like us, but do not let them know that some of these leaders are actually dictators, torturers, murderers, extortionists, and thieves. Some of them even believe that our successes somehow caused their failures, just like some of the less productive in our country believe the same about the more productive people here.

Do not let your friends forget the excellent plan developed by the UN to deal with violations of parole conditions by international criminals such as Saddam Hussein. As you remember, Hussein's gang of thugs heisted the entire country of Kuwait and had to be run out in 1991 by a coalition of forces led by the United States. Mr. Hussein was given certain conditions for staying in power, which he immediately and consistently violated, so the UN was faced with a dilemma. Just what was the UN going to do about one of its many rogue nations that was thumbing its nose at the government of the global village?

> *"Political power grows out of the barrel of a gun."*
>
> —MAO TSE-TUNG

> *"You can do more with a kind word and a gun than with just a kind word."*
>
> —AL CAPONE

> *"It is useless for the sheep to pass resolutions in favor of vegetarianism while the wolf remains of a different opinion."*
>
> —WILLIAM RALPH INGE

The UN's brilliantly simple response was to ignore the misguided advice of Mao and Al (they were already dead anyway) and to send repeated threats to the criminal on parole, Mr. Hussein. Therefore, the representatives of the member nations could feel secure in the knowledge that they had addressed the situation. At the same time, the criminal could feel safe to continue his criminal activities, knowing that the UN would probably write some more resolutions and might play hide-and-seek in the desert for a few years but that it would never take any decisive actions that might disturb the peace. If the allegations are true that the criminal was passing tons of money under the table to make sure that he would not be disturbed, he certainly would feel safe to continue living in peace as he defined it. Everyone stayed happy until an intellectually challenged president of the U.S. came along who did not understand how to play the game. He somehow had the crazy notions that parole conditions should be enforced after twelve years of empty demands and that threats to enforce them should eventually mean something.

Government Control

There are only two options, anarchy vs. total control by Government, so your friends will have to choose. I know that some may say there are other options in between the extremes, such as limited government and using the natural tendency of competition in a free market economy to create an additional layer of control, but what fool believes that?

The concept of limited government as promoted by the Founders of our country is now well over two hundred years old and is extremely dated. It could never be effective in the enlightened twenty-first century. Everyone knows that all successful businessmen are crooked and all government officials (certainly all of those in my political party) are saints.

Competition does not begin to control those criminals who call themselves businessmen. They all need to be thrown in jail, especially anyone who is rich. Everyone knows that while all poor people are honest, it is impossible for any rich person to be the same. It is imperative that we recognize the infallibility of Government bureaucrats and pass more laws giving them total control.

Individual Actions and Responsibilities

Your friends need to know that no one should ever again try to take an individual action. Only the enlightened people with Government jobs have the ability to think, and only they should control our actions.

> *"We must stop thinking of the individual and start thinking about what is best for society."*
>
> —HILLARY CLINTON

> *"We can't be so fixated on our desire to preserve the rights of ordinary Americans..."*
>
> —PRESIDENT BILL CLINTON

> *"Comrades! We must abolish the cult of the individual decisively, once and for all."*
>
> —NIKITA KHRUSHCHEV

> *"Delayed Notice Search Warrants: A Vital and Time-Honored Tool for Fighting Crime"*
>
> —U.S. DEPARTMENT OF JUSTICE'S WEBSITE EXTOLLING THE VIRTUES OF THE USA PATRIOT ACT OF 2003

It Takes a Village...

Your idiot friends probably believe that they and their husbands or wives have the ability to raise their children primarily by themselves but with some assistance from the grandparents, a special neighbor or two, some school teachers, some Sunday school teachers, and a few babysitters.

Believe me, that is not a village. To qualify as a real village, the enlightened people in the U.S. Government must have a significant role in shaping children, and ideally, the incredibly brilliant people in the United Nations must be included as soon as possible. Without the control of these organizations, there is no telling what decisions parents might make concerning the impressionable children in our country.

Free Enterprise Economy

> *"America's abundance was created not by public sacrifices to 'the common good,' but by the productive genius of free men who pursued their own personal interests and the making of their own private fortunes. They did not starve the people to pay for America's industrialization. They gave the people better jobs, higher wages and cheaper goods with every new machine they invented, with every scientific discovery or technological advance—and thus the whole country was moving forward and profiting, not suffering, every step of the way."*
>
> —AYN RAND

Your friends might believe the free enterprise system is the goose that laid the golden eggs that we enjoy. We Controllers know it is not, and we should kill that system so that we can be fair while continuing to enjoy our wealth. The only possible reasons we have abundance while many other countries have poverty is simply because we are very lucky to have a lot of natural resources and stole the rest from others.

I realize that the former Soviet Union had a lot of natural resources, an intelligent populace, a large territory, and an economic system with complete management and controls by a central government, but it still had rampant poverty and a government led by a gang of international thieves. However, all of that is immaterial. Our success has nothing to do with a system that supposedly gave us the motivation to create wealth, and there is certainly no reason to continue the archaic arrangement stemming from that ridiculous concept. We need to get much closer to the system that was tried only from shortly after their 1917 revolution to about 1989 in the Soviet Union—not exactly what anyone would call being given a real chance to prove its worth.

You need to explain to your friends that socialism is the economic system that is chosen by Controllers because it has such good intentions. Socialism clearly states its intention to improve human conditions by dividing all wealth fairly, and if ever given a real chance, it is bound to deliver. It has already shown us how to spread poverty somewhat equally, and eventually it will give us an abundance of "golden eggs" to divide "fairly." Just make sure that your friends keep the promises of fairness and equality at a higher priority than recognition of consequences. Past results of minimal production when the wealth has been divided equally are just history. They are no indication of what the future holds.

By the way, there is one overlooked problem in our economy that we absolutely must get your friends to help us address immediately. We have got to do something to alleviate the horrible suffering of all the ex-employees of the buggy whip manufacturers. These poor people and their helpless children have been on very hard times for a very long time, and it was not their fault that automobiles were invented to replace buggies and eliminate their jobs. We are a rich country; we must control all of the symptoms of every underlying cause, and we should not wait for decades to do so.

Greed

"Politicians never accuse you of 'greed' for wanting other people's money—only for wanting to keep your own money."

—JOSEPH SOBRAN

Greed, as correctly defined in today's enlightened society, means to want to keep more of what you earn. Greed no longer has the outdated meaning of wanting to take away more of what someone else has earned. Your friends probably think that it is greedy and an abuse of the Government's taxing authority for others to accumulate enough votes to confiscate a large percentage of what they earn so that their money can be given to those underachievers who know how to vote.

Somehow, you are going to have to make them realize that income does not belong to those who have earned it, but to the Government, and their families need only to petition the Government to keep some of what they earned. You know them, and you know that their earnings are certainly not due to their abilities and efforts. A great amount of individual preparation and effort is certainly not a factor in their successes. All that they received were gifts, and their efforts were worthless. They either stole their money or were just lucky. They are just plain greedy to want to keep more of what they have and consider theirs to keep or to give to those they choose.

They may also be mistaken in thinking that their obligation to "give some back" would mean back where they got it—that is, from their employers, schools, etc. To be politically correct, they must realize that giving it "back" means back to those who did not give it to them, to those with less luck or less ability to steal.

Of course, the only pure way to give it back is through the Government so that adequate controls can be instituted. Besides, bureaucrats are people too. They need the jobs that are created to administer these Government controls, and they should be allowed to get their cut before passing on whatever is left to both the needy and to those that the uninformed and politically incorrect among us would call the greedy.

Welfare

Once again, there are only two options: abandoning the unfortunate vs. Government controlled and enforced welfare. I know that some people may say there are other options and suggest, for instance, that charitable organizations do a better job of helping the needy and of rejecting the greedy. What fool would believe that? It is imperative to recognize the infallibility of Government programs and pass more laws providing Government a total monopoly in this area.

Guns vs. Butter

"We the People of the United States, in order to...provide for the common defense...do ordain and establish this Constitution for the United States of America."

"The President shall be Commander in Chief of the Army and Navy of the United States, and of the Militia of the several States, when called into the actual Service of the United States..."

"The Congress shall have power to...provide for the common defense...of the United States...To declare War...To raise and support Armies...To provide and maintain a Navy...To make Rules for the Government and Regulation of the land and naval Forces...To provide for calling forth the Militia to execute the Laws of the Union, suppress Insurrections and repel Invasions...To provide for organizing, arming, and disciplining the Militia, and for governing such part of

> *them as may be employed in the service of the United States...to exercise...authority over all places purchased...for the erection of forts, magazines, arsenals, dock-yards, and other needful buildings..."*
>
> —CONSTITUTION OF THE UNITED STATES OF AMERICA

Where in the world did your friends ever get the notion that some of the tax revenues of this country should go to buy military and intelligence equipment and to pay salaries for military and intelligence personnel? When the Founding Fathers said that Congress had the power to impose taxes for the president to spend as commander-in-chief of an army, navy, and militias, surely they did not really mean it.

Doesn't everyone today realize that more money could go into socialistic welfare programs if we would just cut out all of that defense spending? Besides, this is the twenty-first century, and we won "The War to End All Wars" way back in 1918. All of our enemies of the twentieth century and prior eras have been defeated by now, and there are no more evil people left in the world. Other than Americans, that is! If we would just be nice, everyone could live in peace under the benevolent leadership of the honorable dictatorships in the United Nations.

Gun Control

> *"A well regulated Militia, being necessary to the security of a free State, the right of the people to keep and bear Arms, shall not be infringed."*
>
> —SECOND AMENDMENT TO THE CONSTITUTION

Everyone but the Neanderthals of the National Rifle Association knows that guns are never used in self-defense by good people and that the only people with the necessary enlightenment to be entrusted with them are Government employees. (How did the NRA get to be so powerful anyway? Surely, there are not enough intelligent voters in that fringe group of out-of-control crazies to intimidate Congress.)

Make sure that your friends do not have any firearms in their houses. If anyone should break in to rape the women and terrorize the children, God forbid that the intruder be injured in the process by one of these inherently evil instruments of death and destruction. The Government's police will come eventually to deal with the situation properly, and there are excellent Government rape and grief counselors available for the victims.

Besides, Government gun control will make everyone happy. The criminals will get to keep their guns and use them without fear of effective retaliation since the law-abiding people will turn theirs in. The Government bureaucrats will get another area of control. Some of the unemployed will be hired to fill the government jobs needed to administer the laws. We Controllers will be able to rest in the knowledge that we got rid of some of these evil instruments just by writing a few letters to our Congressmen and getting a law passed. We will not need to trouble ourselves with addressing any remaining underlying causes of violence in our communities. With everyone's needs met, what better solution could there possibly be?

And Heaven forbid that the pilot of a commercial airliner ever be given a button enabling him to dump a load of lethal and/or non-lethal weapons into all or parts of the cabin area where the passengers could use them during a terrorist hijacking. The best solution is to find more sharpshooters and anoint them to be official government protectors. Otherwise, we should continue the pre–9-11 plan of either sitting quietly or responding to our attackers with our bare fists. If we ordinary citizens were ever allowed to defend ourselves with evil weapons, thousands of people in the air and on the ground might survive, but the entire concept of individual responses to danger is fatally flawed. Some people would be injured or killed by all of the uncontrolled (non-governmental) use of firepower, and just think of the emotional damage that would be caused during the chaos. Using weapons is simply too messy and uncivilized to consider for any but Government officials. Besides, everyone knows that our enemies would never use anything to hurt us if we would just try to understand their grievances.

The Media

> *"A cynical, mercenary, demagogic press will produce in time a people as base as itself."*
>
> —JOSEPH PULITZER

This is a sticky area for you to control, and you will have to be vigilant. At one time, your friends would have been exposed only to a presentation of news items carefully selected to reinforce politically correct principles. Now, there are a number of rogue publications and programs that are very dangerous and disruptive. Some of them:

- Challenge the sanctity of Government and state that it should not control everything.
- Suggest to us that our Constitution includes limits, checks, and balances because our country's Founders had noticed abuses by all other governments in the past and had a healthy lack of blind faith in any government for the future.
- Allege that some established news sources in effect are putting editorials on the news pages by their methods of choosing which news items to cover and which to omit, and by spinning the stories they do cover to fit a political agenda.
- Allege that some of the leaders of other governments in the UN are thugs.
- Promote free enterprise and individual responsibility.
- Provide examples (probably fictitious) of firearms being used for beneficial self-defense by people other than those who have been anointed with a Government position.
- Maintain that we have a republic and not a democracy.

Schools

> *"Do we really think that a government-dominated education is going to produce citizens capable of dominating their government, as the education of a truly vigilant self-governing people requires?"*
>
> —ALAN KEYES

> *"Drop out of school before your mind rots from exposure to our mediocre educational system."*
>
> —FRANK ZAPPA

There is a very dangerous concept being circulated by those who do not realize how infallible the Government employees are and how incompetent everyone else is. Many people agree that we should use government authority to collect taxes for the necessary money to educate our children, but some want to terminate our Government's virtual monopoly in the delivery of that education. They advocate that Government should raise the funds and then turn them over to the parents in the form of vouchers for them to buy education from the marketplace.

All of the horrors of the law of supply and demand, competition, profit making, free enterprise, and highly questionable innovations will be unleashed on our children by this voucher concept, and it must be squashed. Where is there any Government control with this voucher system? Who will know what our children will be taught and by what methods?

Just because we have mistakenly learned to rely on the marketplace to create and deliver some goods and services, we certainly cannot rely on the marketplace to offer quality educational choices or for parents to choose the best school program for their children. All of the crooked businessmen will just take the money and keep it while providing just enough education to keep making huge profits.

What irresponsible decisions will some parents make? Will children be exposed to the truth instead of being taught political correctness? Will some children be left behind to repeat classes until they learn the material? Will some parents send their children to private, religious schools where the parents' choice of religion is promoted? And worst of all, how many parents will send their children to schools where they will be taught that this country was founded on the beliefs that blind faith in Government ignores the facts and that total Government control is the wrong answer to most problems?

Only Government bureaucrats know what is best for our children. The Government is the only institution with enlightened people and the necessary degree of perfection to educate and indoctrinate our impressionable children. The Government monopoly must be protected. Total control must remain with Government.

Part IV

Messages to the Reader

Perfection?

Would a system based on persuasion and competition be perfect? Will it solve all of our problems? Of course not!

Is our current system based on control perfect? Has it solved all of our problems? Will it do so if extended to its logical conclusion? Of course not!

Humans are not perfect, and none of our systems will ever be perfect. We exhibit destructive behaviors under our present system, and we will continue to exhibit destructive behaviors under any change we make, including a change back to the system that made this country wealthy and great. We humans will never find the perfect balance between the advantages of eliminating unnecessary government controls on adults and the need to protect the children of abusive and neglectful parents. Most of us will never stop being greedy, and some of us will always use any available means of force, including guns and the ballot box, to hurt others.

However, I submit that a system based on persuasion and competition would be much closer to the ideal than our current one, which is based on ignoring the causes of problems and attempting to control the symptoms. It is your choice, and your decision affects your life. Even more so, it affects the lives of your grandchildren.

Come Home, Gentle People

Warning: You need to remain aware that I speak only for myself and my personal opinions of the Libertarian Party. I am not authorized to speak for any political party and certainly not for the Democrats or Republicans. So find your brain and use it to judge whether my opinions are correct or not and choose your associations carefully. Or, if prolonged exposure to government monopoly schools has equipped you only for memorization and not for thinking, just take notes from the recognized authority (me). Incidentally, I can prove that I am an expert because for almost all of you, I am from over one hundred miles away, and the next time we meet, I'll carry a briefcase.

If you generally vote Republican as the lesser evil because you find the Democratic areas of control to be just too oppressive and objectionable, take a look at what Libertarians think. Or, if you generally vote for Democrats as the lesser evil because you find the Republican areas of control to be just too oppressive and objectionable, take a look at what we, Adam Smith, and the Founders of this country hold to be true. We Libertarians maintain that both major parties are comprised of control freaks and that there is a better way.

If you are angry about some government positions that you are forced by majority rule to support with your tax payments, and if you are concerned about the resulting divisiveness in our country today, I urge you to vote for Libertarian leaders who will remove as many issues as possible from the political arena and return them to the marketplace where they belong.

If you prefer to be judged as a member of the world's smallest minority group, an individual, instead of as a member of a different minority group, there is a home for you in the Libertarian Party where all are individuals. For example, I happen to belong to many minority groups including Libertarians, Rotarians, and the Association of Old White Male Chauvinist Pigs, but I prefer to be identified as a person and an American.

If you consider socialism to be an abhorrent injustice against those who have the potential to produce and believe that all of us would benefit from the production of additional wealth, and if you are able to accept the fact that your neighbor may get filthy rich creating and selling valuable goods and services, come home to the Libertarian Party. Surely you are already upset that the Democrats embrace many aspects of socialism openly and that the Republicans only give lip service to opposing it.

If you wish to pursue maximum financial wealth, maximum emotional wealth, and/or maximum spiritual wealth for you and yours, the Libertarian Party is the place to be. We do not place any artificial ceilings on your aspirations or try to force you into any "acceptable" patterns of behavior so long as you do not harm others.

If you do not believe in any God or if you believe in a God great enough to create the universe (or the multiverse) and to take care of Himself or Herself, there is a home for you in the Libertarian Party. There are no Republican Controllers here who will attempt to force any moral beliefs on you. Some of us would like to discuss religion with you, but we have two zillion different opinions, and some of us are not interested in discussing our religious beliefs at all.

If you are a homosexual, you have certainly been rejected by the Republicans, whereas we will welcome you. We will demand only that you do not force yourself on anyone, adult or child. And that is the same standard we impose on heterosexuals.

If you believe in the Constitution, you will find a comfortable place with the Libertarians. We believe that the Founders were truly brilliant and at least 99.99% correct.

If you object to control freaks, you will not find any among the Libertarians. We even think that parents should have some choices in the education of their children without a monopoly of federal, state, and local Controllers.

If you are tired of the "gloom and doom" Democrats and feel even more optimistic about the potential of individuals than most Republicans, come join the most optimistic club, the Libertarians.

If you are disgusted with the way the Democrats and Republicans squander your grandchildren's legacy with counterproductive programs, come join us. Together, we can vote the wasteful spenders out of office and into productive jobs, and we can sue their programs into oblivion.

If you are an African-American, Hispanic, or a member of any other minority group, we will not even notice that fact unless you bring it up. You will not be judged by the color of your skin, but you damn sure will be judged by the content of your character.

If you can accept free speech and peaceful discussion of disagreements, there is a place for you among us. We too are looking for a few good men (and women). Come home and live in peace with us.

However, if you believe in rights without responsibilities, you are a libertine and not a Libertarian. Your party is somewhere else if you agree with the 1960s attitude, "If it feels good, do it." We believe, as George Bernard Shaw said, that "Liberty means responsibility. That is why most men dread it."

If you want to defend yourself and your home, come home to the Libertarian Party. We are at peace with those who wish to bear arms so long as they are used for recreational purposes or in self-defense and not to harm others. Many Republicans accept this viewpoint, but very few Democrats feel that you are to be trusted unless you have been anointed to membership in the sacred order of government bureaucrats. Or, if you prefer nonviolent methods of defending yourself and your home, Libertarians will assist and support you with that decision too.

We already have, however, too many in our party who believe in defending our country with only nonviolent responses to evil. Unless you have some nonviolent responses that will actually work, you can put your own family at risk, but don't risk mine too. The best time for us to disarm unilaterally is right after Hell freezes over.

If you are an advocate of the Neville Chamberlain method of securing "peace in our time" by appeasement, we do not need you either. Unfortunately, we already have too many gutless weasels and/or damn fools in our party who are willing to risk that form of national suicide, only to be forced eventually to fill in the blank with the name of the tyrant of the day and then to repeat the naïve lament that Mr. Chamberlain apparently never actually said, "Everything would have worked if only Hitler had kept his promises." To the contrary, we need to profit from the experience of Cleopatra's death by snakebite. She was committing suicide and knew that it was a snake she was picking up. We also need to realize that we are committing suicide when we embrace the wrong people and ideas.

Discrediting the Author

Will my critics make personal attacks and try to discredit me? That logical fallacy is used so often that it has a name, the ad hominem argument, but it has worked well before, and it sounds to me like a good approach for them to try. Republicans have lambasted Hillary ("Shrillary") Clinton and Howard ("The Scream") Dean for the perceived offense of raising their voices "far" too much at times when presenting their ideas, and Democrats have attacked George W. Bush for offending them by strutting "far" too much when he walks. Surely, there are more important issues to discuss than these purely personal attacks, but logical fallacies never bother some people, and it certainly will be easier to attack me than to refute the ideas I express.

A word of caution! If you are planning to attack my ideas instead of attacking me, you are over two hundred years too late and way out of your league, unless you can show where I have misunderstood Adam Smith and the Founders of our nation. The principles of severely limited governmental powers as expressed in this book could have been challenged a lot easier before 1788 because, back then, they truly were radical and untested. However, more than two centuries have passed since they were first introduced, and the application of these concepts (along with Adam Smith's observations about free enterprise) has made us the wealthiest country in history. In fact, each of your representatives in Washington, D.C., has sworn an oath to defend these concepts because they are not mine, but instead they are all mandates stipulated in the U.S. Constitution. So instead of attacking me or my agreement with the mandates of our Founders, I suggest that you use your freedoms to speak, vote, and file lawsuits to support the ideas I am supporting. It is up to you to force your representatives to honor their oaths and to get our country back to what was working before the Controllers started trying so hard to control the symptoms of the real problems we face.

For those who decide to take the easier route by attacking me instead of attacking my ideas, let me make it easy. I am no mental giant. I am not smart enough to write a document even comparable to the Constitution or *The Wealth of Nations*, and it took me a lifetime to understand that they are what made us so wealthy. I am over sixty years old, so you cannot say that I am too young and immature. You will do better to say that I am too old and am probably showing signs of approaching senility and maybe even dementia. Being a real estate broker from Alabama, you will find it difficult to put me in the category of an impractical, egghead, ivory-tower intellectual, so I suggest that you try to show that I am just a slow-talking, slow-thinking, ignorant redneck Southerner. While you are accusing me of that, it would be just a small stretch for you also to call me a conservative, a liberal, a racist, and/or a male chauvinist pig.

It will be easy to prove that I do not practice everything I preach and that I am certainly not a genius or a saint. I am guilty of being divisive "at a time when we need to come together." I refuse just to be nice and agree that a democracy or a totalitarian form of government is better than the Republic our Founders established. While righteous indignation is okay for Controllers (their motives are so pure), anger from Persuaders is cause for criticism, and I am madder than a hornet at how Controllers have hijacked the direction of our country. You can also accuse me of being a cruel, mean-spirited person for agreeing with the U.S. Constitution that government has no business being in the welfare business. Since government has seized control of a huge percentage of the available welfare funds in the economy, you can emphasize how desperate the poor will be without the government welfare. Of course, you will need to forget that I propose for other institutions to retake responsibility for the field and for government to assist in the change. You will also need to forget that these other institutions will have increased job opportunities for qualified administrators of welfare programs, namely some of the excess government employees.

So, there you have it, Controllers. That should be a good start on how to attack the messenger and impugn my character and motives, and that is all the help I will give you. If that is not enough, you will just have to find your own facts or make them up yourselves. Who knows, you may be able to throw up enough of a smokescreen about me that you will not have to respond to any of the ideas. However, I warn you in advance that I agree fully with the warm sentiment stated by Larry Langford, one of the most likable Controllers in Alabama, "If I have said anything that has offended you, I want you to know from the bottom of my heart that I do not give a damn."

I Dare You!

> *"He who passively accepts evil is as much involved in it as he who helps to perpetuate it."*
>
> —MARTIN LUTHER KING, JR.

> *"If you think you're too small to make a difference, you haven't been in bed with a mosquito."*
>
> —ANITA RODDICK

One of my motivations for writing this book is to counteract the wealth-destroying indoctrination most of us have received from the media and from government monopoly school systems. Another motive is to become one of those "lucky" rich people by selling a lot of books at an "unconscionable" profit. Unfortunately, I have insulted the intelligence of just about everyone on the planet, so I can only hope that you bought this book before you got to the part that made you the maddest. However, whether you bought, borrowed, or stole a copy of this book, I remind you, once again, of the men who wrote our Constitution and of Adam Smith, who wrote *The Wealth of Nations*, and I challenge you to reject the indoctrination you were subjected to. You have been warned, and your grandchildren will curse you if your apathy and inaction sentence them to lives of poverty as virtual servants of the state. I challenge you to:

- Stop relying so heavily on government to "solve" the real problems that we all face daily.
- Stop being so weak and afraid of freedom and the responsibilities that come with it.
- Question whether the government "solutions" are not often worse than the original problems.
- Recognize one of the underlying causes of the divisiveness in our country today and correct the problem by removing as many issues as possible out of politics and back into the marketplace where they belong.
- Submit all of the ideas in this book to the Four Way Test of Rotary International.
  a. Are they the truth?
  b. Are they fair to all concerned?
  c. Will they build goodwill and better friendships?
  d. Will they be beneficial to all concerned?
- Realize that the plan of limited government established by our Founders has not only kept us free but that it has made us partially wealthy since it was combined with a partial acceptance of the principles of free enterprise.
- Remember that we have a constitutional republic and not a democracy.
- Reconsider and support the Libertarian view that "societies and governments infringe on individual liberties whenever they tax wealth, create penalties for victimless crimes, or otherwise attempt to control or regulate individual conduct that harms or benefits no one except the individual who engaged in it."
- Start valuing individual responsibilities along with individuals and individual freedoms.

- Consider the possibility that each individual should be free to do as he or she pleases so long as he or she does not harm others and takes responsibility for the good or bad consequences of those actions.
- Develop tolerance for people who have differing ideas about health, love, sex, recreation, prayer, and other activities so long as they are peaceful and don't infringe on your own freedom.
- Recognize that free-market competition is far better for all of us than central planning by government and tolerate variation in economic success so long as the people who acquire wealth do so by honest production and trade and not by theft, cheating, or political pull.
- Stop getting government to enforce your standards of morality and wealth distribution.
- Stop proving your compassion by forcing others to pay for your pet projects.
- Stop trying to control the symptoms of problems and start persuading others to help you solve the underlying problems causing those symptoms.
- Resist the current wealth-draining trend toward increased government regulation and control.
- Change yourself and those around you so that we can then change our political leadership.
- Stop being a Controller who says that we have a "crisis" and that "there ought to be a law."
- *I challenge you to stop being a Controller so that your grandchildren can be wealthy.*

Conclusion

Now that you have finished reading this book, you can either forget it or you can do your part to improve the world your grandchildren will inherit. If I have not convinced you by now or at least caused you to do some thinking, one of us is hopeless. Now it's time to put out the fire and call in the dogs 'cause this hunt's over. For you unfortunate non-Southerners, that means that this is:

The End

Appendix: Additional Quotations

I couldn't care less whether William Shakespeare or Francis Bacon wrote the works attributed by most reputable scholars to Mr. Shakespeare. Likewise, for almost all of the quotations in this book, I was not there and I cannot guarantee that the speakers were quoted accurately or that the persons quoted were the ones who actually made the statements. However, the words as printed were stated by someone, and I found them to be very thought provoking.

Constitution

- *"Taken seriously, the Constitution would pose a serious threat to our form of government."*

  —JOE SOBRAN

- *"Constitutional rights may not be infringed simply because the majority of the people choose that they be."*

  —SUPREME COURT OF THE UNITED STATES IN WESTBROOK V. MIHALY 2 CAL. 3D 756

- *"The American Constitution, one of the few modern political documents drawn up by men who were forced by the sternest circumstances to think out what they really had to face, instead of chopping logic in a university classroom."*

  —GEORGE BERNARD SHAW

- *"...the Constitution is a limitation on the government, not on private individuals...it does not prescribe the conduct of private individuals, only the conduct of the government...it is not a charter for government power, but a charter of the citizen's protection against the government."*

  —AYN RAND

- *"From the utopian viewpoint, the United States constitution is a singularly hard-bitten and cautious document, for it breathes the spirit of skepticism about human altruism and incorporates a complex system of checks, balances and restrictions, so that everybody is holding the reins on everybody else."*

  —CHAD WALSH

- *"Hold on, my friends, to the Constitution and to the Republic for which it stands. Miracles do not cluster and what has happened once in 6,000 years may not happen again. Hold on to the Constitution, for if the American Constitution should fail, there will be anarchy throughout the world."*

  —DANIEL WEBSTER

- *"No one can read our Constitution without concluding that the people who wrote it wanted their government severely limited; the words 'no' and 'not' employed in restraint of government power occur 24 times in the first seven articles of the Constitution and 22 more times in the Bill of Rights."*

  —EDMUND A. OPITZ

- *"The Constitution only gives you the right to pursue happiness. You have to catch it yourself."*

  —BENJAMIN FRANKLIN

- *"The Constitution is what the judges say it is."*

  —JUSTICE CHARLES EVANS HUGHES

- "The Constitution doesn't claim to be a 'living document.' It is written on paper, not rubber."

  —JOE SOBRAN

- *"The most unresolved problem of the day is precisely the problem that concerned the founders of this nation: how to limit the scope and power of government."*

  —MILTON FRIEDMAN

- *"If the provisions of the Constitution can be set aside by an Act of Congress, where is the course of usurpation to end? The present assault upon capital is but the beginning. It will be but the stepping-stone to others, larger and more sweeping, till our political contests will become a war of the poor against the rich; a war growing in intensity and bitterness."*

  —JUSTICE STEPHEN J. FIELD

Education

- *"The foundation of every state is the education of its youth."*

  —DIOGENES

- *"To educate a man is to unfit him to be a slave."*

  —FREDERICK DOUGLASS

- *"It is precisely because education is the road to equality and citizenship, that it has been made more elusive for Negroes than many other rights. The walling off of Negroes from equal education is part of the historical design to submerge him in second-class status. Therefore, as Negroes have struggled to be free they have had to fight for the opportunity for a decent education."*

  —MARTIN LUTHER KING, JR.

- *"A popular government without popular information or the means of acquiring it is but a prologue to a farce or a tragedy, or perhaps both. Knowledge will forever govern ignorance: And a people who mean to be their own Governors, must arm themselves with the power which knowledge gives."*

  —JAMES MADISON

- *"Human history becomes more and more a race between education and catastrophe."*

  —H. G. WELLS

- *"I have never let my schooling interfere with my education."*

  —MARK TWAIN

- *"Religion, morality, and knowledge being necessary to good government and the happiness of mankind, schools and the means of education shall forever be encouraged."*

  —NORTHWEST ORDINANCE, ARTICLE III, 1787

Fight for Your Principles

- *"I know not what course others may take; but as for me, give me liberty or give me death!"*

  —PATRICK HENRY

- *"Freedom is never voluntarily given by the oppressor; it must be demanded by the oppressed."*

  —MARTIN LUTHER KING JR.

- *"Liberty is always dangerous, but it is the safest thing we have."*

  —HARRY EMERSON FOSDICK

- *"Courage is the first of all the virtues because if you haven't courage, you may not have the opportunity to use any of the others."*

  —SAMUEL JOHNSON

- *"The right to defy an unconstitutional statute is basic in our scheme. Even when an ordinance requires a permit to make a speech, to deliver a sermon, to picket, to parade, or to assemble, it need not be honored when it's invalid on its face."*

  —JUSTICE POTTER STEWART

- "A good offense is the best defense."

  —UNKNOWN, BUT TAKE A PAGE FROM THE ACLU PLAYBOOK AND SUE SOMEONE WHO IS DESTROYING YOUR GRANDCHILDREN'S HERITAGE

- *"A society of sheep must in time beget a government of wolves."*

  —BERTRAND DE JOUVENEL

- *"In Germany, the Nazis first came for the communists, and I didn't speak up because I wasn't a communist. Then they came for the Jews, and I didn't speak up because I wasn't a Jew. Then they came for the trade unionists, and I didn't speak up because I wasn't a trade unionist. Then they came for the Catholics, but I didn't speak up because I was a protestant. Then they came for me, and by that time there was no one left to speak for me."*

  —REVEREND MARTIN NIEMOELLER

- *"A man who won't die for something is not fit to live."*

  —MARTIN LUTHER KING, JR.

- *"The tree of liberty must be refreshed from time to time, with the blood of patriots and tyrants."*

  —THOMAS JEFFERSON

- *"If you love wealth more than liberty, the tranquility of servitude better than the animating contest of freedom, depart from us in peace. We ask not your counsel nor your arms. Crouch down and lick the hand that feeds you. May your chains rest lightly upon you and may posterity forget that you were our countrymen."*

  —SAMUEL ADAMS

- *"It does not require a majority to prevail, but rather an irate, tireless minority keen to set brush fires in people's minds."*

  —SAMUEL ADAMS

- *"First they ignore you, then they laugh at you, then they fight you, then you win."*

  —MAHATMA GANDHI

- *"Whether you think that you can, or that you can't, you are usually right."*

  —HENRY FORD

- *"Liberty lies in the hearts of men and women; when it dies there, no Constitution, no court can even do much to help it."*

  —JUDGE LEARNED HAND

- *"When the going gets tough, the tough get going."*

  —COACH PAUL "BEAR" BRYANT

- *"The hottest places in hell are reserved for those who in a period of moral crisis maintain their neutrality."*

  —DANTE

- *"Non-cooperation with evil is as much a duty as is cooperation with good."*

  —MAHATMA GANDHI

- *"Still, if you will not fight for the right when you can easily win without bloodshed, if you will not fight when your victory will be sure and not so costly, you may come to the moment when you will have to fight with all the odds against you and only a precarious chance for survival. There may be a worse case. You may have to fight when there is no chance of victory, because it is better to perish than to live as slaves."*

  —SIR WINSTON CHURCHILL

- *"We must not confuse dissent with disloyalty. We will not be driven by fear into an age of unreason if we remember that we are not descended from fearful men, not from men who feared to write, to speak, to associate and to defend causes which were, for the moment, unpopular."*

  —EDWARD R. MURROW

- *"Freedom has never been free. Sometimes it costs everything you've got."*

  —ERIC SCHAUB

- *"The mighty oak tree was once a little nut that held its ground."*

  —UNKNOWN

- *"Illegitimi Non Carborundum" (Don't let the bastards grind you down.)*

  —GENERAL JOSEPH W. "VINEGAR JOE" STILWELL

- *"I have always held firmly to the thought that each one of us can do a little to bring some portion of misery to an end."*

  —ALBERT SCHWEITZER

- *"The liberties of our country, the freedom of our civil Constitution, are worth defending at all hazards; and it is our duty to defend them against all attacks. We have received them as a fair inheritance from our worthy ancestors: they purchased them for us with toil and danger and expense of treasure and blood, and transmitted them to us with care and diligence. It will bring an everlasting mark of infamy on the present generation, enlightened as it is, if we should suffer them to be wrested from us by violence without a struggle, or to be cheated out of them by the artifices of false and designing men."*

  —SAMUEL ADAMS

- *"No guts, no glory."*

  —COACH PAUL "BEAR" BRYANT

Free Enterprise

- *"The problem of social organization is how to set up an arrangement under which greed will do the least harm; capitalism is that kind of a system."*

  —MILTON FRIEDMAN

- *"Underlying most arguments against the free market is a lack of belief in freedom itself."*

  —MILTON FRIEDMAN

- *"Are you entitled to the fruits of your labor or does government have some presumptive right to spend and spend and spend?"*

  —RONALD REAGAN

- *"Trade and commerce, if they were not made of Indian rubber, would never manage to bounce over the obstacles which legislators are continually putting in their way."*

  —HENRY DAVID THOREAU

- *"It is not from the benevolence of the butcher, the brewer, or the baker, that we expect our dinner, but from their regard to their own interest."*

  —ADAM SMITH

- *"The way to crush the bourgeoisie is to grind them between the millstones of taxation and inflation."*

  —VLADIMIR ILYICH LENIN

- *"We can't expect the American People to jump from Capitalism to Communism, but we can assist their elected leaders in giving them small doses of Socialism, until they awaken one day to find that they have Communism."*

  —NIKITA KHRUSHCHEV

- *"The more is given the less the people will work for themselves, and the less they work the more their poverty will increase."*

  —LEO NIKOLAEVICH TOLSTOI

- *"Nothing is less productive than to make more efficient what should not be done at all."*

  —PETER DRUCKER

- *"To be controlled in our economic pursuits means to be controlled in everything."*

  —FREDRICH AUGUST VON HAYEK

- *"He profits most who serves best."*

  —ROTARY INTERNATIONAL

- *"A prosperous population has no need of divisive demagogues."*

  —BILL O'REILLY

- *"It has often been found that profuse expenditures, heavy taxation, absurd commercial restrictions, corrupt tribunals, disastrous wars, seditions, persecutions, conflagrations, inundation, have not been able to destroy capital so fast as the exertions of private citizens have been able to create it."*

  —THOMAS BABINGTON

- *"We have no more right to consume happiness without producing it than to consume wealth without producing it."*

  —GEORGE BERNARD SHAW

- *"The Tenth Amendment sends a message to socialists, to egalitarians, to people obsessed with fairness, to American presidential candidates in the year 2000—to everyone who believes that wealth should be redistributed. And that message is clear and concise: Go to Hell."*

  —P. J. O'ROURKE

- *"Every government interference in the economy consists of giving an unearned benefit, extorted by force, to some men at the expense of others."*

  —AYN RAND

Freedom

- *"There have existed, in every age and every country, two distinct orders of men—the lovers of freedom and the devoted advocates of power."*

  —ROBERT Y. HAYNES

- *"Man is not free unless government is limited…As government expands, liberty contracts."*

  —RONALD REAGAN

- *"We can't be so fixated on our desire to preserve the rights of ordinary Americans…"*

  —BILL CLINTON, WHO HAD PLEDGED AN OATH TO DEFEND THE CONSTITUTION

- *"You can't promote freedom and big government at the same time."*

  —NEAL BOORTZ

- *"Democracy is two wolves and a lamb voting on what to have for lunch. Liberty is a well-armed lamb contesting the vote!"*

  —BENJAMIN FRANKLIN

- *"How can man be equal yet also be free to become unequal?"*

  –ZELL MILLER

- *"If you think we are free today, you know nothing about tyranny and even less about freedom."*

  –TOM BRAUN

- *"[T]here exists a very large audience receptive to the never-ending theme: Life is meant, ever and always, to be safe–and you're not safe!...we citizens of the land of the free and the home of the brave have happily traded freedom for every scrap of bogus safety dangled before us. Indeed, we have devoted prodigious energy to inventing threats that demand the sacrifice of liberty, privacy, and even basic human dignity...Small wonder if Osama bin Laden expected the entire American edifice to collapse along with the New York towers the moment he showed us something genuinely scary. We gave him every reason to believe it would...How much freedom would Americans surrender to ease their fear? All of it. Take it! We're afraid of it anyway."*

  –JACK GORDON

- *"The more we do to you, the less you seem to believe we are doing it."*

  –DR. JOSEPH MENGELE

- *"As long as men are free to ask what they must, free to say what they think, free to think what they will, freedom can never be lost and science can never regress."*

  –J. ROBERT OPPENHEIMER

- *"The first step in saving our liberty is to realize how much we have already lost, how we lost it, and how we will continue to lose it unless fundamental political changes occur."*

  –JAMES BOVARD

- *"None are more hopelessly enslaved than those who falsely believe they are free."*

  –JOHANN WOLFGANG VON GOETHE

- *"If men use their liberty in such a way as to surrender their liberty, are they thereafter any the less slaves? If people by a plebiscite elect a man despot over them, do they remain free because the despotism was of their own making?"*

  —HERBERT SPENCER

- *"The people never give up their liberties, but under some delusion."*

  —EDMUND BURKE

- *"As I watch government at all levels daily eat away at our freedom, I keep thinking how prosperity and government largesse have combined to make most of us fat and lazy and indifferent to, or actually in favor of, the limits being placed on that freedom."*

  —LYN NOFZIGER

- *"Is freedom anything else than the right to live as we wish? Nothing else."*

  —EPICTETUS

- *"No matter how noble the original intentions, the seductions of power can turn any movement from one seeking equal rights to one that would deny them to others."*

  —TAMMY BRUCE

- *"Freedom is the right to be wrong, not the right to do wrong."*

  —JOHN G. DIEFENBAKER

- *"Man exists for his own sake and not to add a laborer to the State."*

  —RALPH WALDO EMERSON

- *"The true danger is when liberty is nibbled away, for expedience, and by parts."*

  —EDMUND BURKE

- *"Surely, you can give up a little bit of your freedom so that you can be safe."*

  —TOO MANY POLITICIANS AND ORDINARY CITIZENS TO LIST

- *"It is the first responsibility of every citizen to question authority."*

  —BENJAMIN FRANKLIN

- *"A prohibition law strikes a blow at the very principles upon which our government was founded."*

  —ABRAHAM LINCOLN

- *"Get your laws off my body."*

  —BUMPER STICKER

- *"The system of private property is the most important guaranty of freedom, not only for those who own property, but scarcely less for those who do not."*

  —FREDRICH AUGUST VON HAYEK

- *"Human rights are not a privilege conferred by government. They are every human being's entitlement by virtue of his humanity. The right to life does not depend, and must not be contingent, on the pleasure of anyone else, not even a parent or sovereign.... You must weep that your own government, at present, seems blind to this truth."*

  —MOTHER TERESA

- *"Freedom is the fundamental character of the will, as weight is of matter... That which is free is the will. Will without freedom is an empty word."*

  —GEORG WILHELM FRIEDRICH HEGEL

- *"The human race divides itself politically into those who want to be controlled, and those who have no such desire."*

  —ROBERT A. HEINLEIN

- *"The liberty of the individual is the greatest thing of all, it is on this and this alone that the true will of the people can develop."*

  —ALEXANDER IVANOVICH HERZEN

- *"In the end they will lay their freedom at our feet and say to us, 'Make us your slaves, but feed us.'"*

  —DOSTOEVSKY'S "GRAND INQUISITOR"

- *"By physical liberty I mean the right to do anything which does not interfere with the happiness of another. By intellectual liberty I mean the right to think and the right to think wrong."*

  —ROBERT G. INGERSOLL

- *"The right to be let alone is indeed the beginning of all freedom."*

  —JUSTICE WILLIAM O. DOUGLAS

- *"Perhaps the fact that we have seen millions voting themselves into complete dependence on a tyrant has made our generation understand that to choose one's government is not necessarily to secure freedom."*

  —FREDRICH AUGUST VON HAYEK

- *"I believe that if the people of this nation fully understood what Congress has done to them over the last 49 years, they would move on Washington; they would not wait for an election...It adds up to a preconceived plan to destroy the economic and social independence of the United States!"*

  —GEORGE W. MALONE

- *"I never hurt nobody but myself and that's nobody's business but my own."*

  —BILLIE HOLIDAY

- *"If the words 'life, liberty, and the pursuit of happiness' don't include the right to experiment with your own consciousness, then the Declaration of Independence isn't worth the hemp it was written on."*

  —TERENCE MCKENNA

- *"There is no subjugation so perfect as that which keeps the appearance of freedom for in that way one captures volition itself."*

  —JEAN-JACQUES ROUSSEAU

- *"The worst forms of tyranny, or certainly the most successful ones, are not those we rail against but those that so insinuate themselves into the imagery of our consciousness, and the fabric of our lives, as not to be perceived as tyranny."*

  —MICHAEL PARENTI

- *"Our dependency makes slaves out of us, especially if this dependency is a dependency of our self esteem. If you need encouragement, pats on the back from everybody, then you make everybody your judge."*

  —FRITZ PERLS

- *"I'm in favor of legalizing drugs. According to my value system, if people want to kill themselves, they have every right to do so. Most of the harm that comes from drugs is because they are illegal."*

  —MILTON FRIEDMAN

- *"...no one has a right to coerce others to act according to his own view of truth."*

  —MAHATMA MOHANDAS K. GANDHI

- *"He is free who knows how to keep in his own hand the power to decide, at each step, the course of his life, and who lives in a society which does not block the exercise of that power."*

  —SALVADOR DE MADARIAGA

- *"Liberty lies in the hearts of men and women; when it dies there, no Constitution, no court, can even do much to help it."*

  —JUDGE LEARNED HAND

- *"There is only one success: to be able to spend your life in your own way, and not to give others absurd maddening claims upon it."*

  —CHRISTOPHER DARLINGTON MORLEY

- *"It must never be forgotten...that the liberties of the people are not so safe under the gracious manner of government as by the limitation of power."*

  —RICHARD HENRY LEE

- *"Fascism finds it necessary, at the outset, to take away from the ordinary human being what he has been taught and has grown to cherish the most; personal liberty. And it can be affirmed, without falling into exaggeration, that a curtailment of personal liberty not only has proved to be, but necessarily must be, a fundamental condition of the triumph of Fascism."*

  —MARIO PALMIERI

- *"To the frustrated, freedom from responsibility is more attractive than freedom from restraint. They are eager to barter their independence for relief from the burdens of willing, deciding and being responsible for inevitable failure. They willingly abdicate the directing of their lives to those who want to plan, command and shoulder all responsibility."*

  —ERIC HOFFER

- *"A man may have to die for our country: but no man must, in any exclusive sense, live for his country. He who surrenders himself without reservation to the temporal claims of a nation, or a party, or a class is rendering to Caesar that which, of all things, most emphatically belongs to God himself."*

  —C. S. LEWIS

- *"The history of the world is none other than the progress of the consciousness of freedom."*

  —GEORG WILHELM FRIEDRICH HEGEL

- *"People demand freedom only when they have no power."*

  —FRIEDRICH WILHELM NIETZSCHE

- *"When we have begun to take charge of our lives, to own ourselves, there is no longer any need to ask permission of someone."*

  —GEORGE O'NEIL

- *"I want for our country enough laws to restrain me from injuring others so that these laws will also restrain others from injuring me. I want enough government, with enough constitutional safeguards, so that this necessary minimum of laws will be applied equitably to everybody, and will be binding on the rulers as well as those ruled. Beyond that I want neither laws nor government to be imposed on our people as a means or with the excuse of protecting us from catching cold, or of seeing that we raise the right kind of crops, or of forcing us to live in the right kind of houses or neighborhoods, or of compelling us to save money or to spend it, or of telling us when or whether we can pray. I do not want government or laws designed for any other form of welfarism or paternalism, based on the premise that government knows best and can run our lives better than we can run them ourselves. And my concept of freedom, and of its overwhelming importance, is implicit in these aspirations and ideals."*

  —ROBERT WELCH

Freedom of Speech

- *"If there is a bedrock principle of the First Amendment, it is that the government may not prohibit the expression of an idea simply because society finds the idea itself offensive or disagreeable."*

  —JUSTICE WILLIAM J. BRENNAN

- *"Politically incorrect and proud of it."*

  —BUMPER STICKER

- *"Restriction of free thought and free speech is the most dangerous of all subversions. It is the one un-American act that could most easily defeat us."*

  —JUSTICE WILLIAM O. DOUGLAS

- *"We must protect the right of our opponents to speak because we must hear what they have to say."*

  —WALTER LIPPMANN

- *"Heresy is only another word for freedom of thought."*

  —GRAHAM GREENE

- *"It is error alone which needs the support of government. Truth can stand by itself."*

  —THOMAS JEFFERSON

- *"Only the suppressed word is dangerous."*

  —LUDWIG BÖRNE

- *"The liberty of thinking and publishing whatsoever each one likes, without any hindrances...is the fountainhead and origin of many evils."*

  —POPE LEO XIII, NOT EXACTLY A SUPPORTER OF OUR FIRST AMENDMENT

- *"I am for the First Amendment from the first word to the last. I believe it means what it says."*

  —JUSTICE HUGO L. BLACK

- *"The dominant purpose of the First Amendment was to prohibit the widespread practice of government suppression of embarrassing information."*

  —WILLIAM O. DOUGLAS

- *"In a free society, standards of public morality can be measured only by whether physical coercion violence against persons or property occurs. There is no right not to be offended by words, actions or symbols."*

  —RICHARD E. SINCERE, JR.

- *"If there is any principle of the Constitution that more imperatively calls for attachment than any other it is the principle of free thought—not free thought for those who agree with us but freedom for the thought that we hate."*

  —JUSTICE OLIVER WENDELL HOLMES, JR.

- *"If freedom of speech is taken away, then dumb and silent we may be led, like sheep to the slaughter."*

  —GEORGE WASHINGTON

- *"At no time is freedom of speech more precious than when a man hits his thumb with a hammer."*

  —MARSHALL LUMSDEN

- *"If we don't believe in freedom of expression for people we despise, we don't believe in it at all."*

  —NOAM CHOMSKY

- *"...the whole country is a free speech zone."*

  —BILL NEEL

- *"It is impossible for ideas to compete in the marketplace if no forum for their presentation is provided or available."*

  —THOMAS MANN

- *"The bourgeoisie is many times stronger than we. To give it the weapon of freedom of the press is to ease the enemy's cause, to help the class enemy. We do not desire to end in suicide, so we will not do this."*

  —VLADIMIR ILYICH LENIN

- *"The first principle of a free society is an untrammeled flow of words in an open forum."*

  —ADLAI E. STEVENSON

- *"We are willing enough to praise freedom when she is safely tucked away in the past and cannot be a nuisance. In the present, amidst dangers whose outcome we cannot foresee, we get nervous about her, and admit censorship."*

  —EDWARD M. FORSTER

- *"The justification and the purpose of freedom of speech is not to indulge those who want to speak their minds. It is to prevent error and discover truth. There may be other ways of detecting error and discovering truth than that of free discussion, but so far we have not found them."*

  —HENRY STEELE COMMAGER

- *"We are not afraid to entrust the American people with unpleasant facts, foreign ideas, alien philosophies, and competitive values. For a nation that is afraid to let its people judge the truth and falsehood in an open market is a nation that is afraid of its people."*

  —JOHN F. KENNEDY

- *"I disagree with what you say but will defend to the death your right to be wrong."*

  —TY ROBIN

Government

- *"The enumeration in the Constitution, of certain rights, shall not be construed to deny or disparage others retained by the people. The powers not delegated to the United States by the Constitution, nor prohibited by it to the States, are reserved to the States respectively, or to the people."*

  —THE COMBINED NINTH AND TENTH AMENDMENTS TO THE CONSTITUTION OF THE UNITED STATES

- *"According to the Declaration of Independence, the rights of the people come from God, and the powers of the government come from the people."*

  —JOE SOBRAN

- *"The legitimate powers of government extend only to such acts as are injurious to others."*

  —THOMAS JEFFERSON

- *"The essence of Government is power; and power, lodged as it must be in human hands, will ever be liable to abuse."*

  —JAMES MADISON

- *"It is amazing how many bad ideas began in either the 1930s or the 1960s."*

  —THOMAS SOWELL

- *"To the size of the state there is a limit, as there is to plants, animals and implements, for none of these retain their facility when they are too large."*

  —ARISTOTLE

- *"A government that is big enough to give you all you want is big enough to take it all away."*

  —BARRY GOLDWATER

- *"History, in general, only informs us what bad government is."*

  —THOMAS JEFFERSON

- *"The business of Progressives is to go on making mistakes. The business of Conservatives is to prevent mistakes from being corrected."*

  —GILBERT KEITH CHESTERTON

- *"At the end of a century that has seen the evils of communism, Nazism and other modern tyrannies, the impulse to centralize power remains amazingly persistent."*

  —JOSEPH SOBRAN

- *"The purpose of government is to rein in the rights of the people."*

  —BILL CLINTON, WHO HAD PLEDGED AN OATH TO DEFEND THE CONSTITUTION

- *"Every government degenerates when trusted to the rulers of the people alone. The people themselves, therefore, are its only safe depositories."*

  —THOMAS JEFFERSON

- *"In general the art of government consists in taking as much money as possible from one class of citizens to give to the other."*

  —VOLTAIRE

- *"The last stage but one of every civilization, is characterized by the forced political unification of its constituent parts, into a single greater whole."*

  —ARNOLD J. TOYNBEE

- *"Whenever you have an efficient government you have a dictatorship."*

  —HARRY S. TRUMAN

- *"Giving money and power to government is like giving whiskey and car keys to teenage boys."*

  —P. J. O'ROURKE

- *"Ours was the first revolution in the history of mankind that truly reversed the course of government, and with three little words: 'We the people.' 'We the people' tell the government what to do, it doesn't tell us. 'We the people' are the driver, the government is the car. And we decide where it should go, and by what route, and how fast. Almost all the world's constitutions are documents in which governments tell the people what their privileges are. Our Constitution is a document in which 'We the people' tell the government what it is allowed to do. 'We the people' are free."*

  —RONALD REAGAN

- *"There is danger from all men. The only maxim of a free government ought to be to trust no man living with power to endanger the public liberty."*

  —JOHN ADAMS

- *"In framing a government, which is to be administered by men over men, the great difficulty lies in this: you must first enable the government to control the governed, and in the next place, oblige it to control itself."*

  —JAMES MADISON

- *"A democracy cannot exist as a permanent form of government. It can only exist until the voters discover that they can vote themselves money from the public treasure. From that moment on the majority always votes for the candidates promising the most money from the public treasury, with the result that a democracy always collapses over loose fiscal policy followed by a dictatorship. The average age of the world's great civilizations has been two hundred years. These nations have progressed through the following sequence: from bondage to spiritual faith, from spiritual faith to great courage, from courage to liberty, from liberty to abundance, from abundance to selfishness, from selfishness to complacency, from complacency to apathy, from apathy to dependency, from dependency back to bondage."*

  —ALEXANDER TYLER WRITING ABOUT THE FALL OF THE ATHENIAN REPUBLIC

- *"Nothing whatever but the constitutional law, the political structure, of these United States protects any American from arbitrary seizure of his property and his person, from the Gestapo and the Storm Troopers, from the concentration camp, the torture chamber, the revolver at the back of his neck in a cellar."*

  —ROSE WILDER LANE

- *"Everyone wants to live at the expense of the state. They forget that the state lives at the expense of everyone."*

  —FREDERIC BASTIAT

- *"Congress will ever exercise their powers to levy as much money as the people can pay. They will not be restrained from direct taxes by the consideration that necessity does not require them."*

  —MELANCTON SMITH

- *"All government, in its essence, is organized exploitation, and in virtually all of its existing forms it is the implacable enemy of every industrious and well-disposed man."*

  —H. L. MENCKEN

- *"The State's criminality is nothing new and nothing to be wondered at. It began when the first predatory group of men clustered together and formed the State, and it will continue as long as the State exists in the world, because the State is fundamentally an anti-social institution, fundamentally criminal. The idea that the State originated to serve any kind of social purpose is completely unhistorical. It originated in conquest and confiscation—that is to say, in crime. It originated for the purpose of maintaining the division of society into an owning-and-exploiting class and a propertyless dependent class—that is, for a criminal purpose. No State known to history originated in any other manner, or for any other purpose. Like all predatory or parasitic institutions, its first instinct is that of self-preservation. All its enterprises are directed first towards preserving its own life, and, second, towards increasing its own power and enlarging the scope of its own activity. For the sake of this it will, and regularly does, commit any crime which circumstances make expedient."*

  —ALBERT JAY NOCK

- *"In dealing with the State, we ought to remember that its institutions are not aboriginal, though they existed before we were born; that they are not superior to the citizen; that every one of them was once the act of a single man; every law and usage was a man's expedient to meet a particular case; that they all are imitable, all alterable; we may make as good; we may make better."*

  —RALPH WALDO EMERSON

- *"Men…should do their actual living and working in communities…small enough to permit of genuine self-government and the assumption of personal responsibilities, federated into larger units in such a way that the temptation to abuse great power should not arise. The larger (structurally) a democracy grows, the less becomes the rule of the people and the smaller is the say of individuals and localized groups in dealing with their own destinies. Moreover, love and affection, are essentially personal relationships. Consequently, it is only in small groups that Charity, in the Pauline sense of the word, can manifest itself. Needless to say, the smallness of the group, in no way guarantees the emergence of Charity. In a large undifferentiated group, the possibility does not even exist, for the simple reason that most of its members cannot, in the nature of things, have personal relations with one another."*

—MAHATMA GANDHI

- *"It has been thought a considerable advance towards establishing the principles of Freedom, to say, that government is a compact between those who govern and those that are governed: but this cannot be true, because it is putting the effect before the cause; for as man must have existed before governments existed, there necessarily was a time when governments did not exist, and consequently there could originally exist no governors to form such a compact with. The fact therefore must be, that the individuals themselves, each in his own personal and sovereign right, entered into a compact with each other to produce a government: and this is the only mode in which governments have a right to arise, and the only principle on which they have a right to exist."*

  —THOMAS PAINE

- *"Many now believe that with the rise of the totalitarian State the world has entered upon a new era of barbarism. It has not. The totalitarian State is the only State; the kind of thing it does is only what the State has always done with unfailing regularity, if it had the power to do it, wherever and whenever its own aggrandizement made that kind of thing expedient. Give any State like power hereafter, and put it in like circumstances, and it will do precisely the same kind of thing. The State will unfailingly aggrandize itself, if only it has the power, first at the expense of its own citizens, and then at the expense of anyone else in sight. It has always done so, and always will."*

  —ALBERT JAY NOCK

- *"Here is the Golden Rule of sound citizenship, the first and greatest lesson in the study of politics: You get the same order of criminality from any State to which you give power to exercise it; and whatever power you give the State to do things FOR you carries with it the equivalent power to do things TO you."*

  —ALBERT JAY NOCK

- *"These things I believe: That government should butt out. That freedom is our most precious commodity and if we are not eternally vigilant government will take it all away. That individual freedom demands individual responsibility. That government is (contrary to George W. Bush) not a necessary good but an unavoidable evil. That the executive branch has grown too strong, the judicial branch too arrogant and the legislative branch too stupid. That political parties have become close to meaningless. That government should work to insure the rights of the individual, not plot to take them away. That government should provide for the national defense and work to insure domestic tranquility. That foreign trade should be fair rather than free. That America should be wary of foreign entanglements. That the tree of liberty needs to be watered from time to time with the blood of patriots and tyrants. That guns do more than protect us from criminals; more importantly, they protect us from the ongoing threat of government. That states are the bulwark of our freedom. That states should have the right to secede from the Union. That once a year we should hang someone in government as an example to his fellows."*

  —LYN NOFZIGER

- *"Governing a large country is like frying a small fish. You spoil it with too much poking."*

  —LAO-TZU

- *"That government is best which governs least."*

  —HENRY DAVID THOREAU

- *"Weak people desire strong police."*

  —EDWIN SILBERSTANG

Gun Control

- *"For the first time, a civilized nation has full gun registration! Our streets will be safer, our police more efficient, and the world will follow our lead into the future!"*

  —ADOLF HITLER

  (NOTE: SOME SURVIVORS OF THE HOLOCAUST MIGHT QUESTION JUST HOW SAFE THOSE STREETS BECAME FOR THEM AFTER FULL GUN REGISTRATION.)

- *"Guns do not make you a killer. I think killing makes you a killer. You can kill someone with a baseball bat or a car, but no one is trying to ban you from driving to the ball game."*

  —ANDY ROONEY

- *"One of the basic conditions for the victory of socialism is the arming of the workers (Communist) and the disarming of the bourgeoisie (the middle class)."*

  —VLADIMIR ILYICH LENIN

- *"...task of creating a socialist America can only succeed when those who would resist...have been totally disarmed."*

  —SARAH BRADY

- *"People who object to weapons aren't abolishing violence, they're begging for rule by brute force, when the biggest, strongest animals among men were always automatically 'right.' Guns ended that, and social democracy is a hollow farce without an armed populace to make it work."*

  —SMITH L. NEIL

- *"Foolish liberals who are trying to read the Second Amendment out of the Constitution by claiming it's not an individual right or that it's too much of a safety hazard don't see the danger of the big picture. They're courting disaster by encouraging others to use this same means to eliminate portions of the Constitution they don't like."*

  —ALAN DERSHOWITZ

- *"Certainly one of the chief guarantees of freedom under any government, no matter how popular and respected, is the right of citizens to keep and bear arms.... The right of citizens to bear arms is just one guarantee against arbitrary government, one more safeguard against the tyranny which now appears remote in America but which historically has proven to be always possible."*

  —HUBERT H. HUMPHREY

- *"Another source of power in government is a military force. But this, to be efficient, must be superior to any force that exists among the people, or which they can command; for otherwise this force would be annihilated on the first exercise of acts of oppression. Before a standing army can rule, the people must be disarmed; as they are in almost every kingdom in Europe. The supreme power in America cannot enforce unjust laws by the sword; because the whole body of the people are armed, and constitute a force superior to any band of regular troops that can be, on any pretense, raised in the United States. A military force, at the command of Congress, can execute no laws, but such as the people perceive to be just and constitutional; for they will possess the power, and jealousy will instantly inspire the inclination, to resist the execution of a law which appears to them unjust and oppressive."*

  —NOAH WEBSTER

- *"False is the idea of utility that sacrifices a thousand real advantages for one imaginary or trifling inconvenience; that would take fire from men because it burns, and water because one may drown in it; that has no remedy for evils except destruction. The laws that forbid the carrying of arms are laws of such a nature. They disarm only those who are neither inclined nor determined to commit crimes. Can it be supposed that those who have the courage to violate the most sacred laws of humanity, the most important of the code, will respect the less important and arbitrary ones, which can be violated with ease and impunity, and which, if strictly obeyed, would put an end to personal liberty...and subject innocent persons to all the vexations that the guilty alone ought to suffer? Such laws make things worse for the assaulted and better for the assailants; they serve rather to encourage than to prevent homicides, for an unarmed man may be attacked with greater confidence than an armed man. They ought to be designated as laws not preventive but fearful of crimes, produced by the tumultuous impression of a few isolated facts, and not by thoughtful consideration of the inconveniences and advantages of a universal decree."*

—CESARE BECCARIA

Individuals

- *"It is thus necessary that the individual should finally come to realize that his own ego is of no importance in comparison with the existence of the nation, that the position of the individual is conditioned solely by the interests of the nation as a whole."*

  —ADOLF HITLER

- *"When will the world learn that a million men are of no importance compared with one man?"*

  —HENRY DAVID THOREAU

- *"Fascist ethics begin...with the acknowledgment that it is not the individual who confers a meaning upon society, but it is, instead, the existence of a human society which determines the human character of the individual. According to Fascism, a true, a great spiritual life cannot take place unless the State has risen to a position of pre-eminence in the world of man. The curtailment of liberty thus becomes justified at once, and this need of rising the State to its rightful position."*

  —MARIO PALMIERI, "THE PHILOSOPHY OF FASCISM," 1936

- *"The main plank in the National Socialist program is to abolish the liberalistic concept of the individual..."*

  —ADOLF HITLER

- *"All our lives we fought against exalting the individual, against the elevation of the single person, and long ago we were over and done with the business of a hero, and here it comes up again: the glorification of one personality. This is not good at all."*

—VLADIMIR LENIN

- *"The smallest minority on earth is the individual. Those who deny individual rights cannot claim to be defenders of minorities."*

  —AYN RAND

- *"The man who craves disciples and wants followers is always more or less of a charlatan. The man of genuine worth and insight wants to be himself; and he wants others to be themselves, also."*

  —ELBERT HUBBARD

- *"All the people I know who are driving for a form of national service, primarily want it to be compulsory. They realize that's a terrible problem politically, so they're not willing to say it. It is endangerment of freedom and the potential for indoctrination that skeptics do not like in the national service concept. However benign the program, some think it will not succeed on any meaningful scale unless it is compulsory."*

  —MARTIN ANDERSON, SENIOR FELLOW OF THE HOOVER INSTITUTION

Luck

- *"A little government and a little luck are necessary in life; but only a fool trusts either of them."*

  —P. J. O'ROURKE

- *"All of us have bad luck and good luck. The man who persists through the bad luck—who keeps right on going—is the man who is there when the good luck comes—and is ready to receive it."*

  —ROBERT COLLIER

- *"I believe in luck: how else can you explain the success of those you dislike?"*

  —JEAN COCTEAU

- *"Some folk want their luck buttered."*

  —THOMAS HARDY

- *"I believe in luck. The harder I work the luckier I get."*

  —SAM SHOEN

- *"Men of action are favored by the Goddess of luck."*

  —GEORGE S. CLASON

- *"Diligence is the mother of good luck."*

  —BENJAMIN FRANKLIN

- *"Men have made an idol of luck as an excuse for their own thoughtlessness."*

  —DEMOCRITUS

- *"The champion makes his own luck."*

  —RED BLAIK

- *"Luck is not something you can mention in the presence of self-made men."*

  —E. B. WHITE

- *"Shallow men believe in luck."*

  —RALPH WALDO EMERSON

- *"Luck is a dividend of sweat. The more you sweat, the luckier you get."*

  —RAY KROC

- *"I am a great believer in luck, and I find the harder I work, the more I have of it."*

  —THOMAS JEFFERSON

- *"Depend on the rabbit's foot if you will, but remember it didn't work for the rabbit."*

  —R. E. SHAY

- *"The only sure thing about luck is that it will change."*

  —WILSON MIZNER

- *"Fortune favors the bold."*

  —TERENCE 190–159 BC

Media Bias

- *"Nothing can now be believed which is seen in a newspaper. Truth itself becomes suspicious by being put into that polluted vehicle."*

  —THOMAS JEFFERSON

- *"In the United States there is no phenomenon more threatening to popular government than the unwillingness of newspapers to give the facts to their readers"*

  —NELSON ANTRIM CRAWFORD

- *"Whoever controls the media, controls the mind."*

  —JIM MORRISON

- *"I wouldn't call it fascism exactly, but a political system nominally controlled by an irresponsible, dumbed down electorate who are manipulated by dishonest, cynical, controlled mass media that dispense the propaganda of a corrupt political establishment can hardly be described as democracy either."*

  —ZEHR

Persuasion vs. Force

- *"The creation of the world is the victory of persuasion over force...Civilization is the maintenance of social order, by its own inherent persuasiveness as embodying the nobler alternative. The recourse to force, however unavoidable, is a disclosure of the failure of civilization, either in the general society or in a remnant of individuals..."*

  —PLATO

- *"...the intercourse between individuals and between social groups takes one of these two forms: force or persuasion. Commerce is the great example of intercourse by way of persuasion. War, slavery, and governmental compulsion exemplify the reign of force."*

  —ALFRED NORTH WHITEHEAD

- *"Our life is what our thoughts make it. A man will find that as he alters his thoughts toward things and other people, things and others will alter towards him."*

  —JAMES ALLEN

- *"Between Jesus Christ and every other person in the world there is no possible term of comparison. Alexander, Caesar, Charlemagne, and I founded empires...upon force. Jesus Christ founded His empire upon love; and at this hour millions of people would die for Him."*

  —NAPOLEON BONAPARTE

- *"Justice without force is impotent, force without justice is tyranny."*

  —BLAISE PASCAL

- *"One of the fondest expressions around is that we can't be the world's policeman. But guess who gets called when somebody needs a cop."*

  —COLIN POWELL

- *"Force is not a remedy."*

  —JOHN BRIGHT

- *"Wars are caused by undefended wealth."*

  —GENERAL DOUGLAS MACARTHUR

- *"I will fight no more forever."*

  —CHIEF JOSEPH

Politicians and Bureaucrats

- *"Politicians are the same all over. They promise to build a bridge even where there is no river."*

  —NIKITA KHRUSHCHEV

- *"Sure there are dishonest men in local government. But there are dishonest men in national government too."*

  —RICHARD M. NIXON

- *"Pork is a bipartisan taste."*

  —ROBERT NOVAK

- *"Death solves all problems. No man, no problem."*

  —JOSEF STALIN, A POLITICIAN WHO WAS AT LEAST AS EVIL AS ADOLF HITLER

  (HOWEVER, HITLER WAS A DESPICABLE MEMBER OF THE RIGHT WING OF CONTROLLERS INTERNATIONAL AND RECEIVED FAR MORE UNFAVORABLE PRESS THAN STALIN, WHO WAS A DESPICABLE MEMBER OF THE LEFT WING OF THIS CATEGORY OF MISGUIDED PEOPLE. I MAINTAIN THAT THE DISPARITY IN TREATMENT OF THESE TWO TYRANTS IS NOT JUST A COINCIDENCE AND THAT BIAS IS ALIVE AND WELL IN THE MEDIA AND THE HISTORY BOOKS OF OUR GOVERNMENT MONOPOLY SCHOOLS.)

- *"That politician will doublecross that bridge when he comes to it."*

  —OSCAR LEVANT

- *"…there is no free lunch, even though politicians get elected promising free lunches and calling them 'rights.'"*

  —THOMAS SOWELL

- *"The reason there are so few female politicians is that it is too much trouble to put makeup on two faces."*

  —MAUREEN MURPHY

- *"Politics is supposed to be the second oldest profession. I have come to realize that it bears a very close resemblance to the first."*

  —RONALD REAGAN

- *"Hell hath no fury like a bureaucrat scorned."*

  —MILTON FRIEDMAN

- *"By and large, our country is run by passive men who don't want to offend anyone by saying no."*

  —VERNE BECKER

- *"The trade of governing has always been monopolized by the most ignorant and the most rascally individuals of mankind."*

  —THOMAS PAINE

- *"Every bureaucrat has a constitutional right to fuzzify, profundify and drivelate. It's a part of our freedom of speech…If people can understand what is being said in Washington, they might want to take over their own government again."*

  —JIM BOREN

- *Q: "Why won't you accept typed names on the car title form instead of requiring them all to be hand printed and therefore less legible?"*

  —THE AUTHOR

  A: "It's the law."

  —UNNAMED ALABAMA BUREAUCRAT AT (334) 242-9102 ON 6 FEBRUARY 2004

- *"As long as Americans obsess over a basketball star, the politicians are free to pursue their own goals unnoticed."*

  —NEAL BOORTZ

- *"The problem with political jokes is they get elected."*

  —HENRY CATE VII

- *"The only good bureaucrat is one with a pistol at his head. Put it in his hand and it's good-by to the Bill of Rights."*

  —H. L. MENCKEN

- *"The people can demand square circles if they want. But that doesn't mean that they will get them. What they are more likely to get is the illusion of a solution by someone seeking their vote."*

  —THOMAS SOWELL

- *"If their (kings and ministers) own extravagance does not ruin the state, that of their subjects never will."*

  —SMITH ADAM

- *"Bait and switch advertising is illegal when unscrupulous businesses engage in it. But it is standard operating procedure in politics, especially during election years."*

  —THOMAS SOWELL

- *"...the bureaucrats in the administration don't think the government belongs to the people."*

  —RALPH NADER

- *"The threat of people acting in their own enlightened and rational self-interest strikes bureaucrats, politicians and social workers as ominous and dangerous."*

  —W. G. HILL

- *"Bureaucracy defends the status quo long past the time when the quo has lost its status."*

  —LAURENCE J. PETER

- *"We hang the petty thieves and appoint the great ones to public office."*

  —AESOP

- *"Reader, suppose you were an idiot. And suppose you were a member of Congress. But I repeat myself."*

  —MARK TWAIN

- *"When buying and selling are controlled by legislation, the first things to be bought and sold are legislators."*

  —P. J. O'ROURKE

- *"The world is governed by very different personages from what is imagined by those who are not behind the scenes."*

  —BENJAMIN DISRAELI

- *"Beware the leader who bangs the drums of war in order to whip the citizenry into a patriotic fervor, for patriotism is indeed a double-edged sword. It both emboldens the blood, just as it narrows the mind. And when the drums of war have reached a fever pitch and the blood boils with hate and the mind has closed, the leader will have no need in seizing the rights of the citizenry. Rather, the citizenry, infused with fear and blinded by patriotism, will offer up all of their rights unto the leader and gladly so. How do I know? For this is what I have done. And I am Caesar."*

  —UNKNOWN BUT ALMOST DEFINITELY NOT GAIUS JULIUS CAESAR

- *"Decency, security, and liberty alike demand that government officials shall be subjected to the same rules of conduct that are commands to the citizen…If the government becomes a lawbreaker, it breeds contempt for law; it invites every man to become a law unto himself; it invites anarchy."*

  —JUSTICE LOUIS D. BRANDEIS

"A bureaucrat is the most despicable of men, though he is needed as vultures are needed, but one hardly admires vultures whom bureaucrats so strangely resemble. I have yet to meet a bureaucrat who was not petty, dull, almost witless, crafty or stupid, an oppressor or a thief, a holder of little authority in which he delights, as a boy delights in possessing a vicious dog. Who can trust such creatures?"

—MARCUS TULLIUS CICERO

- *"I have come to the conclusion that politics is too serious a matter to be left to the politicians."*

  —CHARLES DE GAULLE

- *"I'm not going to have some reporters pawing through our papers. We are the president."*

  —HILLARY CLINTON

Power

- *"Power never takes a back step—only in the face of more power."*

  —MALCOLM X

- *"Since everyone has his own definition of fairness, that word is a blank check for the expansion of government power."*

  —THOMAS SOWELL

- *"Abuse of power isn't limited to bad guys in other nations. It happens in our own country if we're not vigilant."*

  —CLINT EASTWOOD

- *"Human beings will generally exercise power when they can get it, and they will exercise it most undoubtedly in popular governments under pretense of public safety."*

  —DANIEL WEBSTER

Republic vs. Democracy

"When the people find they can vote themselves money, that will herald the end of the republic."

—BENJAMIN FRANKLIN

- *"The principle that the majority have a right to rule the minority, practically resolves all government into a mere contest between two bodies of men, as to which of them shall be masters, and which of them slaves..."*

  —LYSANDER SPOONER

- *"The very purpose of a Bill of Rights was to withdraw certain subjects from the vicissitudes of political controversy, to place them beyond the reach of majorities and officials and to establish them as legal principles to be applied by the courts. One's right to life, liberty, and property, to free speech, a free press, freedom of worship and assembly, and other fundamental rights may not be submitted to vote; they depend on the outcome of no elections."*

  —JUSTICE ROBERT H. JACKSON

- *"In questions of power, then, let no more be said of confidence in man, but bind him down from mischief by the chains of the Constitution."*

  —THOMAS JEFFERSON

- *"An elective despotism was not the government we fought for, but one which should not only be founded on true free principles, but in which the powers of government should be so divided and balanced among general bodies of magistracy, as that no one could transcend their legal limits without being effectually checked and restrained by the others."*

  —THOMAS JEFFERSON

- *"When it becomes dominated by a collectivist creed, democracy will inevitably destroy itself."*

  —FREDRICH AUGUST VON HAYEK

Responsibility

"Remember, the Constitution gives you the right to be a moron...But sometimes there is a price to be paid."

—BILL O'REILLY

- *"None can love freedom heartily, but good men; the rest love not freedom, but license."*

  —JOHN MILTON

- *"Freedom is the freedom to say that two plus two make four. If that is granted, all else follows."*

  —GEORGE ORWELL

- *"The proverb warns that 'You should not bite the hand that feeds you.' But maybe you should if it prevents you from feeding yourself."*

  —THOMAS SZASZ

- *"A people that values its privileges above its principles soon loses both."*

  —DWIGHT D. EISENHOWER

- *"Because we fear the responsibility of our actions, we have allowed ourselves to develop the mentality of slaves. Contrary to the stirring sentiments of the Declaration of Independence, we now pledge 'our Lives, our Fortunes and our sacred Honor' not to one another for our mutual protection, but to the state, whose actions continue to exploit, despoil, and destroy us."*

  —BUTLER D. SHAFFER

- *"I will not surrender responsibility for my life and my actions."*

  —JOHN ENOCH POWELL

- *"The only thing necessary for the triumph of evil is for good men to do nothing."*

  —EDMUND BURKE

State/Church

- *"The First Amendment has erected a wall between church and state. That wall must be kept high and impregnable. We could not approve the slightest breach."*

  —HUGO L. BLACK

- *"All religions united with government are more or less inimical to liberty. All, separated from government, are compatible with liberty."*

  —HENRY CLAY

- *"No citizen enjoys genuine freedom of religious conviction until the state is indifferent to every form of religious outlook from Atheism to Zoroastrianism."*

  —HAROLD J. LASKI

- *"This is a Christian country. Either accept it or leave."*

  —POSITION STATEMENT OF THE MILITANT WING OF THE RELIGIOUS RIGHT

- *"Never allow the enemy to block you. Get around them, run over top of them, destroy them—whatever you need to do so that God's word is the word that is being practiced in Congress, town halls, and state legislatures."*

  —BILL THOMPSON OF THE CHRISTIAN COALITION

- *"As the government of the United States of America is not in any sense founded on the Christian Religion..."*

  —GEORGE WASHINGTON

- *"If there is any fixed star in our constitutional constellation, it is that no official, high or petty, can prescribe what shall be orthodox in politics, nationalism, religion, or other matters of opinion or force citizens to confess by word or act their faith therein."*

  —ROBERT H. JACKSON

- *"The government must pursue a course of complete neutrality toward religion."*

  —JOHN PAUL STEVENS

- *"Freedom of religion means the right of the individual to choose and to adhere to whichever religious beliefs he may prefer, to join with others in religious associations to express these beliefs, and to incur no civil disabilities because of his choice..."*

  —JOSEPH L. BLAU

- *"Our civil rights have no dependence on our religious opinions, any more than our opinions in physics or geometry."*

  —THOMAS JEFFERSON

- *"The humans running some religious institutions try hard to give the Creator of the universe a bad name."*

  —DURHAM ELLIS

- *"Let's go risk being killed to waste some Jews and Muslims for the glory of our God of love and peace."*

  —APPROXIMATE STATEMENT MADE BY ONE UNKNOWN CRUSADER TO ANOTHER IN 1096

- *"Let's go blow ourselves up to waste some Jews and Christians for the glory of Allah, some blood money for our families, and those 72 virgins."*

  —APPROXIMATE STATEMENT MADE BY ONE UNKNOWN ISLAMIC TERRORIST TO ANOTHER IN 2004 AFTER 908 YEARS OF ENLIGHTENED PROGRESS IN CIVILIZATION AND THEOLOGY SINCE THE FIRST CRUSADE

- *"We hold it for a fundamental and undeniable truth, that religion, or the duty we owe our Creator and the manner of discharging it, can be directed only by reason and conviction, not by force or violence. The religion then of every man must be left to the conviction and conscience of every man; and it is the right of every man to exercise it as these may dictate. This right is in its nature an unalienable right."*

  —JAMES MADISON

"If you want to make an apple pie from scratch, you must first create the universe."

—CARL SAGAN

- *"All religion comes from the same Manufacturer; there are just different distributors, wholesalers, and retailers."*

  —LYNN DAVIS

- *"God who gave us life gave us liberty. And can the liberties of a nation be thought secure if we have removed their only firm basis: a conviction in the minds of men that these liberties are the gift of God? That they are not to be violated but with His wrath? Indeed, I tremble for my country when I reflect that God is just; that His justice cannot sleep forever."*

  —THOMAS JEFFERSON

- *"The truth is that Christian theology, like every other theology, is not only opposed to the scientific spirit; it is also opposed to all other attempts at rational thinking. Not by accident does Genesis 3 make the father of knowledge a serpent—slimy, sneaking and abominable. Since the earliest days the church as an organization has thrown itself violently against every effort to liberate the body and mind of man. It has been, at all times and everywhere, the habitual and incorrigible defender of bad governments, bad laws, bad social theories, bad institutions. It was, for centuries, an apologist for slavery, as it was the apologist for the divine right of kings."*

  —H. L. MENCKEN

- *"Believing with you that religion is a matter which lies solely between man and his God, I contemplate with solemn reverence that act of the whole American people which declared that their legislature should 'make no law respecting an establishment of religion or prohibiting the free exercise thereof' thus building a wall of separation between Church and State."*

  —THOMAS JEFFERSON

- *"Anyone who knows history, particularly the history of Europe, will, I think, recognize that the domination of education or of government by any one particular religious faith is never a happy arrangement for the people."*

  —ELEANOR ROOSEVELT

Taxes

- *"The power to tax involves the power to destroy."*

  —JOHN MARSHALL

- *"To tax the community for the advantage of a class is not protection, it is plunder."*

  —BENJAMIN DISRAELI

- *"The collection of taxes which are not absolutely required, which do not beyond reasonable doubt contribute to the public welfare, is only a species of legalized larceny. The wise and correct course to follow in taxation is not to destroy those who have already secured success, but to create conditions under which everyone will have a better chance to be successful."*

  —CALVIN COOLIDGE

- *"They are not to lay taxes ad libitum for any purpose they please; but only to pay the debts or provide for the welfare of the Union."*

  —THOMAS JEFFERSON

Truth

- *"Truth: the most deadly weapon ever discovered by humanity. Capable of destroying entire perceptual sets, cultures, and realities. Outlawed by all governments everywhere. Possession is normally punishable by death."*

  —JOHN GILMORE

- *"The simple step of a courageous individual is not to take part in the lie. One word of truth outweighs the world."*

  —ALEXANDER SOLZHENITSYN

- *"Truth does not change because it is, or is not, believed by a majority of the people."*

  —GIORDANO BRUNO

- *"There are two kinds of statistics: the kind you look up and the kind you make up."*

  —REX STOUT

- *"If you cannot convince them, confuse them."*

  —HARRY S. TRUMAN

- *"When in doubt, tell the truth."*

  —MARK TWAIN

- *"The truth will set you free. But, first it's going to piss you off."*

  —SOLOMON SHORT

- *"He who dares not offend cannot be honest."*

  —THOMAS PAINE

- *"Many people today don't want honest answers insofar as honest means unpleasant or disturbing. They want a soft answer that turneth away anxiety."*

  —LOUIS KRONENBERGER

- *"The secret of life is honesty and fair dealing. If you can fake that, you've got it made."*

  —GROUCHO MARX

- *"It should be called Social Security Bust Fund. There is no trust and there are no funds..."*

  —JIM MARTIN

- *"A truth that's told with bad intent beats all the lies you can invent."*

  —WILLIAM BLAKE

- *"We cannot afford to differ on the question of honesty if we expect our republic permanently to endure. Honesty is not so much a credit as an absolute prerequisite to efficient service to the public. Unless a man is honest, we have no right to keep him in public life; it matters not how brilliant his capacity."*

  —THEODORE ROOSEVELT

- *"One of the saddest lessons of history is this: If we've been bamboozled long enough, we tend to reject any evidence of the bamboozle. We're no longer interested in finding out the truth."*

  —CARL SAGAN

Welfare

- *"If pigs could vote, the man with the slop bucket would be elected swineherd every time, no matter how much slaughtering he did on the side."*

  —ORSON SCOTT CARD

- *"A government that robs Peter to pay Paul can always depend upon the support of Paul."*

  —GEORGE BERNARD SHAW

- *"Welfare's purpose should be to eliminate, as far as possible, the need for its own existence."*

  —RONALD REAGAN

- *"The state is the great fiction by which everybody seeks to live at the expense of everybody else."*

  —FREDERIC BASTIAT

- *"I believe the money I make belongs to me and my family, not some governmental stooge with a bad comb-over who wants to give it away to crack addicts for squirting out babies."*

  —ANDY ROONEY

- *"And here we encounter the seeds of government disaster and collapse—the kind that wrecked ancient Rome and every other civilization that allowed a sociopolitical monster called the welfare state to exist."*

  —BARRY GOLDWATER

- *"Whoever claims the right to redistribute the wealth produced by others is claiming the right to treat human beings as chattel."*

  —AYN RAND

- *"I think the best possible social program is a job."*

  —RONALD REAGAN

- *"The democracy will cease to exist when you take away from those who are willing to work and give to those who would not."*

  —THOMAS JEFFERSON

- *"Well, you can't make people give, that's not giving."*

  —TED TURNER

- *"You cannot bring about prosperity by discouraging thrift. You cannot help small men by tearing down big men. You cannot strengthen the weak by weakening the strong. You cannot lift the wage-earner by pulling down the wage-payer. You cannot help the poor man by destroying the rich. You cannot keep out of trouble by spending more than your income. You cannot further the brotherhood of man by inciting class hatred. You cannot establish security on borrowed money. You cannot build character and courage by taking away men's initiative and independence. You cannot help men permanently by doing for them what they could and should do for themselves."*

  —WILLIAM BOETCKER

- *"Congress has not unlimited powers to provide for the general welfare, but only those specifically enumerated."*

  —THOMAS JEFFERSON

- *"We are sure living in a peculiar time. You get more for not working than you will for working, and more for not raising a hog than for raising it."*

  —WILL ROGERS

- *"I cannot undertake to lay my finger on that article of the Constitution which granted a right to Congress of expending, on the objects of benevolence, the money of their constituents."*

  —JAMES MADISON

- *"I predict future happiness for Americans if they can prevent the government from wasting the labors of the people under the pretense of taking care of them."*

  —THOMAS JEFFERSON

- *"...the smallness of the group, in no way guarantees the emergence of Charity. In a large undifferentiated group, the possibility does not even exist for the simple reason that most of its members cannot, in the nature of things, have personal relations with one another."*

  —MAHATMA MOHANDAS K. GANDHI

Well-Meaning Controllers

- *"I am not questioning their compassion or their patriotism. I am challenging their wisdom."*

  —NOT EXACTLY WHAT SENATOR ZELL MILLER SAID BUT CLOSE ENOUGH TO MAKE THE POINT. I TOO AM ANGRY AT WHAT IS GOING ON IN THE HALLS OF CONGRESS

- *"The greatest dangers to liberty lurk in insidious encroachment by men of zeal, well-meaning but without understanding."*

  —JUSTICE LOUIS D. BRANDEIS

- *"There is no right not to be offended by words, actions or symbols."*

  —RICHARD E. SINCERE, JR.

- *"The consumer must be protected at times from his own indiscretion and vanity."*

  —RALPH NADER

  NOTE: THIS CONTROLLER IS DUE THE LION'S SHARE OF THE CREDIT FOR GETTING TRUTH IN ADVERTISING FOR SOME AREAS OF OUR SOCIETY (NO TRUTH YET IN GOVERNMENT), BUT THEN LOOK AT WHAT HE SAYS. HE OBVIOUSLY BELIEVES THAT YOU ARE TOO STUPID TO MAKE GOOD DECISIONS EVEN AFTER GETTING THE FACTS AND THAT THE POLITICIANS AND BUREAUCRATS ARE MUCH WISER THAN YOU ARE. I DO NOT THINK THAT YOU ARE STUPID. ONCE YOU GET ACCURATE FACTS, I BELIEVE YOU CAN RUN YOUR LIFE BETTER IN HOMETOWN, USA, THAN A DISTANT PLANNER IN WASHINGTON, D.C.

- *"If there were some way to add up all the costs imposed by busybodies—on everyone from farmers to people wanting organ transplants—it would probably be greater than the national debt."*

  —THOMAS SOWELL

- *"Tyranny, restrictions on human freedom, come primarily from governmental restrictions that we ourselves have set up."*

  —MILTON FRIEDMAN

- *"I believe a self-righteous liberal or conservative with a cause is more dangerous than a Hell's Angel with an attitude."*

  —ANDY ROONEY

- *"If you see a man approaching you with the obvious intent of doing you good, you should run for your life."*

  —HENRY DAVID THOREAU

- *"...the great mantra of 'affordable housing' rings out across the land, often proclaimed by those who are making housing unaffordable, even by the affluent."*

  —THOMAS SOWELL

- *"Good intentions will always be pleaded for every assumption of authority. It is hardly too strong to say that the Constitution was made to guard the people against the dangers of good intentions. There are men in all ages who mean to govern well, but they mean to govern. They promise to be good masters, but they mean to be masters."*

  —DANIEL WEBSTER

- *"If the Fed had a war on abortion like its war on poverty or war on drugs, within 5 years men would be having abortions!"*

  —HARRY BROWNE

- *"Nowhere have illusions been more abundant than in discussions of housing—especially that ever-elusive 'affordable housing' that so many people wring their hands over—often while passing laws that make it virtually impossible to achieve."*

  —THOMAS SOWELL

- *"Every form of addiction is bad, no matter whether the narcotic be alcohol or morphine or idealism."*

  —CARL GUSTAV JUNG

- *"...nothing has done so much to destroy the juridical safeguards of individual freedom as the striving after this mirage of social justice."*

  —FREDRICH AUGUST VON HAYEK

- *"What has always made the state a hell on earth has been precisely that man has tried to make it his heaven."*

  —F. HOELDERLIN

- *"The holier-than-thou activists who blame the population for not spending more money on their personal crusades are worse than aggravating. They encourage the repudiation of personal responsibility by spreading the lie that support of a government program fulfills individual moral duty."*

  —PATRICK COX

- *"I believe in only one thing: liberty; but I do not believe in liberty enough to want to force it upon anyone."*

  —H. L. MENCKEN

- *"You and I are told we must choose between a left or right, but I suggest there is no such thing as a left or right. There is only an up or down. Up to man's age-old dream—the maximum of individual freedom consistent with order—or down to the ant heap of totalitarianism. Regardless of their sincerity, their humanitarian motives, those who would sacrifice freedom for security have embarked on this downward path."*

  —RONALD REAGAN

- *"Protection, therefore, against the tyranny of the magistrate is not enough; there needs protection against the tyranny of the prevailing opinion and feeling, against the tendency of society to impose, by other means than civil penalties, its own ideas and practices as rules of conduct on those who dissent from them."*

  —JOHN STUART MILL

- *"The public must be put in its place, so that it may exercise its own powers, but no less and perhaps even more, so that each of us may live free of the trampling and the roar of a bewildered herd."*

  —WALTER LIPPMANN

- *"Because of the innumerable problems caused by busybodies who devote 'a most unnecessary attention' to things that would be better without them, the rest of us should devote some very necessary attention to these busybodies and their sloppy arguments."*

  —THOMAS SOWELL

- *"The road to Hell is paved with good intentions."*

  —UNKNOWN

- *"When government accepts responsibility for people, then people no longer take responsibility for themselves."*

  —GEORGE PATAKI

- *"The real destroyer of the liberties of the people is he who spreads among them bounties, donations and benefits."*

  —PLUTARCH

- *"Yes, the way to identify a tree or a person is by the kind of fruit that is produced."*

  —JESUS OF NAZARETH

- *"The only purpose for which power can be rightfully exercised over any member of a civilized community, against his will, is to prevent harm to others. His own good, either physical or moral, is not sufficient warrant."*

  —JOHN STUART MILL

- *"The shepherd always tries to persuade the sheep that their interests and his own are the same."*

  —STENDHAL

- *"It will be found an unjust and unwise jealousy to deprive a man of his natural liberty upon the supposition he may abuse it."*

  —OLIVER CROMWELL

- *"The State...has had a vested interest in promoting attitudes that would tend to make us skeptical of our own abilities, fearful of the motives of others, and emotionally dependent upon external authorities for purpose and direction in our lives."*

  —BUTLER D. SHAFFER

- *"True, it is evil that a single man should crush the herd, but see not there the worse form of slavery, which is when the herd crushes out the man."*

  —ANTOINE DE SAINT-EXUPÉRY

- *"The whole point of the liberal revolution that gave rise to the 1960s was to free us from somebody else's dogma, but now the same people...are striving to impose on others a secularized religion...disguising it behind innocuous labels like 'diversity training' and 'respect for difference.'"*

  —RICHARD BERNSTEIN

- *"Tolerance is a better guarantee of freedom than brotherly love; for a man may love his brother so much that he feels himself thereby appointed his brother's keeper."*

  —EVERETT DEAN MARTIN

- *"...higher minimum wages mean higher levels of unemployment."*

  —THOMAS SOWELL

- *"It is the theory of all modern civilized governments that they protect and foster the liberty of the citizen; it is the practice of all of them to limit its exercise, and sometimes very narrowly."*

  —H. L. MENCKEN

- *"I know no class of my fellowmen, however just, enlightened, and humane, which can be wisely and safely trusted absolutely with the liberties of any other class."*

  —FREDERICK DOUGLASS

- *"Absolute power corrupts even when exercised for humane purposes. The benevolent despot who sees himself as a shepherd of the people still demands from others the submissiveness of sheep."*

  —ERIC HOFFER

- *"The most odious of all oppressions are those which mask as justice."*

  —JUSTICE ROBERT H. JACKSON

- *"To liberals, 'compassion' means giving less productive people the fruits of the efforts of more productive people. But real compassion means enabling less productive people to become more productive themselves. That way, the poor have not only more material things but also more self-respect, as well as more respect from others, and the society as a whole has a higher standard of living and less internal strife."*

  —THOMAS SOWELL

- *"Of all tyrannies, a tyranny sincerely exercised for the good of its victim may be the most oppressive. It may be better to live under robber barons than under omnipotent moral busybodies. The robber baron's cruelty may sometimes sleep, his cupidity may at some point be satiated, but those who torment us for our own good will torment us without end for they do so with the approval of their own conscience."*

  —C. S. LEWIS

- *"Now those who seek absolute power, even though they seek it to do what they regard as good, are simply demanding the right to enforce their own version of heaven on earth, and let me remind you they are the very ones who always create the most hellish tyranny."*

  —BARRY GOLDWATER

- *"Sometimes the law defends plunder and participates in it. Thus the beneficiaries are spared the shame and danger that their acts would otherwise involve...But how is this legal plunder to be identified? Quite simply. See if the law takes from some persons what belongs to them and gives it to the other persons to whom it doesn't belong. See if the law benefits one citizen at the expense of another by doing what the citizen himself cannot do without committing a crime. Then abolish that law without delay...No legal plunder; this is the principle of justice, peace, order, stability, harmony and logic."*

  —FREDERIC BASTIAT

- *"The mania for giving the Government power to meddle with the private affairs of cities or citizens is likely to cause endless trouble, through the rivalry of schools and creeds that are anxious to obtain official recognition, and there is great danger that our people will lose our independence of thought and action which is the cause of much of our greatness, and sink into the helplessness of the Frenchman or German who expects his government to feed him when hungry, clothe him when naked, to prescribe when his child may be born and when he may die, and, in time, to regulate every act of humanity from the cradle to the tomb, including the manner in which he may seek future admission to paradise."*

  —MARK TWAIN

- *"Watch out for the fellow who talks about putting things in order! Putting things in order always means getting other people under your control."*

  —DENIS DIDEROT

- *"Any fool can make a rule, and any fool will mind it."*

  —HENRY DAVID THOREAU

- *"If you want a Big Brother, you get all that comes with it."*

  —ERICH FROMM

Wisdom

- *"What luck for the rulers that men do not think."*

  —ADOLF HITLER

- *"And ye shall know the truth, and the truth shall make you free."*

  —JESUS OF NAZARETH

- *"If a million people say a foolish thing, it is still a foolish thing."*

  —ANATOLE FRANCE

- *"A nation of well informed men who have been taught to know and prize the rights which God has given them cannot be enslaved. It is in the region of ignorance that tyranny begins."*

  —BENJAMIN FRANKLIN

- *"There is more stupidity than hydrogen in the universe, and it has a longer shelf life."*

  —FRANK ZAPPA

- *"If stupidity got us into this mess, then why can't it get us out?"*

  —WILL ROGERS

- *"Facts do not cease to exist because they are ignored."*

  —ALDOUS HUXLEY

- *"Truth is like the sun. You can shut it out for a time, but it ain't goin' away."*

  —ELVIS PRESLEY

- *"When all think alike, no one is thinking very much."*

  —WALTER LIPPMANN

- *"The most formidable weapon against errors of every kind is reason. I have never used any other, and I trust I never shall."*

  —THOMAS PAINE

- *"Finding the occasional straw of truth awash in a great ocean of confusion and bamboozle requires intelligence, vigilance, dedication and courage. But if we don't practice these tough habits of thought, we cannot hope to solve the truly serious problems that face us—and we risk becoming a nation of suckers, up for grabs by the next charlatan who comes along."*

  —CARL SAGAN

- *"Thus it happens in matters of state; for knowing afar off (which it is only given a prudent man to do) the evils that are brewing, they are easily cured. But when, for want of such knowledge, they are allowed to grow so that everyone can recognize them, there is no longer any remedy to be found."*

  —NICCOLO MACHIAVELLI

- *"All political theories assume, of course, that most individuals are very ignorant. Those who plead for liberty differ from the rest in that they include among the ignorant themselves as well as the wisest."*

  —FREDRICH AUGUST VON HAYEK

- *"The more I truly learn, the less I truly know."*

  —ERIC SCHAUB

- *"Great spirits have always found violent opposition from mediocrities. The latter cannot understand it when a man does not thoughtlessly submit to hereditary prejudices but honestly and courageously uses his intelligence."*

  —ALBERT EINSTEIN

- *"To be absolutely certain about something, one must know everything or nothing about it."*

  —OLIN MILLER

- *"We must abandon the prevalent belief in the superior wisdom of the ignorant."*

  —DANIEL BOORSTIN

- *"Men willingly believe what they wish."*

  —GAIUS JULIUS CAESAR

- *"The house of delusions is cheap to build but drafty to live in."*

  —A. E. HOUSMAN

- *"There is no slavery but ignorance. Liberty is the child of intelligence."*

  —ROBERT G. INGERSOLL

- *"Integrity without knowledge is weak and useless, and knowledge without integrity is dangerous and dreadful."*

  —SAMUEL JOHNSON

- *"Knowledge is power."*

  —SIR FRANCIS BACON

- *"Whenever the people are well informed, they can be trusted with their own government; that whenever things get so far wrong as to attract their notice, they may be relied on to set them to rights."*

  —THOMAS JEFFERSON

- *"Minds are like parachutes. They only function when they are open."*

  —SIR JAMES DEWAR

- *"Those who do not learn from history are doomed to repeat it."*

  —PROVERB

- *"The wise learn from the experience of others, most from their own experience, and fools not at all."*

  —PROVERB

- *"The wise do freely, early and in good time, what fools do later out of necessity."*

  —PROVERB

- *"All truth passes through 3 stages. First, it is ridiculed. Second, it is violently opposed. Third, it is accepted as being self-evident."*

  —ARTHUR SCHOPENHAUER

- *"The power of accurate observation is commonly called cynicism by those who have not got it."*

  —GEORGE BERNARD SHAW

- *"Truth has always been found to promote the best interests of mankind."*

  —PERCY BYSSHE SHELLEY

- *"There are a thousand hacking at the branches of evil to one who is striking at the root."*

  —HENRY DAVID THOREAU

- *"The illiterate of the 21st century will not be those who cannot read and write, but those who cannot learn, unlearn, and relearn."*

  —ALVIN TOFFLER

- *"Whenever you find you are on the side of the majority, it is time to pause and reflect."*

  —MARK TWAIN

- *"Any formal attack on ignorance is bound to fail because the masses are always ready to defend their most precious possession—their ignorance."*

  —HENDRICK VAN LOON

- *"To act without clear understanding, to form habits without investigation, to follow a path all one's life without knowing where it really leads—such is the behavior of the multitude."*

  —MENCIUS

- *"Reason and Ignorance, the opposites of each other, influence the great bulk of mankind. If either of these can be rendered sufficiently extensive in a country, the machinery of Government goes easily on. Reason obeys itself; and Ignorance submits to whatever is dictated to it."*

  —THOMAS PAINE

Miscellaneous

- *"Good people do not need laws to tell them to act responsibly, while bad people will find a way around the laws."*

  —PLATO

- *"Any man who is under 30, and is not a liberal, has no heart; and any man who is over 30, and is not a conservative, has no brains."*

  —SIR WINSTON CHURCHILL

- *"Get all the fools on your side and you can be elected to anything."*

  —FRANK DANE

- *"Over the years, the United States has sent many of its fine young men and women into great peril to fight for freedom beyond our borders. The only amount of land we have ever asked for in return is enough to bury those that did not return."*

  —COLIN POWELL

- *"The things that will destroy us are: politics without principle; pleasure without conscience; wealth without work; knowledge without character; business without morality; science without humanity; and worship without sacrifice."*

  —MAHATMA MOHANDAS K. GANDHI

- *"We often give our enemies the means to our own destruction."*

  —AESOP

- *"Resistance to the organized mass can be effected only by the man who is as well organized in his individuality as the mass itself."*

  —CARL GUSTAV JUNG

- *"Unless they can pass the same test that immigrants must pass to become citizens, people shouldn't be allowed to vote. The idea that there is some public benefit in ignoramuses and morons pulling levers next to names on a ballot is one of the evil myths of post-modern America. The purpose of voting, in our country, is to select men and women with the competence and integrity to operate the mechanics of government fixed by our Constitution. For this process to have any public benefit requires that the choices be made on an intelligent, knowledgeable and reasoned basis."*

  —CHARLEY REESE

- *"The ends do not justify the means."*

  —UNKNOWN

- *"The means is the end in the process of becoming."*

  —JAMES DOUGLASS

- *"As I grow older, I pay less attention to what men say. I just watch what they do."*

  —ANDREW CARNEGIE

- *"Moral indignation is in most cases 2% moral, 48% indignation and 50% envy."*

  —VITTORIO DE SICA

- *"Give a small boy a hammer and he will find that everything he encounters needs pounding."*

  —ABRAHAM KAPLAN

- *"History is written by the victor."*

  —LATIN PROVERB

- *"I would not mind straight people if they just would not act straight in public."*

  —BUMPER STICKER

- *"If destruction be our lot, we must ourselves be its author and finisher. As a nation of freemen, we must live through all time, or die by suicide."*

  —ABRAHAM LINCOLN

- *"What becomes of the surplus of human life? It is either, 1st destroyed by infanticide, as among the Chinese and Lacedemonians; or 2nd it is stifled or starved, as among other nations whose population is commensurate to its food; or 3rd it is consumed by wars and endemic diseases; or 4th it overflows, by emigration, to places where a surplus of food is attainable."*

  —JAMES MADISON

- *"Those are my principles. If you don't like them I have others."*

  —GROUCHO MARX

- *"You got their peckers in your pocket, their hearts and minds will follow."*

  —LYNDON JOHNSON

- *"The highest patriotism is not a blind acceptance of official policy, but a love of one's country deep enough to call her to a higher standard."*

  —GEORGE MCGOVERN

- *"To die for an idea: it is unquestionably noble. But how much nobler it would be if men died for ideas that were true."*

  —H. L. MENCKEN

- *"All men are frauds. The only difference between them is that some admit it. I myself deny it."*

  —H. L. MENCKEN

- *"Petty laws breed great crimes."*

  —OUIDA

- *"These are the times that try men's souls.... Tyranny, like hell, is not easily conquered; yet we have this consolation with us, that the harder the conflict, the more glorious the triumph."*

  —THOMAS PAINE

- *"Those who cannot remember the past are condemned to repeat it."*

  —GEORGE SANTAYANA

- *"You won't find average Americans on the left or on the right. You'll find them at Kmart."*

  —ZELL MILLER

- *"While birds can fly, only humans can argue. Argument is the affirmation of our being. It is the principal instrument of human intercourse. Without argument the species would perish. As a subtle suggestion, it is the means by which we aid another. As a warning, it steers us from danger. As exposition, it teaches. As an expression of creativity, it is the gift of ourselves. As a protest, it struggles for justice. As a reasoned dialogue, it resolves disputes. As an assertion of self, it engenders respect. As an entreaty of love, it expresses our devotion. As a plea, it generates mercy. As charismatic oration it moves multitudes and changes history. We must argue—to help, to warn, to lead, to love, to create, to learn, to enjoy justice, to be."*

  —GERRY SPENCE

- *"Find out just what the people will submit to and you have found out the exact amount of injustice and wrong which will be imposed upon them; and these will continue until they are resisted with either words or blows, or with both. The limits of tyrants are prescribed by the endurance of those whom they oppress."*

  —FREDERICK DOUGLASS

- *"Guns will make us powerful; butter will only make us fat."*

  —HERMANN GOERING

- *"The doctrine of blind obedience and unqualified submission to any human power, whether civil or ecclesiastical, is the doctrine of despotism, and ought to have no place among Republicans and Christians."*

  —ANGELICA GRIMKE

- *"There is as far as I know, no example in history, of any state voluntarily ceding power from the centre to its constituent parts."*

  —CHARLES HANDY

- *"The plea of necessity, that eternal argument of all conspirators."*

  —WILLIAM HENRY HARRISON

- *"The ultimate decision about what is accepted as right and wrong will be made not by individual human wisdom but by the disappearance of the groups that have adhered to the 'wrong' beliefs."*

  —FREDRICH AUGUST VON HAYEK

- *"Justice, like liberty and coercion, is a concept which, for the sake of clarity, ought to be confined to the deliberate treatment of men by other men."*

  —FREDRICH AUGUST VON HAYEK

- *"Now that no one buys our votes, the public has long since cast off its cares; the people that once bestowed commands, consulships, legions, and all else, now meddle no more and long eagerly for just two things—bread and circuses."*

  —JUVENA

- *"There is no king who has not had a slave among his ancestors, and no slave who has not had a king among his."*

  —HELEN KELLER

- *"It is an injustice, a grave evil and a disturbance of the right order, for a larger and higher organization, to arrogate to itself functions which can be performed efficiently by smaller and lower bodies."*

  —POPE LEO XIII

- *"Money, it has been said, is the cause of good things to a good man, of evil things to a bad man."*

  —PHILO

- *"We will never have true civilization until we have learned to recognize the rights of others."*

  —WILL ROGERS

- *"God made the Idiot for practice, and then He made the School Board."*

  —MARK TWAIN

- *"Live your life that the fear of death can never enter your heart. Trouble no one about his religion. Respect others in their views and demand that they respect yours. Love your life, perfect your life, beautify all things in your life. Seek to make your life long and of service to your people. Prepare a noble death song for the day when you go over the great divide. Always give a word or sign of salute when meeting or passing a friend, or even a stranger, if in a lonely place. Show respect to all people, but grovel to none. When you rise in the morning, give thanks for the light, for your life, for your strength. Give thanks for your food and for the joy of living. If you see no reason to give thanks, the fault lies in yourself. Abuse no one and nothing, for abuse turns the wise ones to fools and robs the spirit of its vision. When your time comes to die, be not like those whose hearts are filled with fear of death, so that when their time comes they weep and pray for a little more time to live their lives over again in a different way. Sing your death song, and die like a hero going home."*

  —TECUMSEH (1768–1813), SHAWNEE CHIEF